Karl Barth

KARL BARTH
Studies of his Theological Method

EDITED BY

S. W. SYKES

Clarendon Press · Oxford
1979

Oxford University Press, Walton Street, Oxford OX2 6DP

OXFORD LONDON GLASGOW

NEW YORK TORONTO MELBOURNE WELLINGTON

KUALA LUMPUR SINGAPORE JAKARTA HONG KONG TOKYO

DELHI BOMBAY CALCUTTA MADRAS KARACHI

NAIROBI DAR ES SALAAM CAPE TOWN

*Published in the United States
by Oxford University Press, New York*

British Library Cataloguing in Publication Data
Karl Barth.
1. Barth, Karl
I. Sykes, Stephen Whitefield
209′.2′4   BX4827.B3   79–41095

ISBN 0–19–826649–9

Text set in 11/12 pt VIP Baskerville, printed and bound
in Great Britain at The Pitman Press, Bath

Preface

This book is the result of three extremely lively meetings which took place in my house in Durham over the space of eighteen months. The participants, all of whom are teachers of systematic theology, felt a need for some friendly but searching theological argument; they found it in the subject of this inquiry. In the course of the discussion considerable efforts were made to respond to objections arising out of the initial papers that were written, and to correlate the differing approaches to Barth's method. The disagreement which remained, even after some exhausting sessions, may be attributed to (and most certainly reflect) the variety of contemporary styles of theological argument, as well as the complexity of Barth's own work.

As is well known, some of the most important sections of Barth's work are intellectually very demanding; and it is only fair to warn the reader that so are some of these essays. We shall not regard him as altogether lacking in seriousness if at a relatively early stage he turns to the question, Is Barth a fraud? with which Dr Ford opens Chapter 6 ('Conclusion: Assessing Barth'). None the less, the authors of this book, 'non-Barthian' though they may be, are in complete agreement about the value and importance of the study of Barth's massive achievement. Our aim is to convey to the reader something of that improved quality and depth in understanding the *Church Dogmatics*, which was the outcome of our meetings.

To Mrs Julie Ramsbottom we express our gratitude for the preparation of the indexes and for other help.

S.W.S.

The College,
Durham.

Contents

Abbreviations of Barth's Works

REFERENCES TO the works listed below are directly followed by a numeral, giving the page reference, except in the case of the *Church Dogmatics*, where the column and part number (roman and arabic numerals respectively) are directly followed by numerals giving page references. Of the *Church Dogmatics* I/1 there is an earlier translation (Thompson, 1936) and a later (Bromiley, 1975). Bromiley's is cited except where explicitly indicated.

Chr. D   *Prolegomena zur Christlichen Dogmatik* (Munich, 1927)

CD   *Church Dogmatics* (Edinburgh, 1936–74)

ER   *The Epistle to the Romans* (Oxford, 1935)

ET   *Evangelical Theology* (London, 1965)

FQI   *Anselm: Fides Quaerens Intellectum* (London, 1960)

PT   *Protestant Theology in the Nineteenth Century* (London, 1972)

RD   *The Resurrection of the Dead* (London, 1933)

TC   *Theology and Church* (London, 1962)

WW   *The Word of God and the Word of Man* (London, 1928)

Busch   E. Busch, *Karl Barth* (London, 1976)

1

The Study of Barth

S. W. SYKES

University of Durham

I

THE PROBLEM for the student of theology in confronting the massive theological achievement of Karl Barth (1886–1968) is, evidently, time—time, moreover, in the entirely practical sense of finding enough time to read enough of his work. Barth himself would certainly have appreciated the point. 'To study theology', he wrote, 'means not so much to examine exhaustively the work of earlier students of theology as to become *their* fellow student.'[1] However, we clearly stand at the threshold of a period of evaluation of Barth's significance for Christian theology, which will most certainly be more exhaustive in extent than anything known hitherto. The projected publication of numerous volumes containing virtually everything Barth committed to paper will mean a still more herculean task for any one setting out to master his thought.

There remains, however, a useful intermediate task for someone who is dissatisfied with more facile ways in which his theological position is still summarized and discussed. That task is to acquire a sufficient understanding of Barth's *method* of theological argument, so as to be able to use Barth's *Dogmatics* intelligently as a source of theological stimulation. This is what the essays in this book set out to achieve. The authors of them do not suppose that the reader is just about to begin the ten-month, eight-to-ten-hours-per-day, exercise of reading through the volumes of the *Dogmatics*, of which one American Professor speaks.[2] But if any well-informed theological inquirer of our day may reasonably be expected to have read a certain amount of Barth for himself, that reading will

[1] *ET*, p. 161.
[2] A. B. Come, *An Introduction to Barth's Dogmatics for Preachers* (London, 1963), p. 9.

only make sense if it is accompanied and supported by some idea of what Barth is attempting to do *as a whole*.

Plausible as that may sound, there is an obvious problem. It is the problem of a man entering for the first time into a magnificent architectural site, like the palace at Mycenae. The question at once arises, through whose eyes is he going to see it? Is he going to consult first the speculative reconstruction of what the buildings may once have looked like? Or will he inspect each stone with the aid of an archaeological guide, and try to separate layer upon layer of different periods? And who is to help him relate all that was once said and done in these places to his own twentieth-century dwellings and culture? And what is he to make of the controversies which have raged, and still rage, about the origin and fate of this civilization? The decisions the visitor makes, or has made for him, on these matters very substantially affect the quality and depth of his response to what he sees about him.

No less vulnerable to predetermined ways of seeing Barth is the theological student; and no less significant for the ultimate quality of his experience of the writings will be the strengths and weaknesses, percipience and prejudice, of the guides he chooses, or chances upon, in his innocence. What happens in this book is, in effect, that a number of writers, convinced that such guides to Barth as are available in English are not as helpful as they should be, have tried to reveal what they believe to be the fundamental methods he employs. The result is, predictably and, I believe, helpfully, diverse. Nothing in the history of the interpretation of Barth hitherto should lead one to suppose that any one scholar has the 'key to Barth' secreted in his robes. A more explicit guide to the guides will be offered in Section III of this Introduction.

A further point is of importance. The English reader of Barth, like the English tourist in Greece, is very unlikely to survey his task with an innocent eye. 'Nobody', said John Baillie in 1939, 'seems to be able to talk theology these days without mentioning him.'[3] Still fewer have mentioned him without conveying a strong opinion about him, one way or another. It seems to be the case that most English-speaking theological students have been brought up on stories and jokes

[3] J. Baillie, *Our Knowledge of God* (London, 1939), p. 17.

about Barth, often involving the supposed arrogance of claiming inside knowledge of God's way of viewing mankind, and on one-sentence dismissals of his efforts. Of this latter genre my favourite is (it is the one on which *I* was reared), 'The theology of Barth lacks nothing—except a basis'; this being a way of referring to Barth's refusal to provide a natural theology of the traditional kind for his own dogmatics.

The prevalence of such canards suggests that more than ordinary care should be taken in this Introduction to outline something of the history of the English-speaking world's reception of Barth's thought.

II

Literary comment on Barth, as distinct from reviews of his books, begins, it seems, some time in 1923. Barth himself records with some amusement that he had received a copy of a magazine, called *The Watchman*, from a layman in Iowa, which contained an account of his recent public exchange of letters with Adolf von Harnack.[4] This controversy had been conducted in the pages of *Christliche Welt* from January to May of 1923, and is one of the most instructive episodes in the history of Barth's break with liberal Protestantism. After this there are a number of clear indications that the English-speaking public were beginning to attend to the new movement of thought. In the *Expositor* for 1925 two articles appeared under the heading of 'The theology of Crisis'.[5] In 1926 Union Theological Seminary in New York entertained a German visitor, Professor Gustav Krüger of Giessen, who lectured on the Theology of Crisis, treating Gogarten, Barth, and Brunner, and whose lectures were published in the *Harvard Theological Review*.[6] Krüger also urged the translation of *Das Wort Gottes und die Theologie*, which Barth had issued in 1925; but it seems that the impulse which led Douglas Horton, a Congregationalist Minister, to undertake the work was entirely independent. By 1928 this translation had been published,

---

[4] As Barth reports in his letter to Thurneysen, of 20 December 1923, K. Barth and E. Thurneysen, *Revolutionary Theology in the Making* (London, 1964), p. 161.

[5] A. Keller, 'The Theology of Crisis I', *Expositor*, 9th series, III, no. 3 (March, 1925), pp. 164–75, and 'The Theology of Crisis II', op. cit., III, no. 4 (April 1925), pp. 245–60.

[6] *Harvard Theological Review*, XIX, 3, 227–58.

and reviews and articles became more frequent. Among them are contributions by Reinhold Niebuhr, H. R. Mackintosh, and J. K. Mozley among others.[7]

If this seems somewhat meagre, it must be remembered that Barth himself in the period 1920 to 1930 was in the first decade of his professorial theological activity. Harnack had indeed complained early in the 1920s that Barth seemed to be more of an object of academic theology than a subject.[8] Although the second edition of his *Commentary on Romans* (1921), and the first volume of his *Christliche Dogmatik in Entwurf* (1927) *(Christian Dogmatics in Outline;* no English translation) lay behind him, there were many unsettled questions and signs of strain in the initial circle of 'dialectical theologians'. All the more perceptive, therefore, was the observation of J. K. Mozley when he remarked in 1929:

> The extraordinary unlikeness of Barth's theology to anything we usually meet in Anglican or Free Church circles makes it all the more worthy of study. Barth does not fit in either with the orthodoxy or with the liberalism which are familiar to us or with any current attempt to combine the two . . . Barth's methods of thought and speech and his characteristic emphases are far removed from ours. But if we neglect him we shall miss a great deal.[9]

But from 1929 onwards it cannot reasonably be said that Barth was neglected in English-language theological writing. Quite a number of works on Barth or on dialectical theology were produced of a popular or semi-popular kind from which the appropriateness of Mozley's comment might have been appreciated.[10] Brunner's own *Theology of Crisis* appeared in

---

[7] H. R. Mackintosh, 'Leaders of Theological Thought: Karl Barth', *Expository Times*, XXXIX, 12 (Sept. 1928), pp. 536–40. J. K. Mozley, 'The Theology of Karl Barth', *Review of the Churches*, VI, 4 (Oct. 1929).

[8] Cited in E. Busch, *Karl Barth* (London, 1976), p. 192.

[9] J. K. Mozley, op. cit.

[10] Among these are the following:

R. B. Hoyle, *The Teaching of Karl Barth* (London, 1930), 286 pp.

J. A. Chapman, *The Theology of Karl Barth* (London, 1931), 47 pp.

W. Pauck, *Karl Barth, Prophet of a New Christianity?* (New York, 1932), 228 pp.

W. Lowrie, *Our Concern with the Theology of Crisis* (New York, 1932), 214 pp.

E. Lewis, *A Christian Manifesto* (London, 1934), 254 pp.

G. W. Richards, *Beyond Fundamentalism and Modernism: The Gospel of God* (New York,1934), 333 pp.

J. McConnachie, *The Significance of Karl Barth* (London, 1931), 288 pp. and *The Barthian Theology and the Man of Today*, 335 pp.

1929. In the same year an Anglican country clergyman, C. J. Shebbeare (Rector of Stanhope in County Durham), gave a perceptive account of Barth's views in *Romans* in the course of an essay on the Atonement.[11] We find a passing reference to Barth in Gore's Gifford Lectures for 1929 to 1930, *The Philosophy of the Good Life* (1930), where, together, with Rudolf Otto, he is accused of laying so heavy an emphasis on divine transcendence 'as to suggest that they have overlooked that the voice of God from without or above must correspond with His voice from within the heart of man in his conscience and reason'.[12]

This passing indictment, both as to manner and substance, becomes a virtual habit in the theology of the 1930s. Oliver Quick, admitting that he had not studied Barth in the original, devoted ten pages to a criticism of ' "Barthianism" as commonly presented' on much the same grounds.[13] The Congregationalist, A. E. Garvie, defends 'human religion' against the Barthian attack with a footnote ascribing to a witty French preacher the remark that 'the Barthian theology' provides God with a great key, but not with a keyhole in man.[14] W. R. Matthews, noting it as 'a curious illustration of the remoteness of English theology from that of Europe that Barth is welcomed as an ally by some Anglo-Catholics', gives another frequently heard dismissal of Barth as 'at least in part . . . a portent of disillusionment and dissatisfaction'.[15] Temple likewise, in his Gifford Lectures, *Nature, Man and God* (1934), finds the 'Barthian school of theology' obviously in error in denying to reason and conscience their proper role as vin-

---

In the volume of essays presented to Barth on his 50th birthday, John McConnachie contributed a brief sketch of Barth's impact on British theology and church life, 'Der Einfluss Karl Barths in Schottland und England', E. Wolf (ed), *Theologische Aufsätze* (Munich, 1936), pp. 529–70. The essay records general agreement that Barth's influence hitherto had been indirect and generalized, rather than direct and particular.

[11] C. J. Shebbeare, 'The Atonement and some Tendencies of Modern Thought', in L. W. Grensted (ed.), *The Atonement in History and Life* (London, 1929).

[12] Everyman edn, p. 213

[13] O. C. Quick, *The Ground of Faith and the Chaos of Thought* (London, 1931), pp. 96–107.

[14] A. E. Garvie, *The Christian Belief in God* (London, 1933), p. 29.

[15] W. R. Matthews, *Essays in Construction* (London, 1933), pp. 19 f.

dicators of the claim of revelation.[16] He, moreover, is responsible for one of the notable, one-sentence dismissals of Barth,
voiced, it is said, on observing a cat washing its face; 'How in
the face of *that* can they [i.e. the Barthians] deny the existence
of natural theology?'[17]

These expressions of distant dissent from the older leaders
of English theistic philosophy of religion are hardly surprising;
they entirely coincide with Barth's own observations on the
alienating effect of his style of theology on his British friends,
when on his first visit to England in June 1930.[18] The same
visit took him to Scotland where he received an honorary
doctorate at Glasgow University as 'the most-discussed
theologian of Germany'.[19] In 1933 appeared Sir Edwyn Hoskyns's magnificent translation of the sixth edition of Barth's
Romans, and in the summer of 1935 Barth was himself invited
to give the Gifford Lectures at the University of Aberdeen. We
step in the later thirties into a changed atmosphere. In 1935
George Hendry delivered a powerful onslaught on the tradition of natural theology represented by W. R. Matthews, with
numerous references to Luther, Barth, and Brunner and the
explicit statement that Scottish theology had its true affinity
with continental Protestantism, rather than with England and
America.[20] From now onwards it is in Scotland that Barth is
taken with the greatest seriousness in the English-speaking
world, a fact of which the crowning monument is the
unbroken association of the Edinburgh publishers, T. and T.
Clark, with the translation of Barth's *Church Dogmatics*, the
first volume of which appeared in 1936.

But it would be false to depict the Scottish reception of
Barth as in any way uncritical. H. R. Mackintosh
(1870–1936), who, as Professor of systematic theology at
Edinburgh, was chiefly responsible for encouraging students
to study Barth, bequethed to many generations of students in
his posthumously published *Types of Modern Theology* (1937) a
rather cautiously positive response to Barth's work hitherto.

[16] W. Temple, *Nature, Man and God* (London, 1934), p. 396.
[17] F. A. Iremonger, *William Temple* (London, 1948), p. 608.
[18] Busch, p. 204.
[19] Ibid.
[20] G. S. Hendry, *God the Creator* (London, 1937), p. viii; this represents the Hastie
Lectures in the University of Glasgow for 1935.

Both John and Donald Baillie, whose important contributions to theology cover more than thirty years of Scottish university life, were independent and criticial observers of Barth's influence. Especially in *Our Knowledge of God* (1939), John Baillie shows himself both well informed on, and sharply critical of, both Barth's and Brunner's views on nature and grace, as exemplified in their pamphlet war of 1934.[21] In his posthumously published Gifford Lectures of 1961 to 1962, 'the devastating Baillie',[22] as Barth referred to him, offered his retrospective summary of Barth's influence:

He has changed the face of protestant theology far more radically than any other theologian during my life-time. He has also made more difference than anybody else to my own attempts at theologizing. Whatever the measure of our agreements or disagreements with him, we have all to reckon with him. I have often said that there can be no hopeful forward advance beyond his teaching, as I fervently hope there will be, if we attempt to go *round* it instead of *through* it. There are already many signs of a reaction towards a more liberal outlook, but it must be a liberalism which, while regaining some of the lost pre-Barthian ground, has been much chastened by the many valuable things he has taught us.[23]

A complicating factor in the assessment of the reception of Barth in English-speaking theology is the coupling of Barth with Brunner under the term 'Barthianism'. Emil Brunner (1889–1966), however, had a quite separate, and, to a large extent, more immediate impact on the English-speaking scene. Brunner spent a brief time in England before the First World War, and during this period made the acquaintance of William Temple. Shortly after the war he was offered a year's fellowship for study at Union Theological Seminary, an experience which he spoke of as providing the basis for his 'particularly fruitful contacts with the English-speaking world' for the rest of his life.[24] *Der Mittler* (1927), Brunner's major Christological work, first appeared in an English translation in 1934 with warmly commendatory forewords by

---

[21] E. Brunner, *Natur und Gnade* (Tübingen, 1934; 2nd edn., 1935); K. Barth, *Nein!* (Munich, 1934).

[22] Busch, p. 395.

[23] J. Baillie, *The Sense of the Presence of God* (London, 1962), pp. 254.

[24] 'Intellectual Autobiography' in C. W. Kegley (ed.), *The Theology of Emil Brunner* (New York, 1962), p. 8.

J. K. Mozley and H. R. Mackintosh. From then onwards Brunner's major works were translated into English as soon as he wrote them, and their cumulative effect was considerable. Ahlstrom in his history of American religion comments that Brunner understood the American situation much better than Barth, and that until the Second World War he was the most influential of the dialectical theologians.[25]

None the less a recent piece of careful research on modern American Protestantism reaches a firmly negative conclusion of the extent of the true penetration of American theology by Barth and Brunner. Even those who considered themselves in realist reaction from the dominant liberalism and idealism of the earlier decades were unwilling to accept Barth himself, and by 1939 the term 'Barthianism' had become the code-word, even among the neo-orthodox for 'an unacceptable transcendentalism, anti-intellectualism, and ignoring of social responsibility'.[26] In a survey of American religion published in 1945, the Dean of Harvard Divinity School, wrote Barth off as a reactionary and 'much to sophisticated for the average American layman'.[27]

This broadly based rejection is entirely consistent with the reaction against liberal theology, characteristic of the early 1940s. Despite the fact that the movement broadly knows as 'Biblical theology' was powerful in Britain and that the influence of Reinhold Niebuhr's form of 'Christian realism' was at its height, Barth was still liable to be rejected out of hand. For this, it must be said, the publication of his sharp dispute with Brunner over 'natural theology' is much to blame. In a revealing comment, which passes over into irony towards its close, Alan Richardson wrote:

We in Britain find it hard to understand the dialectical theology of Barth and Brunner because we live in a very different spiritual and mental climate from theirs. We do not feel their problems as our problems or their burdens as our burdens. The whole pattern of our civilization has not been shattered, as theirs has, by war and economic upheaval. Post-Kantian philosophy has not undermined

[25] S. E. Ahlstrom, *A Religious History of the American People* (New Haven, 1974), p. 934.

[26] W. R. Hutchison, *The Modernist Impulse in American Protestantism* (Cambridge, Mass., 1976), p. 300.

[27] W. L. Sperry, *Religion in America* (Cambridge, England 1945) p. 156.

our belief in reason and conscience, and we have not been driven to choose between nihilism and some form of existentialism. We were not brought up on a theology dominated by Schleiermacher and 'the consciousness of religion' [sic]; if Feuerbach laughs, we do not feel he is laughing at us. If Barth and Brunner disagree with each other about the details of their erroneous view of the *imago Dei*, we do not get excited. We are insular, we live in a different world. *Cuius regio eius theologia*. We cannot see through the dialectical spectacles. Consequently we dismiss Barthianism or existentialism with a remark about passing post-war neurosis, and our complacency is undisturbed.[28]

Niebuhr, likewise, occasionally emphasized in the course of his frequent and rhetorically effective raids upon Barth or Barthianism, the essential foreignness of his whole thought-world. Contrasting American optimism with what he termed 'Lutheran pessimism' (were there no Lutherans in America?), he opined that

Karl Barth actually reduced Lutheran pessimism to a new level of consistency and made it even more difficult for the Christian conscience to express itself in making the relative decisions which are so necessary for the elaborations of justice in the intricacies of politics and economics. Karl Barth's present position of uncompromising hostility to Nazism cannot change the fact that his system of thought helped at an earlier date to vitiate the forces which contended against the rising Nazi tyranny.[29]

With the publication in 1957 of the second volume of the *Dogmatics* the history of the English-speaking reception of Barth enters a transitional phase. By 1955 Barth himself had completed ten volumes of the *Dogmatics*, and the English translators found themselves faced with the task of closing a gap of seventeen years which had opened up between the writing of I/2 and its translation. Dimly aware that Barth was developing his work along sometimes unexpected and always highly sophisticated lines, professional theologians in England

[28] *Theology* (1948), p. 30. In his *Christian Apologetics* (London, 1947), Professor Richardson had already explained with explicit reference to Barth's attack on apologetics that he considered that twentieth-century theologians had the task of refuting negative strictures upon reason, much in the style of Hooker's refutation of the Puritans.

[29] 'Germany and the Western World' in R. Niebuhr, *Christianity and Power Politics* (New York, 1940), p. 58. Compare Niebuhr's qualification of this view in 'An Answer to Karl Barth', *The Christian Century* (23 Feb. 1949), p. 236.

and America were forced to bring to an end the long tradition of amateurish comment based on a few dips in the literature, and faced with the alternative of a lot of hard work or silence. For the most part they chose silence. In 1947 those who were keeping pace with developments published their tribute to Karl Barth on his sixtieth birthday, *Reformation Old and New*. Edited by another English country parson, F. W. Camfield, the list of contributors contained only one person currently teaching in a British University.[30] In the period until 1962 the only major work on Barth to appear in English, G. C. Berkouwer's *The Triumph of Grace in the Theology of Karl Barth* (1956), was translated from Dutch. Otherwise, for a really able contextualization of Barth in English there was only an extraordinarily fine essay on the background to the thought of H. Richard Niebuhr by an American, Hans Frei, who had done a doctorate on Barth's early theological writing.[31]

In 1962 Professor T. F. Torrance produced two important contributions to the interpretation of Barth, an essay of fifty-four pages introducing a series of Barth's early papers on *Theology and Church*, and a carefully researched survey of Barth's early theology, up to the writing of the first volume of the *Dogmatics*, *Karl Barth: An Introduction to His Early Theology 1910—1931*. Three characteristics of these writings may be remarked on. First, and most obviously, is Torrance's enthusiasm for one spoken of as 'the greatest theological genius that has appeared on the scene for centuries'.[32] Secondly, Torrance insists that, although Barth is very much a European in that he carries on a running debate with post-Kantian thought, he is fundamentally to be seen as a catholic theologian wrestling with the whole history of Christian thought in the light of the Nicene faith that God communicates *himself* in his revelation.[33] The plausibility of the view

[30] The name of Professor H. A. Hodges, of Reading University. The other contributers were J. McConnachie, T. F. Torrance (at the time a parish minister), G. Hendry, H. F. Lovell Cocks, D. T. Jenkins, and W. A. Whitehouse (at the time Chaplain of Mansfield College, Oxford).

[31] Hans W. Frei, 'Niebuhr's Theological Background' in P. Ramsey (ed.), *Faith and Ethics* (New York, 1957). Frei's exposition of how Richard Niebuhr wrestled with the problem of academic theology bequeathed by Troeltsch and Barth is particularly illuminating. Frei's unpublished Yale thesis is entitled 'The Doctrine of Revelation in the Thought of Karl Barth, 1909–1922', New Haven, 1956.

[32] 'Introduction' to K. Barth, *Theology and Church* (London, 1962), p. 7.

[33] Ibid., p. 25; *Karl Barth*, p. 30.

that in Barth we are dealing with more than a minor variant of Protestantism is given considerable force by the fact, to which Torrance refers, that Barth had by this time been the subject of major works by von Balthasar, Bouillard and Küng.[34] The third remark to be made is that Torrance himself felt compelled to lay special emphasis, in his interpretation of Barth, on the methodological affinity of Barth's theology to that of an exact science. Specifically against the English critics who accused Barth of either Kantian subjectivism or irrationalism Torrance argued that 'Karl Barth belongs to the very centre of the great European tradition which has sought to give reason its fullest place in exact and careful thinking.'[35] Theology is 'better described as *theological science* than as sacred philosophy'.[36]

Torrance's work marks the beginning of a new and more sophisticated era for English-language reception of Barth. The climate of theological opinion, however, cannot be said to have responded to Torrance's evident enthusiasm for his subject. The 1960s saw the *Honest to God* debate and the *Death of God* theologies, for both of which Bonhoeffer's *Letters and Papers from Prison* are more responsible than any writing of Barth's. Even in 1969, Robert Jenson, the author of a study of Barth, could complain that 'almost nothing of what people have spoken of in America or England as "Barthianism" has much to do with the thought of the man from Basel.'[37]

However, a curious phenomenon became apparent at this time. It emerged that a number of the most radical of the younger theologians had done doctoral work on the theology of Karl Barth as students, and had even published a first book of a markedly 'Barthian' character. The effect of a close acquaintance with Barth's work was not invariably to create lifelong disciples. Although Dr John Robinson had not himself been a close student of Barth (his doctoral studies were on

[34] Hans Urs von Balthasar, *Karl Barth: Darstellung und Deutung seiner Theologie* (Cologne, 1951).

Henri Bouillard, *Karl Barth*, vol. I, *Genèse et Évolution de la Théologie dialiectique*; vols. II and III, *Parole de Dieu et Existence Humaine* (Paris, 1957).

Hans Küng, *Rechtfertigung: Die Lehre Karl Barths und eine katholische Besinnung* (Einsiedeln, 1957); Eng. Trans., *Justification* (London, 1964).

[35] *Karl Barth*, p. 32.

[36] Introduction to *Theology and Church*, p. 40.

[37] R. Jenson, *God after God* (Indianapolis, 1969), p. 6.

Buber), his attempt to achieve a reformation of the concept of God provoked the following perceptive comment from Alastair MacIntyre:

At first sight Barth's starting-point in theology is at the opposite pole from that of Dr Robinson. And certainly as Barthian theology has developed systematically, it has remained a keystone of orthodoxy, by now a major influence among Roman Catholics as well as among Protestants. But Barthian Theology none the less contains the materials for its own self-transformation. For if the Word of God cannot be identified with *any* frail human attempt to comprehend it, the way is open for sympathy with those who reject human theologies which have attempted to substitute for the Divine Word (and perhaps Barthian theology among them). So Barth has always had an interest in Ludwig Feuerbach.[38]

The Feuerbachian reaction to Barth, in the variety of 'theologies' celebrating man's coming of age, look, even a bare ten years later, distinctly ephemeral. Far from ephemeral, on the other hand, is the *problem*—some would say the *refutation*—with which any theology is confronted in the works of Feuerbach and Marx; and one pervasive reason why the study of Barth is likely to continue to provide an admirable theological education for those with the tenacity to pursue it is the fact that Barth himself tried to confront that problem directly.

Much more justice would need to be done to the indirect influence exerted by Karl Barth on the theological work of the last fifty years, if a survey of this kind were to claim any kind of comprehensiveness. However, its purpose will have been fulfilled if it has shown that certain aspects of the contemporary situation in which the present book has been written have a powerful, and some cases predeterminative effect, on a student's approach to Barth's work. Among these aspects should be mentioned the following: a tradition of amateurish comment on Barth, based largely on the negative impact made by some of his early works; a willingness to use the terms 'Barthian' or 'Barthianism' to characterize certain presuppositions which are supposed to run counter to a long tradition of Anglo-Saxon theology; a powerful counter-

---

[38] 'God and the Theologians', reprinted from *Encounter*, Sept. 1963. in A. MacIntyre, *Against the Self-Images of the Age* (London, 1971), p. 15.

movement of approval of Barth, which sees him as standing in the select company of the unquestionable geniuses of the history of Christian theology; and a legacy of disillusionment among those who once would have counted themselves as disciples of Barth. At the very least the study of Barth poses some considerable puzzles.

III

What, then, do the essays in this book seek to do? In the first place, as already stated, they are essays about Barth's methods of doing theology. Two of the authors, Dr Roberts and Dr Ford, have written doctoral theses which are, in effect, analyses of the strategies pursued by Barth chiefly in his *Church Dogmatics*. Dr Roberts takes the theme of time and eternity, and uses it as a tool for the systematic analysis of Barth's view of the structure of reality. The category of time, he argues, has become in effect a surrogate for that of 'substance', as used in traditional theology. Dr Ford, on the other hand, explores Barth's persistent emphasis upon the theme of story and of narration, and tries to bring out the way in which his use of Scripture is structured by a fundamental pattern provided by the sequence of Good Friday, Easter, and Pentecost.

These are by no means the only attempts at analysis of the method of Barth's dogmatics, as Dr Ford acknowledges in his essay. They are usefully brought together here, however, because they illustrate very clearly what is involved once a response to Barth is pursued beyond the superficial level characteristic of so much English writing. Dr Ford, taking up Barth's own insistence on listening to what Scripture is saying and on repeating what is heard, concentrates on the use of Scripture. This is a theme which has long puzzled English readers, who have been at a loss how to interpret Barth's apparently conservative reliance upon the Bible, but patent unwillingness to return to the strict letter of pre-critical orthodoxy. Dr Ford's enlightening use of the literary genre of realistic narrative to elucidate what Barth is attempting to achieve carries out, as he indicates (p. 76), some suggestions of Professor Hans Frei.

To take narrative as the means whereby the character of God is rendered in story-form is, of course, only the introduction to a complex of problems, the most conspicuous of which is inevitably that of time and eternity. In this respect Dr Roberts's philosophical probe into the basic procedures of the *Church Dogmatics* is obviously complementary to that of Dr Ford. If their essays tend to point to different conclusions that is chiefly because the authors seem to have reached rather different, provisional conclusions about what Christian theology itself can hope to achieve. Thus Dr Roberts uses against Barth a strong alternative concept of 'natural reality' (p. 110) or 'the shared reality of human existence' (p. 114) or 'experience and intersubjective reality' (p. 131). Measured against the force of such a criterion Barth's theology might even be depicted, he believes, as 'the most profound and systematically consistent theological alienation of the natural order ever achieved' (pp. 124f). This view of Barth, it should be noted, can clearly account for the phenomenon of disillusionment noted in some of Barth's erstwhile disciples.

Dr Ford's analysis, on the other hand, is undergirded by a different kind of critical drive. While asking whether 'some theological weight' might not be given to 'factors such as the natural and human sciences, historical criticism, and other religions' (p. 83), his own method is to undermine the apparently take-it-or-leave-it quality of Barth's demand. This he achieves by making Barth's method more amenable to discussion and criticism in the very act of comparing it to that of a known literary genre, that of realistic narrative. This in effect undermines the doctrine, on which Barth insists, and which he propounds in *Anselm: Fides Quaerens Intellectum*, that strictly speaking there can be no analogies for the necessity which the object of theology lays upon the theologian.

No less critical is Dr Williams's essay, though both here and in the case of my own essay, we have more to do with an inquiry into the success of Barth's own prescription of his theological method. If theology is rooted in acknowledgement of the self-revealing God, its form and structure must be that of Trinitarian theology—so Barth. The question Dr Williams pursues is whether or not Barth's view of revelation is determined simply by the structure of the saving events;

against Barth he argues that a prior ideological motive is apparent, that of the sovereign effectiveness of the acts of God, Calvin's irresistible grace rendered into epistemological terms (p. 158). Furthermore, the content of Barth's Trinitarian theology shows certain signs of strain, primarily a weakness in respect of the doctrine of the Holy Spirit, and a development towards greater pluralism in the later volumes of the *Church Dogmatics* (especially in relation to the Cross)—signs which indicate an inherent problem in the form of the initial, Trinitarian ground-plan. This, Dr Williams argues, may be connected with a certain view of language as self-expression, which accounts for Barth's insistence on the unity of the revelatory event and for the way in which disclosure and apprehension are seen as part of the single act of God in a duality of modes.

Thus a unifying, critical theme in the book emerges in this identification of a certain lack of interest in Barth in the phenomenon of human diversity and the processes of human growth. My own essay, which like Dr Williams's, proceeds largely along lines clearly indicated by Barth himself in his references to 'the centre of theology', has, as its chief conclusion, an express dissatisfaction with the absence of welcome for theological pluralism. It offers, as a reason for this lack, certain obvious features of the ecclesial life of the Reformed Churches, as compared with those of a more clearly Catholic liturgical tradition. The problem which we all see, in one way or another, is the problem of the account Barth gives of the unitary character of the revelatory event and our human experience of the irreducible plurality of things. There is a certain irony in this criticism. For Karl Barth came upon the theological scene as a self-proclaimed realist in a world of idealists, and as such made a deep appeal to a number of philosophically acute observers.[39] The criticisms which are passed in this book do not represent a return to one form or another of idealism; rather they raise the question whether

[39] Among them, Professor D. M. MacKinnon, whose inspiration as a theological teacher and friend all the authors of these essays wish warmly to acknowledge. On the philosphical influence of Barth on him as an undergraduate see his essay 'Philosophy and Christology', reprinted in *Borderlands of Theology* (London, 1968), pp. 55–81. See also P. G. Wignall, 'D. M. MacKinnon: An introduction his Early Theological Writings', *New Studies in Theology*, 1 (London, 1980).

Barth was enough of a realist. It is out of consistency with this standpoint that both Dr Roberts and Dr Williams question whether Barth is finally free of the constructivist urge characteristic of one deeply influenced by Hegel's pan-logism and his dialectical identification of the ideal with the actual. Those, therefore, whose interpretation of the contemporary theological situation leads them to stress the plasticity of the world to human perspective, and the capacity of man to respond to the Christian tradition in such a way as to see in it the potential for the enhancement of life, ought to derive no comfort from the mere fact that we are critical of Barth. It is, we believe with John Baillie, by working through Barth and not by going round him that a pathway exists to constructive contemporary theological endeavour; working through him, moreover, in a direction in which he endeavoured to point.

2

Barth on the Centre of Theology

S. W. SYKES

University of Durham

I

IN THIS essay the focus of attention will be upon Barth's writing on 'the centre of theology', an idea which he uses in the *Church Dogmatics*, and which repeatedly turns up at other points in his substantial literary output. When a major theologian takes the bother to write explicitly on the principle of the organization of his efforts ought, it seems to me, to be given careful analysis. So far as I am aware, this has not yet been done. Yet the tradition in which Barth stands in this talk of a 'centre' is long, complex, and fascinating, and provides useful insight into a thologian's basic methods.

Here, of course, all that can be done is to set Barth in relation to some of the other major writers of the past who have, in one way or another, provided answers to the question of the centre of theology (Section I); to review Barth's use of the idea before the writing of the *Dogmatics* (Section II); to analyse the sections of the *Dogmatics* where this idea is employed (Section III); and to offer a criticism of the position at which Barth has arrived (Section IV). That is to say, in this essay Barth's fundamental theological method is being taken at its face value, placed in context, analysed, and criticized, as though Barth himself had identified this method with complete accuracy. This is one way to read Barth, or, indeed any author who offers a view of his own basic intellectual procedures.

But there is another way, which is to attempt to penetrate beneath the surface and to trace ways of thinking or lines of argument which are not explicitly acknowledged or even recognized by the author as belonging to his principles of

method. Other chapters of this work pursue this latter course
and provide substantial analyses and interpretations of
Barth's theology, which depend to some degree on a distinction between what Barth says he is doing and what he does.
These different inquiries are obviously complementary, and it
will be possible in this chapter to provide signposts to the
investigations pursued at greater depth in other chapters;
here, to repeat, the crucial question is not whether Barth
actually carries out the method he prescribes, but rather *what*
he prescribes, and why, and, especially, whether it is a
satisfactory prescription.

The first question to ask is, obviously enough, why anyone
should bother to speak of a 'centre' to theology. It is not, after
all, a cabbage or a cricket ball, or a circle or other geometrical
figure. Why should it have a centre? Barth, who repeatedly
employs the term 'centre' (as do other modern theologians,
among them Ernst Käsemann), knows perfectly well that he is
using a metaphor. But it is important that we do not lose sight
of this simpleminded inquiry. Although theologians are not
the only ones to confuse themselves with their own metaphors,
it must be admitted that theological history contains numerous examples of thinkers being misled by the irrelevant
connotations of the metaphors they employ. The inquiry after
the 'centre' is, after all, a way of trying to identify the most
important element or elements in a particular intellectual
endeavour. Nevertheless, that which is most important is still
only relatively important—relative, that is, to the other parts
of the material. There is no good reason why what is most
important should consist of one point. On the contrary, there
is every reason to suppose that in an intellectual discipline,
such as theology, quite different sorts of things may be of
prime importance for different reasons. If one is not to be
misled by the metaphor of centrality, one must always be
ready to question any assumption that 'the centre' is singular.

There are two helpful ways of avoiding too rigid an
approach to the inquiry after a centre in theology. One is to
observe the variety of ways in which, in the New Testament,
certain things are picked out for special emphasis as fundamental. These turn out to be very different sorts of things, at
one moment Christ himself (1 Cor. 3:11–13), at another Peter

(Matt. 16:18) or the twelve apostles (Rev. 21:14, 19f.), and at another a series of doctrines regarded as elementary and which have to be put behind in the advance towards spiritual maturity (Heb. 5:11–6:3). It is at once evident that the term 'fundamental', which is another way of drawing attention to the relatively more important parts of the Christian tradition, is not being used in the same way on each occasion.

Or again, we could consider the diversity of ways in which the New Testament speaks of faith itself. Nothing remotely so sharply defined as a corpus of propositions to which the believer must assent appears in the literature, and the whole process of breaking out of darkness to walk in the light, or entering the kingdom, or yielding one's allegiance is a richly complex movement of heart and mind, resistant to acute simplification.

A further way of freeing oneself from rigidity in pursuit of a centre of theology is to pose the question of great theologians who did not express themselves in those terms. So far as I know, neither Thomas Aquinas, nor Luther, nor Calvin ever spoke of the centre of theology; all the more reason, therefore, for asking what they would have made of the idea. There are further advantages to be gained by prefacing the presentation of Barth's work on the subject with examples drawn from these three writers; since we find not merely that he himself writes in conscious dialogue with them, but also that their modern commentators are often conscious of the contemporary interest in identifying centres in the theological work of their authors and present their work in this light. For both of these reasons, we shall seek in this first section to elucidate the question—What is the centre of theology?—as it might have been answered respectively by Thomas Aquinas, by Luther, and by Calvin.

In the case of Thomas we could do no better than examine the first question of the *Summa*, namely, *de sacra doctrina, qualis sit et ad quae se extendat* (on what sort of teaching Christian theology is and what is covers). In this question he argued that Christian theology is a single science, that 'all things whatsoever that can be divinely revealed share in the same formal objective meaning' (*in una ratione formali*).[1] The unity of

---

[1] *Prima Pars*, 1, 3. Blackfriars edn., vol. 1 (London, 1964), pp. 12–15.

Christian theology is given precisely in the imprint on us of the divine knowing 'which is the single and simple vision of everything'. Hence what makes theology cohere is its necessary relation to God. *Omnia autem tractantur in sacra doctrina sub ratione dei* (all things are dealt with in holy teaching in terms of God); 'therefore God is truly the object of this science.'[2]

Although this is not talk about a centre of theology in so many words, it prescribes with brevity, and, as the *Summa* unfolds, with astonishing precision, the principle of cohesion in Thomas's theology. The theologian is not a collector of stray facts about the Word; he is not just a narrator of the events of salvation; he is one who disciplines his thought to the supreme effort of seeing things *sub ratione dei*, not in the sense of how they might appear to him, the theologian, in relation to God, but in such a way as actually to approximate to God's own knowledge in which we share by the beatific vision. The centre of theology is God, and the theologian strives to centre his theology in tracing the continuity between vision, faith, and reason, held together by their each being a *scientia*, sure, articulate, and intellectual knowledge about objective reality.

Fundamental, therefore, to the new kind of coherence Thomas gains for theology is the elaboration of a thorough explanation of what sort of knowing these different knowings are; and this is achieved solely by a new treatment of the theological doctrine of man. Where previously theologians had contented themselves with an account of the states of man—that is, successively, man before the Fall, man after the Fall, and man restored by grace—Thomas offers us an understanding of human nature as such, including a theory of cognition and an epistemology.[3] In other words, the coherence of the theologian's theology, centred upon God, lies in the elaboration of a doctrine of man, faithful to the scriptural analysis of his 'states', but going far beyond Scripture in philosophical penetration, a doctrine of man by which every

---

[2] *Prima Pars*, 1,7. Blackfriars edn., pp. 26–7. In commenting on this passage, Barth notes that Thomas Aquinas co-ordinates the effects of God's working in grace and nature, and thus fails to mean by *sub ratione dei* what Barth would gloss by *sub ratione verbi dei*, *CD* I/2, 866.

[3] Thus M. -D. Chenu, *Toward Understanding Saint Thomas* (Chicago, 1964), pp. 301–18. Compare the remark: 'That a system requires a science of human nature is not open to question,' (p. 317.)

aspect of the *scientia fidei* (the knowledge of faith) can be shown to cohere both with natural knowledge on the one hand, and the beatific vision on the other.

Barth's study of Book I of Thomas's *Summa* was serious[4] and his formulation of dissent from Thomas's position was careful and deliberate; though it should be noted that the adequacy of his understanding of Thomas has been repeatedly challenged.[5] Barth's failure to be persuaded by this version of the source of coherence in theology is due especially to his conviction that man, when truly perceptive of the grace of God, knows himself as contradicted. No realistic philosophizing about man which does not begin with this truth is, in his view, appropriate to its object. Whether Barth has returned to an earlier state of confusion and uncertainty, or whether he has mapped out a securer basis, or whether he has imported an unacknowledged source of coherence—that is a question for other essays in this volume. What at least is certain is that he has provided a different account of his own method, one which follows more closely the procedures of Luther and, expecially, Calvin, to both of whom we now turn.

In one sense Luther would have well understood the question as to the centre of theology. He is, after all, frequently to be found encapsulating the Gospel in some pithily-worded sentence. For example, in his Sermons on the Catechism of 1528, which present the 'elements and fundamentals of Christian knowledge', he says of the second article: 'The whole gospel is contained in this article, for the gospel is nothing else but the preaching of Christ, who was conceived, born . . .' (etc. etc.).[6] Attempts to express 'the whole gospel' in a brief statement are of very long standing in Christian instruction, from the New Testament onwards; and, as we shall see, Barth has views on the effect on theology of importing the distinction between fundamental and non-fundamental articles from catechetics into dogmatics. This, however, is not Luther's major contribution to the quest for a

---

[4] The Seminar of the winter Semester 1928–9 was spent on it, and Barth invited the Jesuit theologian, Erich Pryzywara (1889–1972), who taught at Munich to debate questions with him. Busch, p. 182f.

[5] See, above all, the third part of Hans Urs von Balthasar's, *Karl Barth* (Cologne, 1951).

[6] *Luther's Works*, vol. 51, Sermons : 1 (Philadelphia, 1959), p. 164.

centre in theology. It is one of Luther's modern interpreters, Gerhard Ebeling, who answers the question for us more penetratingly. Ebeling well understands the modern attempts which have been made to represent one particular idea (such as, repentance, love, the Kingdom of God, or whatever) as the centre of Luther's thought, or the principle by which his system was ordered. None of these proposals is successful, in his opinion, not even the popular but superficial view that Luther gave pride of place to justification by faith. He writes:

Christian faith [does not] of its nature require one to orientate oneself towards a particular idea, or even towards a profusion of specific ideas. Luther does in fact lay great weight upon the doctrine of justification, but his purpose is not to give preference to one Christian doctrine amongst many others, but to make possible a thorough approach to all Christian doctrines, or, to use more radical language, to make possible a proper treatment of all conceivable doctrine. The proper function of the doctrine of justification is that of giving a true significance to all other doctrines. But it can only be understood as Luther saw it if it is identical with what is implied by the distinction between the law and the gospel as the basic guiding principle of theological thought, and therefore as the decisive standard of theological judgement.[7]

The idea that the *distinction* between law and Gospel is the basic guiding principle is hard to grasp unless we realize with Luther that theology is not a self-sufficient enterprise, but one carried out in relation to *preaching* the Word of God. 'Christian preaching *is* the process in which the distinction between the law and the gospel takes place', the ground on which the issue between law and Gospel is joined and becomes ever and again actual.[8]

What Luther is saying, according to Ebeling, is that anything which is Christian Gospel, which, by definition, has actually brought about faith in God, honouring God as God, trust in him, self-abandonment to God, and freedom from oneself, has already thereby partaken of the distinction between law and Gospel. 'The understanding of the gospel as justification through the word alone, through faith alone, is

[7] G. Ebeling, *Luther* (London: Fontana edn., 1972), p. 113.
[8] Ibid., p. 117.

identical with the distinction between the law and the gospel, and to lose sight of the distinction between the law and the gospel is to lose sight of the pure gospel.'[9] One distinguishing feature of this view, and one which Barth adopted, as we shall see, in express disagreement with Adolf von Harnack, is the close relationship established with the occurrence of preaching. Preacher and theologian alike stand faced with the impossibility of speaking of God; for both alike the only possibility of doing so is rooted in the power of the resurrection. 'Jesus Christ in the power of His resurrection is present wherever men really speak really of God.'[10] Barth's clarification of his relationship to Luther on this point is of far-reaching consequence, involving as it does the affirmation of the freedom of God, of revelation, and of faith over against all human talk of God (themes further expounded in Dr Williams's essay). And this, as we shall see, brings Barth to the point of asserting as a principle of his thought a particular view about theology's centre.

It is again a modern commentator who understands the interest we have in the question as to the centre of theology in relation to the work of Calvin. François Wendel comments that it is only with great reservation that we can speak of a 'system' in Calvin's *Institutio* at all, 'because of the plurality of themes that impose themselves simultaneously upon its author's thinking'. He continues:

It is because they have failed to realise this, that the majority of historians have tried to reconstruct the Calvinist dogmatic from the standpoint of one central idea supposed to dominate it as a whole. For a long while, as we know, predestination was held to be that idea. Some proposed to discard this in favour of the Glory of God; others exchanged it for the sovereignty of God, or even for eschatology. Still more recently the divinity of Jesus Christ has been presented as the central thesis of Calvinism . . . But this is not the central idea of his system from which all the rest of it could be deduced . . . It would be better, we think, to confess that Calvin's is not a closed system elaborated around a central idea, but that it

[9] Ibid., p. 122.

[10] *CD I/2*, 752. In this context, Barth discusses the apparently appalling claim of Luther that a preacher must not say the Lord's Prayer, nor ask forgiveness of sins, when he has preached (if he is a true preacher), but must boldly say, *Haec dixit dominus* (ibid., p. 747.)

draws together, one after another, a whole series of Biblical ideas, some of which can only with difficulty be logically reconciled.[11]

The reason for these paradoxes, as Wendel calls them is not far to seek. They arise precisely out of Calvin's fidelity to Scripture; 'one could even say that his fidelity is proved by the fact that he allowed them to remain.'[12] The *Institutio* is a very different sort of literature from Thomas's *Summa*, and the reason lies in the fact that Calvin regarded the *Institutio* and the commentaries on Scripture as complementary to each other. In Calvin's prefatory Letter to the Reader of 1539 he states that his intention in the work was to provide a statement of 'the sum of religion in all its parts', such that a student of Scripture would the more easily be able both to know what to look for and to relate its different parts to each other.[13] When Calvin says he wishes to arrange his material 'systematically' (*ordine*), he means that he intends his book to present the *loci theologici*, the theological topics, which together comprise the sum of Christianity's content.

This theological method was first employed in Protestant theology by the German Reformer, Melanchthon, explicitly on the basis of Aristotelian method. Melanchthon's *Loci communes rerum theologicarum* of 1521 is intended as a collection of basic concepts (such as Law, Sin, Grace, the Sacraments, and so forth) in which the discipline of theology is comprehended. As compared with Melanchthon, however, who pursued his method even in his commentaries, Calvin proposes that the method of the *Institutio* (which is that of a suitable arrangement of *Loci communes*, without long exegetical excurses) shall differ from the method of the commentaries (which centres solely upon the text). Both are complementary; neither is a dispensable preparation for, or amplification of, the other.[14]

If this is truly Calvin's method, then there is indeed no central theological doctrine. The commentaries pursue their

[11]   F. Wendel, *Calvin* (London: Fontana edn., 1965), pp. 357 f.
[12]   Ibid., p. 359.
[13]   Cited by T. H. L. Parker, *Calvin's New Testament Commentaries* (London, 1971), p. 53. Revised for the 1559 edition; see *Institutes of the Christian Religion*, vol. I (LCC edn., London, 1961), pp. 4f.
[14]   See Parker, pp. 51ff.

way relentlessly through every verse of Scripture, because in the understanding of the text lies the opportunity of understanding the mind of the Spirit who inspires it. The *Institutio* gathers and arranges what in Scripture is scattered and occasional, helping the commentator to a perspective on the whole in the context of which he can set his understanding of each particular. Now it is highly significant for the purposes of this essay that Barth explicitly states that Melanchthon's and Calvin's method of *Loci* 'is the only truly scholarly method in dogmatics' (*CD* I/2, 820), and this for the reason that it alone makes clear that the basic dogmatic tenets derive from no higher source of systematization than from the Word of God itself. Barth's 'rediscovery' of Calvin is well known. In 1921 as he began his professional activity, he was directed to lecture on the Reformed tradition. This necessarily involved him in a more thorough study of the Reformed confessions than he had previously undertaken; and he naturally found himself devoting a series of lectures to Calvin himself. Of the experience of immersing himself in Calvin he wrote, 'I just don't have the organs, the suction cups, even to assimilate this phenomenon, let alone to describe it properly.' (Busch, p. 138.) Forty years later he was able to say: 'Unlike Luther, Calvin was not a genius, but a conscientious exegete . . . He is a good teacher, of a kind which has been rare in the church—who does not hand over to an understanding reader the results of his study, but asks him to take it up and discover new results in his footsteps.' (Busch, p. 439.) Consistent with this acknowledgement of Calvin's influence is Barth's conviction which we are to examine, that while there is a centre in theology, there is no central doctrine, concept, or idea. Furthermore, it explains why Barth so decisively seeks to break with the hundred-year-long tradition of relating the writing of dogmatic theology to a definition of the 'essence of Christianity'.

However, the matter is not quite finished. For we can very well ask of Calvin a further question about his view of man. Is there anything in his work which corresponds to Thomas's theological doctrine of man, or to Luther's distinction between law and Gospel? It seems that if there is an answer to this question it lies in Calvin's understanding of faith as knowledge. Faith, Calvin says in the *Institutio*, is 'a firm and sure

knowledge of God's benevolence towards us, founded upon
the truth of the freely given promise in Christ, both revealed to
our minds and sealed upon our hearts by the Holy Spirit'.[15]
Commenting on this, Professor Torrance asserts that Calvin
means that, through the Spirit, we are carried beyond the
cognitive forms we bring with us in our attempt to understand
God.[16] This is what Torrance calls the epistemological relevance of the Holy Spirit, the fact that it is through the action
of the Spirit alone that the Word of God, the text of the
Scriptures, becomes for us a 'firm and sure knowledge of God';
that in the human documents, set forth in human thoughts
and language as befits the poverty and crudity of the human
mind (man's rude and stupid wit),[17] man is addressed by
God, and is enabled to set out on the road leading to the
blessed life, which is a resting in the knowledge of God.[18] Just
how important this view is for Barth we shall come in due
course to see. It is sufficient for the moment to remark on the
combination of two features; first, the consistency of this
position with the essentially unsystematic character of the *Loci*
method, and, secondly, the strength of the claim made for real
knowledge of God. When we find Barth making what, to
modern ears, sound like extremely strong claims for statements which, again to modern ears, sound contradictory, and
resisting the obvious demands to drop one or other in the
interests of systematic consistency, we shall be correct in
seeing in Calvin his principal precursor, though it remains the
case that he develops the epistemological basis more explicitly
and with greater thoroughness.

II

Barth's treatment of dogmatic method, which contains his
answer to the question about the centre of theology and which

[15] *Institutes* III, ii, 7. LCC edn., vol. i, p. 551.

[16] 'Our forms of thought and speech are opened up and reshaped from an objective
ground in God'; so that just as all scientific constructs or theories have to be kept
'infinitely open' if they are to serve advances in knowledge, so 'through the Spirit we
are cast upon the inexhaustible Reality of God in an infinite depth of objectivity.'
(*Theology in Reconstruction* (London, 1965), p. 96.) The comparison with scientific
method emphatically turns the interpretation of Calvin in the direction of Torrance's
own engagement with Barth's revolution in theological methodology.

[17] *Institutes* I, xi, 7. LCC edn., vol, i, p. 99.

[18] *Institutes* I, v, 1. LCC edn., vol. i, pp. 51f.

we are to examine, is found in the second half-volume of the *Doctrine of the Word of God*, and was published in German in 1938. The twenty years of public theological activity before that time contain, as one might expect, a number of observations on theological method of considerable importance if the story of the evolution of his thought were to be fully told. Of these we shall examine only two occurrences, Barth's controversy with Harnack, and his depiction of and self-differentiation from Schleiermacher. The first is a relatively self-contained episode, issuing in a public exchange of letters in 1923 and hardly important, except illustratively, thereafter.[19] It is a somewhat painful event, involving the separation of master and pupil, and demonstrating, as other of Barth's controversies do, a certain unwillingness to express the points at issue with maximum analytic clarity. But for our purposes it is a valuable moment, since both Harnack and Barth speak of 'the centre of the gospel' in sharply contrasting ways.

The principal subject of dispute was the nature of academic theology. Harnack, who had been one of Barth's most revered teachers during his student days at Berlin, had increasingly found Barth's new style of theology impossibly enthusiastic, and had likened him, in a review of *Romans*, to Thomas Münzer (Busch, 113). In the correspondence, which Harnack opened, without great premeditation in January of 1923, he posed the 'despisers of scientific theology' fifteen questions, the fourteenth of which read:

If the person of Jesus Christ stands at the centre of the gospel, how else can the basis for reliable and communal knowledge of this person be gained but through critical-historical study so that an imagined Christ is not put in place of the real one? What else besides scientific theology is able to undertake this study?[20]

Barth's answer contained the following sentences:

The reliability and communality of the knowledge of the person of Jesus Christ as the centre of the gospel can be none other than that of God-awakened *faith*. Critical-historical study signifies the

---

[19] Published in H. Martin Rumscheidt, *Revelation and Theology, An Analysis of the Barth–Harnack Correspondence of 1923* (Cambridge, 1972).
[20] Op. cit., p. 31

deserved and necessary end of *those* 'foundations' of this knowledge which are no foundations at all since they have not been laid by God himself.[21]

Both the question and its answer turn on the relationship, which is still a matter of acute controversy, between historical reconstruction of the circumstances of Jesus' ministry and teaching, the standpoint of the resurrection *vis-à-vis* the whole of New Testament theology, and the discipline of dogmatic or systematic theology. Harnack, finding himself in the uneasy position of a moderate, caught between conservatives who refused critical methods, and radicals who used critical methods to reach theologically destructive conclusions, argued that historical criticism was the ally of a constructive theology which, if not orthodox by the (to him obsolete) standards of pre-critical eras, was an intellectually sound basis for a modern Christian. In his famous *History of Dogma*, and the lectures on the Essence of Christianity, he had bent all his powers as a scholar to the task of using the material thrown up by the history of the Christian tradition as a source from which to distil the very heart of religion, which was, he believed, none other than the essence of Christianity.[22] This essence was the Gospel itself, its centre was Jesus Christ, and it was comprehensible by wise and simple alike, provided only that there was an inner, spiritual openness to receive the truth. Waspishly Barth protested:

What I must defend myself against is not historical criticism but rather the foregone conclusiveness with which—and this is charac-teristic also of your present statements—the task of the theology is *emptied*, that is to say, the way in which a so-called 'simple gospel', discovered by historical criticism *beyond* the 'Scriptures' and *apart from* the 'Spirit', is given the place which the Reformers accorded to the 'Word' (the correlation of 'Scripture' and 'Spirit').[23]

The disagreement between Harnack and Barth as to the meaning of the centrality of the person of Jesus Christ is many-sided. But its most obvious source is a disagreement as to content. Where for Harnack, Jesus Christ is the centre

---

[21] Op. cit., p. 35

[22] Agnes von Zahn–Harnack, *Adolf von Harnack* (Berlin, 1951), p. 104, cited by Rumscheidt, op. cit., p. 133.

[23] Op. cit. p. 42.

primarily as the teacher of the Gospel, and secondarily as its personal exemplification, for Barth the doctrine of the Incarnation is primary. The Gospel is an action of its content, and the Scriptures bear witness to the genuine novelty of the fact that the Word became flesh, died, and rose again. 'The historical reality of Christ (as revelation, as "centre of the gospel") is not "the historical Jesus" . . . [but] the Christ who is *witnessed to* as the risen one.'[24] Of this centre Barth denies that there is any direct historical comprehension. Acceptance of the witness is by faith, worked in us by the Holy Spirit—here Barth appeals directly to both Luther and Calvin—a working to be distinguished from all immanent potentialities of the human spirit, including, and especially, its alleged capacity for 'religious experience'. Harnack's supposedly scientific theology, Barth terms 'spectator theology', and regards it as basically estranged from its own essence.

But perhaps the most significant of Barth's attempts to account for the contrast between his and Harnack's approaches to theology is to be found in his repeated insistence that for him the *object* of theology is determinative of the method, not vice versa, as he believed had become the case since the Enlightenment and Schleiermacher. This reversal had already been a theme of an address given in 1919, where he had spoken of the unhelpful domination of recent theology by considerations of formal types of godliness in religious experience. Religious experience, however, is not adequate to the new truth of the Incarnation. 'No mental apprehension of the *form* of this truth, however subtle that apprehension may be, can replace or obscure the true transcendence of its *content*.' (*WW*, 286.) The disagreement with Harnack as to content has, therefore, fundamental implications as to methodology, the precise working out of which was to occupy him for some years to come.

The second occurrence illustrating an important element of Barth's development of an answer to the question of the centre of theology is his process of self-differentiation from Schleiermacher. Unlike the separation from Harnack, this is very far from being merely an episode in Barth's intellectual pilgrimage. From the moment he came to believe that the idea of

[24] Op. cit. p. 46.

'religious experience' and of 'religion' itself was vulnerable to theological criticism, it was apparent that he would have to set himself against Schleiermacher's legacy. Schleiermacher he himself began to study intensively as soon as he took up his first academic appointment in 1921. In 1928 Barth published two essays on Schleiermacher written in 1924 and 1926. In 1932 to 1933 he gave a course on the history of Protestant theology, which was eventually published after the war in 1946, and which included a revised treatment of Schleiermacher. The *Church Dogmatics* contain numerous references to Schleiermacher's work in a variety of its aspects, and in 1968 he summed up his fifty-year-long engagement in a delightful essay published as a *Nachwort* to a collection of extracts from Schleiermacher's work.[25]

Schleiermacher is one of the theologians who gave a strong impetus to the tradition of defining the essence of Christianity, and using the definition as a way of holding Christian theology true to itself. The essence of Christianity for Schleiermacher was redemption through Jesus of Nazareth; by 'redemption' Schleiermacher means the passage of a man from a condition of bondage to a higher self-consciousness, a new condition of liberation. Implicit in the definition is Schleiermacher's thesis about the nature of man.

In the second edition of his *Christian Faith* (1830) Schleiermacher builds up in his hundred-page Introduction a method for his dogmatics rooted in a theory of human religiosity. This preparatory material, which includes a wide-ranging series of 'borrowings' from related disciplines (such as philosophical psychology, what amounts to the sociology of religion, and the philosophy of religions), amounts in effect to a theological anthropology. In other words, the theological understanding of man, including a theory of cognition and an epistemology for which he is to a degree dependent on contemporary philosophy once again become the source of coherence in the strictly doctrinal sections.

Not surprisingly Barth sees the proposal as a version of the error of Roman Catholic dogmatics, that is, the attempt to articulate a way of knowing which is apart from or above the work of dogmatics. Against Schleiermacher specifically, he

[25] H. Bolli (ed.), *Schleiermacher–Auswahl* (Munich, 1968).

affirms that there is no possibility of a prolegomenon to dogmatics which is not itself part of dogmatics. Schleiermacher's understanding of piety, the higher self-consciousness, and the Church as a fellowship for the purposes of promoting piety, are all of them (contrary to Schleiermacher's belief that they do not constitute part of dogmatics), highly dogmatic utterances with their origins in English Congregationalism—and in that sense heretical dogmatics.[26] The only proper way is to integrate the apparently formal prolegomena with the material of the subsequent sections. For Barth this means that the whole doctrine of the Trinity and the essentials of Christology are particularly involved. 'We cannot pose the question of formal dogma without immediately entering at these central points upon material dogma. Indeed what is thought to be formal dogma is itself highly material in fact.' (*CD* I/1, 44.)

It will be observed that Barth's objection to Schleiermacher at this point is not to what he has done, but to what he has *said* he has done. Schleiermacher was in fact, according to Barth, deceived in thinking that his prolegomena were non-dogmatic, when they were, as they should have been, dogmatic—that is, integrally related to the content of Christian theology. It says much for the quality and breadth of Barth's mind that he repeatedly re-examined this aspect of Schleiermacher's work. From the lectures of 1932 to 1933 up to the essay of 1968, when he declared himself finally undecided on the question, Barth carefully considered whether Schleiermacher's understanding of man which informed his whole view of piety and religion could not in fact be regarded as a way of making the doctrine of the Holy Spirit central to dogmatics (*PT*, 459). We shall briefly take up the question for the light it sheds on Barth's understanding of the centre of theology.

[26] *CD* I/1, 38. This fascinating conjecture refers expressly to Articles 20, 23, and 24 of the Platform of the Savoy Declaration of 1658, but, so far as I know, there is no documentary evidence in Schleiermacher's work to support it. Schleiermacher's inclination towards Congregationalism is quite apparent in the speeches *On Religion*, and no doubt Moravian ecclesiology has Congregationalist leanings. Barth's attitude to English Congregationalism had changed by 1948, when, in an address to the Amsterdam Assembly of the World Council of Churches he specifically commended this movement as 'too little noticed' and 'too quickly rejected'. (K. Barth, *God Here and Now* (London, 1964), p. 84.)

Barth interpreted Schleiermacher's whole approach to Christian theology in terms of what he called 'the principle of the centre' which he, Barth, found profoundly influential in Romantic thought from Herder and Novalis. According to this principle, the function of a proper view of the world is to overcome irreconcilable contradictions by identifying and embracing the truth which lies in the middle, at the point of peace and reconciliation. In feeling itself there is peace and reconciliation between the infinite and the finite; it is, moreover, 'the victorious centre between knowledge and action' (*PT*, 454), and piety, the essence of which is feeling, is the centre of all religion whatsoever. Barth has no doubt that, for Schleiermacher, man determined by pious self-awareness is 'the central subject of his theological thought'. But this centre is not undifferentiated; it contains within it, as a kind of secondary motif, the reference to the revelation of God in Christ. This is what distinguishes Schleiermacher's theology from pure metaphysics or mysticism. Barth finds Schleiermacher guilty of an inversion; where the Reformers taught a doctrine of the Word of God in correlation with faith as the work of the Holy Spirit in man, Schleiermacher reverses the order, putting man and faith first. But that does not necessarily mean that a proper theology, taking the Holy Spirit as its starting-point, could not be built up on the basis of this reversal. And Barth recognizes Schleiermacher's intention to make the reference to revelation a second centre alongside his original one (*PT*, 460). The ambiguity about whether Schleiermacher's is, in Barth's eyes, a legitimate theological endeavour arises from the fact that Schleiermacher, true to his principle of mediation, did not really want to grant that there might be both an Incarnation of the Word and an outpouring of the Holy Spirit in the faith of the believer. The tendency, therefore, of his thought is to seek to turn these two centres of his theology into a single centre dominated by the notion of a 'higher life' of pious self-awareness, constituting the true essence of humanity (*PT*, 464).

The contribution of this continuous wrestling with Schleiermacher has not yet been given a fully sophisticated assessment. I shall suggest that, in a sense other than that in which he defined it, Barth did not himself escape from the powerful attraction of the Romantic 'principle of the centre'. Moreover, Barth's very determination to remove all traces of ambiguity from his own methodology, making the content of dogmatics wholly determinative for its formal method, leaves in its wake a whole trail of unanswered questions. But, there can be no question of the very great penetration of the analysis of the enigmatic structure of Schleiermacher's theological system; and from this engagement Barth's own work has profited considerably.

III

We come now to the presentation and analysis of Barth's explicit treatment of the question of a centre of theology. In the first place we must notice that he differentiates himself from two earlier traditions of theological thought which appear to be striving for the same objective, namely the tradition which defines the fundamental articles of the Christian faith (later Protestant orthodoxy) and the neo-Protestant attempt to define the essence of Christianity. The former tradition he sees as a departure from the greatly to be preferred method of *Loci*, practised, as we have seen, by Melanchthon and Calvin. Barth's objection is to the attempt to identify a *fundamentum dogmaticum*, a structure of formulae set up 'in a sort of aseity' above other dogmas, articles, and formulae.[27] This involves distinctions between primary, secondary, and non-fundamental articles of faith which are artificial and arbitrary.

Once the doctrine of *articuli fundamentales* was recognised, who or what was to stop the Pietists and Rationalists of the early 18th century from drawing the line of demarcation between fundamental and non-fundamental very differently from the older generation, in accordance with their different views? What still looked most imposing in Quenstedt and Turretini was to end one day in the thin formulae by which later Neo-Protestantism thought it could grasp the so-called 'essence of Christianity'. We ought never to have entered that path. (*CD* I/2, 866.)

The true objection to the identification of *articuli fundamen-*

---

[27] For the discussion of A. Quenstedt's distinction between the *fundamentum fidei substantiale*, the *fundamentum organicum*, and the *fundamentum dogmaticum*, see *CD* I/2, 863f.

tales is even more remarkable than this quotation suggests. The fundamental articles proposed by orthodox dogmaticians of the late seventeenth century were anything but 'thin formulae'. What Barth objects to is, in fact, the principle of making such a choice, 'because it involves a definition, limitation and restriction of the Word of God', which itself must be left entirely free. 'In dogmatics we cannot presume to know and declare in advance, as a more than hypothetical certainty, what is and what is not fundamental.' 'Traditional notions as to what is fundamental or not, central or peripheral, more or less important, have to be suspended, so that they can become a matter for vital new decision by the Word of God itself.' (*CD* I/2, 865.)

Now this is very striking. Barth does not dispute that, for the purposes of confession, a Church at a particular time and place makes (and is bound to make) a selection from the wealth and diversity of the biblical witness—he writes, it must be remembered, in the testing circumstances of 1938. Nor does he dispute that dogmatics must pay due respect to Church confession, and also be the confession of the individual theologian. To this extent selection is unavoidable, and selection means the distinguishing of more important from less important. Dogmatics itself, however, is not a confession of a Church or of an individual, but a confronting of the Church's proclamation with the Word of God. In this way Barth puts the theologian in the position of *having* to claim that the dogmatics he writes is subject to, and the result of, a new divine initiative, a decision of the Word of God himself. He may not shelter behind the statement that the fundamental truths of doctrine have been irrevocably and unalterably revealed; nor may he, with a show of modesty, merely claim that he is offering his own view of the matter. He must claim, and clearly seek to make good his claim by constant reference to the Scriptures, that in his work the Word of God is itself newly challenging the Church's proclamation. Preoccupation with 'mere creeds and dogmas' is not a substitute for this living, open relationship to the Word of God. Barth's self-differentiation from the tradition of high dogmatic orthodoxy is, by intention at least, far-reaching and profound.

Similarly far-reaching, on the other side, is his rejection of the neo-Protestant method of essence-definition, which reached a pinnacle of confusion and controversy in the discussion of Harnack's celebrated lectures, *What is Christianity?*.[28] Barth's objection to the thin formula of the so-called, simple Gospel, we have already examined. But even in the case of definitions of the essence more closely faithful to the doctrine of the Incarnation than was Harnack's, Barth finds difficulty, the same difficulty of methodological arbitrariness as he found in the case of the tradition of fundamental articles. 'A dogmatic system', he roundly declares, 'is in any case an impractical idea, because in it it is not the Word of God but the presupposed fundamental view of things that will become the object of dogmatics.' (*CD* I/2, 861.)

The Word of God may not be replaced even vicariously by any basic interpretation of the 'essence of Christianity', however pregnant, deep, and well founded. The simple reason for this is that while its content is indeed the truth, it is the truth of the reality of the work and activity of God taking place within it. As such it is not to be condensed and summarized in any view, or idea, or principle (*CD* I/2, 862).

The objection to a theological system, dominated by an *a priori* principle of interpretation, comes here to expression. It is part of what we have already seen to be Barth's objection to the domination of content by form, characteristic of neo-Protestant dogmatics. It is illustrated by Schleiermacher's tendency, as Barth sees it, to allow the 'centre' of his theology to be determined, not by revelation (in the form of Trinitarian doctrine, centred on the Holy Spirit) but by the human possibility of religious self-consciousness.

In contrast to these rejected alternatives, Barth's own positive view has to do with what he once referred to as the *Centrum Paulinum*, in a reference to the eighteenth-century Pietist, J. A. Bengel. 'Faith, therefore, is never identical with "piety", however pure and however delicate . . . Faith lives of its own, because it lives of God.' (*ER*, 40.) The methodological revolution which Barth hoped to accomplish could only be achieved by an account of faith radically different from that

[28] See, on Troeltsch's response to the questions of method involved, my essay 'Troeltsch on Christianity's Essence' in J. P. Clayton (ed.), *Troeltsch and the Future of Theology* (Cambridge, 1976), pp. 139–71.

offered by the liberal Protestants, who, in the interests of a 'scientific' treatment of theology, were in danger of assimilating it to some general category of human, especially religious, experience. As compared with the terms of our reference to the *Summa* of Thomas Aquinas, Barth's understanding of the *scientia fidei* was to embody a radical disjunction between all forms of natural knowing and the knowledge which is by faith.

At this point we must simply emphasize the fundamental importance for the whole of Barth's work of the argument about theological rationality which he conducts in his book on Anselm. In a well-known sentence in the Preface to the second edition he complains that most of his critics had failed to see that here he was working with 'a vital key, if not the key, to an understanding of that whole process of thought that has impressed me more and more in my *Church Dogmatics* as the only one proper to theology' (*FQI*, 11). In a section on the 'manner' of theology, Barth is attempting to expound the meaning of understanding, *intellectus*. Observing that Anselm speaks of God himself as, in himself, *ratio veritatis*, ultimate Truth, he argues that all other forms of rationality are bestowed by God. Thus to know, rationally, an object in the creation is to know it in accordance with a prior decision of the truth, God himself (*FQI*, 46). This condition applies above all to the rationality of faith. Here, so Barth argues, divine decision enters, not simply as to whether the object of faith is the *ratio veritatis*, but whether it can be recognized as such. (In so far as the *ratio* of the object of faith and the use which man makes of his capacity to think and judge conform to Truth (by virtue of Truth's own decision) its true rationality is determined and the *intellectus* that is sought occurs.' (*FQI*, 47.)

This claim, of course, places man in at once an extremely weak and an extremely strong position; weak, inasmuch as he can only await a decision by the Truth to reveal itself (hence the relationship of knowledge to grace and to prayer), and strong, inasmuch as once the Truth has been revealed, then it is not seen as a human invention or creation but as something which could not be conceived of otherwise. That last fact is expounded with considerable obscurity and compression in a series of propositions about the relation of 'ontic necessity' (the impossibility of the object of faith being other than it is) to 'noetic necessity' (the impossibility for thought to conceive the object of faith as not existing or existing differently) (*FQI*, 49ff.). Barth summarizes the propositions himself in the following way: 'The "rational" knowledge of the object of faith is derived from the object of faith and not *vice versa*. That means to say that the object of faith and its knowledge are ultimately derived from Truth, that is, from God and from his will.' (*FQI*, 52.)

The same conviction can be put—indeed must be put—autobiographically, as it is by Professor T. F. Torrance in the Preface to his work, *Theological Science*. Torrance states: 'I find the presence and being of God bearing upon my experience and thought so powerfully that I cannot but be convinced of His overwhelming reality and rationality. To doubt the existence of God would be an act of sheer irrationality, for it would mean that my reason had become unhinged from its bond with real being.'[29] Theological activity, is thus strictly scientific and rational when it seeks to allow 'God's own eloquent self-evidence to sound through to us in His Logos so that we may know and understand Him out of His own rationality and under the determination of His divine being'.[30]

A conviction of the quality of 'self-evidence' is, none the less, faith, even if it is faith under authority; 'faith', says Barth, 'is always "faith under authority".' (*FQI*, 48.) In the movement towards true rationality in theological matters faith under authority is a stage on the one divine road to attaining knowledge by reason alone (*FQI*, 48). When Anselm proposes to probe the *rationem fidei* he is trying, says Barth, to construe this necessity, this impossibility that the object of faith might not exist or might exist otherwise than it does. That the object of faith has such a basis that it is impossible for it not to exist or to exist differently is for him given in revelation and is certain in faith. His starting-point is therefore not to seek 'what can be' but to seek 'what is' and in fact to seek 'what cannot fail to be'. It is precisely as 'what cannot fail to be' that he tries to conceive 'what is'. Corresponding to the basis in

---

[29] *Theological Science* (London, 1969), p. ix.
[30] Ibid.

faith there has to be a reason in knowledge; to the ontic a corresponding noetic necessity (*FQI*, 52).

The cruciality of this argument is obvious enough, and is equally stressed in the other essays in this volume. Knowledge, whose truth and rationality shines in its own light and which must simply be acknowledged when made plain is an overwhelming experience; and a Christian who claims to speak in the light of this knowledge is, at least, interesting. Barth speaks of the event of such knowing as happening from time to time; but also of it as happening to some extent, *aliquatenus* (*FQI*, 47). That is to say, it is conceivable that even one subjectively convinced of the self-evident quality of the truth which has grasped him may yet not, in practice, have seen more than part of the whole. No third party is obliged, merely on hearing the strong claim made, to accept or reject it *in toto*. It may indeed be the right kind of claim to make, inasmuch as it focuses attention on the object of theology, rather than on the knowing subject—but no third party is thereby delivered from making a judgement for himself about the extent to which the truth has been correctly recognized.

The question of the responsibility of any third party on hearing imposing statements about the self-evident character of theological truth is commonly, and rightly, connected with the function of tradition and the Church. The authority of the individual *credo* and of the Church's *Credo* is indissolubly linked, as Barth acknowledges it in Anselm himself (*FQI*, 27). The Creed of the Church is the very rock on which the Church itself is built; the soundest way of refuting an error is to refer the question to the Pope himself (*FQI*, 23). Although, as Barth notes, we are not, in the eleventh century dealing with a modern Roman Catholic concept of ecclesial authority, none the less 'Anselm's subjective *credo* has an objective *Credo* of the Church as its unimpeachable point of reference—that is, a number of propositions formulated in human words' (*FQI*, 24.)

We are, to be sure, in a different atmosphere in Volumes One and Two of the *Church Dogmatics*. Although the influence of the argument attributed to Anselm is everywhere apparent, there is a constant criticism of preoccupation with 'mere creeds and dogmas', which represents a substantial departure from Anselm himself, and necessarily too, an increased reliance on the personal and contemporary aspect of God's revelatory activity. Although Barth often affirms that past traditions, including the Creeds and dogmatic definitions of the early Church, must be treated with respect, literally nothing must be allowed to impede the freedom of the Word. Obedience to the Word brooks no competitor. There is no final propositional security. The objective *Credo* of the Church lies hidden in the inexpressible depth of the Truth of God himself, to which dogma can only approximate.

We have reached, it seems, an impasse. On the one hand, confident *a priori* formulations of the fundamentals of dogmatics or of the essence of Christianity have been criticized for their usurpation of the position accorded to the Word of God; on the other, emphatic denials have been issued of the possibility of doing conceptual justice to the reality of divine revelation. But this is precisely the position on the centre of theology which Barth wishes to maintain. In accurate correspondence with the position outlined in his methodological sections, Barth opens the fourth volume of the *Church Dogmatics*, which deals with the doctrine of reconciliation, with the following words:

1. God with us

We enter that sphere of Christian knowledge in which we have to do with the heart of the message received by and laid upon the Christian community and therefore with the heart of the Church's dogmatics: that is to say, with the heart of its subject-matter, origin and content. It has a circumference, the doctrine of creation and the doctrine of the last things, the redemption and consummation. But the covenant fulfilled in the atonement is its centre. From this point we can and must see a circumference. But we can see it only from this point. A mistaken or deficient perception here would mean error or deficiency everywhere. (*CD* IV/1, 3.)

Here Barth accepts the logic of his position that the Word of God itself determines the stance of the faithful theologian. The standpoint of the theologian cannot, therefore, be a matter of indifference. The proposition standing at the head of the paragraph states that the content of the message received and proclaimed by the Christian community is 'the free act of the faithfulness of God in which he takes the lost cause of men . . . and makes it his own in Jesus Christ'. This act of God is the centre of theology; and about it we must make four points.

(1) Barth strives to make clear a distinction between the idea of a real or actual centre of dogmatics, and a systematic centre. A systematic centre would be an idea or a principle, which would then govern the presentation of the whole, in the sense that all other parts would be related to it as either presuppositions or consequences. But such systematization is, he holds, illegitimate. By contrast the Atonement must be said to be the actual or real centre, in the sense that it is a report about the act, and hence the being, of God.

The whole being and life of God is an activity, both in eternity and in worldly time, both in Himself as Father, Son and Holy Spirit, and in His relation to man and all creation. But what God does in Himself and as the Creator and Governor of man is all aimed at the particular act in which it has its centre and meaning. And everything that He wills has its ground and origin in what is revealed as His will in this one act. (*CD* IV/1, 7.)

The centrality of the Atonement is thus not the centrality of a doctrine of the Atonement, but the centrality of the act of Atonement in which God is God. From the above quotation two things are clear; first, that there is a narrative to be rehearsed in which God's act in Atonement is told (as Dr Ford expounds it), and secondly, that there is a thesis to be explored which relates the time of the act to the eternity in which God is God, in and for himself (as Dr Roberts makes clear).

(2) We must link what is said here about the centrality of the covenant fulfilled in the Atonement to what is said, and presupposed, everywhere in Barth's works about Christology.

A church dogmatics must, of course, be christologically determined as a whole and in all its parts, as surely as the revealed Word of God, attested by Holy Scripture and proclaimed by the Church, is its one and only criterion, and as surely as this revealed Word is identical with Jesus Christ. If dogmatics cannot regard itself and cause itself to be regarded as fundamentally Christology, it has assuredly succumbed to some alien sway and is already on the verge of losing its character as church dogmatics. (*CD* I/2, 123.)

By 'christologically determined' Barth does not mean what is sometimes meant by the term 'Christocentric', which is applicable to Schleiermacher, Ritschl, and even to Harnack. 'One cannot subsequently speak christologically, if Christology has not already been presupposed at the outset'—this is Barth's way of attempting to guarantee not merely incarnational Christology, but also that Jesus Christ is Way, Truth, and Life, the *ratio fidei* as well as the *ratio veritatis*.[31] This 'necessity', as we have seen Barth speak of it in his examination of Anselm, has to include a statement about the Christology of the New Testament. That the eternal Word of God chose to assume human nature, in order as very God and very man, to become the Word of reconciliation, is said to be 'the sole point in which New Testament witness originates' (*CD* I/2, 124). But this is not a statement we can derive or prove from some higher standpoint, for example from the standpoint of historical science, as Barth's opposition to Harnack's contention has shown. Ultimately this is not a denial that there might be, or is, a variety of Christologies in the New Testament. The variety is, on the contrary, testimony to the one reality which constitutes the mystery of revelation.

It can scarcely be denied, at this point, that Barth is led into the midst of Christological *doctrine*; that is, that there are specific Christological theses, which he defends and others which he opposes. Barth's argument demands a special Christology, which, although it is comparatively unspecific compared with the degree to which two-nature Christology was eventually developed in the post-patristic era, is none the less identifiably non-Docetic, non-Ebionistic, and non-Arian. But if this is the case then surely a doctrine has determined the dogmatics? Can it be said by Barth that the Christological determination of all dogmatics does not constitute its determination by a specific Christological doctrine? That, surely, would amount to the very systematization which he wishes to avoid. There are signs that he would prefer to be able to continue to insist that the centre of theology is not a theological doctrine. For example, he writes that all Christologies

[31] 'Die Grundformen theologischen Denkens' (1936), republished in *Theologische Fragen und Antworten* (Zurich, 1957), pp. 282ff. There is a brief account of this essay in T. F. Torrance, *Karl Barth: An Introduction to His Early Theology, 1910–1931* (London, 1962), pp. 195ff.

which are other than the incarnationist one he articulates
constitute a transformation of Christology into a non-mystery,
which has nothing in common with revelation (*CD* I/2, 124f.
and 132). Or again, he suggests that dogmatics as a whole is
Christology, understood in the most comprehensive sense (*CD*
I/2, 883). These two examples show that Barth would prefer
to be able to avoid the suggestion that a specific Christological
doctrine informs and underlies his work by the devastating
tactic of stating that dogmatics as a whole is Christology, and
what is not Christology in this sense cannot be dogmatics.
Christology is nothing more (and nothing less!) than the
theologian's orientation towards the being and act of God.
That this is not satisfactory, however, is shown by other
aspects of the treatment of Christology. In an image which is
strictly at variance with the main image which which the
centre of theology is compared (which we are to examine
next), Christology is likened to an inner circle surrounded by
a host of other concentric circles in each of which the truth of
the fulness of the deity of the Word is repeated (*CD* I/2, 133).
The centrality of a specific Christology is to be treated further
below in my assessment of Barth's achievement in theological
method.

(3) As promised, we must now expound Barth's metaphor-
ical elucidation of the concept of the centre. Having
repeatedly affirmed that there can be no presupposed basic
view of things, having insisted that the very obedience
required of the dogmatician to the Word of God cannot be
turned into a conception of the Word of God, Barth now states
that 'the position which in a system is occupied by the
fundamental principle of interpretation can only remain basically open in Church dogmatics, like the opening in the centre
of a wheel' (*CD* I/2, 867). This image, introduced appropriately enough 'from a human point of view', is designed to
render in pictorial form the openness to allow the object to
speak for itself, which Barth insists is the only responsible
stance of the Christian. It was an image he had used earlier in
the *Commentary on Romans*, as characteristic of a man who has
come to himself to ask what he is to do in the fact of his
awareness of his rebellion against God. The questioning
which then ensues is essential to his life, and must never be cut

short by simplified answers. 'May the cavity at the cartwheel's centre, which Lao-Tse perceived long ago, be delimited by a ring of questions! In that central void the answer to our questioning is hidden; but since the void is defined by questions, they must never for one moment cease.'[32] More specifically in relation to the knowledge of God, openness and questioning are brought together in the recognition that 'God is the one whose being can be investigated only in the form of a continuous question as to His action.' (*CD* II/1, 61.) God's free grace must be allowed to operate even upon the very insights and first principles of dogmatics, questioning them both as a whole and in detail and exposing their temporary character and incompleteness (*CD* I/2, 868).

Extending the metaphor somewhat, Barth continues:

The unfolding and presentation of the Word of God must take place fundamentally in such a way that the Word of God is understood as the centre and foundation of dogmatics and of Church proclamation, like a circle whose periphery forms the starting-point for a limited number of lines which in dogmatics are to be drawn to a certain distance in all directions. The fundamental lack of principle in the dogmatic method is clear from the fact that it does not proceed from the centre but from the periphery of the circle or, metaphor apart, from the self-positing and self-authenticating Word of God. (*CD* I/2, 869.)

The 'limited number of lines' are, in Barth's dogmatics, the four subdivisions, the doctrine of God, the doctrine of creation, the doctrine of reconciliation (incomplete in the event), and the doctrine of redemption (which was not begun). They are limited because they cannot and may not lay claim to completeness. More lines always could be drawn and they could be drawn in more exhaustive detail. No dogmatics could do all that might be done, nor may it lay claim to any kind of conclusive declaration concerning the work of God. But it must, and does, dare to comprehend and to present as a whole God's revelation, and in doing so is peculiarly threatened by the danger of systematization (*CD* I/2, 883). But this 'daring' is itself subject to the emphatic qualification ensured by the

[32] *ER*, 254. Sir Edwyn Hoskyns added the explanatory reference to the Tao-Teh-King, Ch. xi: 'The thirty spokes of a chariot wheel and the nave to which they are attached would be useless, but for the hollow space in which the axle turns.'

centre of dogmatics. The focal point and foundation themselves determine that in dogmatics strictly speaking there are
no comprehensive views, no final conclusions and results.
There is only the investigation and teaching which take place
in the act of dogmatic work and which, strictly speaking, must
continually begin again at the beginning in every point. The
best and most significant thing that is done in this matter is
that again and again we are directed to look back to the centre
and foundation of it all (*CD* I/2, 868).

It will now be apparent that Barth's purpose in so emphatically insisting both that there is a centre in theology and that
it consists, objectively, in the reconciling act of the Word of
God and, subjectively, in openness to that Word, is to ensure
that nothing man-devised or arbitrary interposes to hamper
and restrict the obedience of faith. *Omnis recta cognitio Dei ab
oboedientia nascitur* (all true knowledge of God is born out of
obedience). Barth cites from Calvin, specifically in answer to
the interpretative pretensions of modern theologies (*ET*, 22).
And it is the theme of obedience which is the material for our
fourth point.

(4) Harnack believed, and with reason, that the development of historical scholarship had delivered men from
ecclesiastical tyranny exercised in the name of dogma. There
has, therefore, to be a compromise between the Church and
the science of theology, by which the 'spirit of dogma' is
appropriately limited. But this, Harnack believed, was ultimately in the interests of a highly developed religious faith,
which is antithetical to 'authoritarian faith'.[33] In Barth's
attitude to historical research, Harnack believed that he
detected the renewed opening of a gateway to 'theological
dictatorship', which 'dissolves the historical ingredient of our
religion and seeks to torment the conscience of others with
one's own heuristic knowledge'.[34] Barth was perfectly aware
of the charge of being a sort of theological Godfather. His
appeal to powerful historical precedent in the persons of
Paul, Luther, or Calvin, impressively justified though it

---

[33] The references are to an essay, 'Religiöser Glaube und freie Forschung', in *Aus
Wissenschaft und Leben*, vol. 1 (Giessen, 1911), p. 270, cited by Rumscheidt in *Revelation
and Theology*, pp. 100f.

[34] Rumscheidt, p. 39.

might be, does not excuse bullying tactics; and, in any case, there is enough evidence to show that he might well feel estranged by the tone of Reformation polemics.[35] How then does Barth present the demand of his own dogmatics?

The obedience of the dogmatician to the work of God in his Word is not a matter of obedience to an objective law external to the subject. It is, rather, a free and wholehearted obedience, and, ultimately, a gift of grace and of the Holy Spirit. And for this a man can only pray.[36] He may not insist that, because he has, objectively, been obedient to the Word, all that is set forth in his dogmatics has the force of the Word of God itself. The theologian must be one who allows himself to be drawn into the sphere of the operation of God in his Word. The dogmatics that is written in the context of such obedience is a witness to others of the absolute character of the demand for obedience. What is written, therefore, ought to carry the weight of a serious challenge. 'But at bottom it can only be a challenge, a suggestion, a *consilium*, not an ultimately and absolutely binding command.' (*CD* I/2, 859.)

The apparent modesty of this stance stands in apparent contrast to the claim for noetic necessity, which we examined in relation to Barth's book on Anselm. It leads one to re-emphasize the importance of the qualification contained in the word *aliquatenus* (to some extent) which Barth adds as a practical acknowledgement of the limit of the authority and certitude claimable on the basis of faith (*FQI*, 47, as mentioned above p. 38). Moreover, *nothing* is exempt from the qualification. It is not the case that whereas central doctrines are absolutely certain, other more peripheral ones are speculative. That is a gambit which other theologians who are attached to the 'fundamental articles' tradition might play, but not Barth. For Barth it must be the *whole* of his theological edifice which is to be interpreted as a *consilium*, the sharpest polemics against Christological heresy no less than the relatively modest proposals to do with intra-Protestant disputes. It is entirely conceivable, on the basis of Barth's own formulation of his position, that he has done justice to the truth of the

---

[35] For example, on the matter of infant baptism, *CD* IV/4, 170.

[36] On the theologian as a man of prayer see *FQI*, 35; *CDI*/1, 23; *CD* I/2, 695; *CD* IV/3, 882ff.; *ET*, 150. On its Christological basis see *CD* I/1, 885.

divine self-revelation, *aliquatenus*. No critic of Barth, in other words, is in any way in a position merely of choosing between unconditional endorsement or unconditional rejection, and those who have argued so have fundamentally misinterpreted him.

IV

In this final section of the essay I propose to examine certain major aspects of the position which has been outlined, and in particular to take advantage of the critical room which the above conclusion has provided. The first point to be made is an acknowledgement of the thoroughness and the sophistication of Barth's treatment of this theme. It is apparent that a substantial element in the motivation is his abhorrence of the weakness which neo-Protestant systematic theology manifested in the early twentieth century in the face of an increasingly independent and aggressive humanism. The cause of this weakness he traced to a methodological shift from content to form, corresponding to the Enlightenment's turn to, and interest in, the subject. Barth was anything but blind to the complexity of the issues in which he was immersing himself, in his attempt to turn the tables upon a form-centred theology and write a consistently content-and object-centred dogmatics. No one who writes with the concentrated respect and attention which Barth devoted to Schleiermacher (and to Anselm) can be accused, as so many of Barth's lesser imitators can be, of running a methodological bus through issues of great delicacy. None the less, the whole impact of the centre talk has its force from the attempt to be rigorously consistent in respect of method. The only antidote to the weakness he observed in liberal Protestantism was the vigorous exclusion from the principles of theology of any kind of independent status for human rationality or potentiality. To write a dogmatics *sub ratione dei* must mean the development and observance of a comprehensive theory of theological obedience; and this very comprehensiveness, definiteness, and coherence is obviously next door to systematization. This too Barth realizes perfectly well, and in a typical note distinguishes between 'unauthorised systematisation' (which might generate itself spontaneously out of the theologian's very obedience) and 'authorised systematisation', consciously and vigorously pursued (*CD* I/2, 868f.). The difference between these two lies in the fact that, according to Barth, if theology is subject to systematization the freedom of the Word to decide its own priorities has been lost. That is the objective situation. Subjectively what has happened is that the theologian has chosen a principle or principles arbitrarily. Of course, the theologian has to choose and there are no external guarantees to prevent him from choosing arbitrarily. What, however, he is *not* to do is to claim protection for his theological work by attempting to show that it operates with a method validated by its use in another (human) discipline. That would guarantee the weakening of the message of the Gospel, whose power is contained within itself. 'Openness' is, subjectively speaking, the only possible position for a theologian who wishes his theology to do justice to that which is the power of God unto salvation to everyone that believes.

The second point, however, which I want to examine further here concerns the precise relation with the Christology of the New Testament which Barth envisages. On the essential nature of the witness of the New Testament to the risen Christ Barth will brook no opposition. Yet what he says about it is not in the form of a historical statement about its contents. That, as his own writing testifies, would have to do justice to divergences and differences of Christological emphasis which have no direct bearing on the fundamental statement which is made.

Here we are in need of greater precision than that with which Barth immediately provides us. For it is not, and cannot be the case, that the Christological testimony of the New Testament writers is irrelevant to Barth's position. What, however, is its relevance? On the basis of the assertion of a shared faith (shared, that is, with the writers themselves) it is stated that all the New Testament authors attempt to do justice to a mystery which is beyond historical description and beyond direct articulation in theological doctrine. There are, then, three elements in the situation; a shared faith, the mystery itself, and the New Testament witnesses. Historical study of the New Testament has the last as a datum, but has no direct access to either of the first two elements. The first, a shared faith, is, indeed, irrelevant to its purposes; the documents are themselves historical to the extent that they yield a meaning to believer and unbeliever alike. To the elucidation of 'the mystery itself' the historian has a significant contribution in that he may make suggestions regarding the provenance of such doctrinally-loaded concepts as 'the Son of Man' or 'the Lord'. Moreover, he may, and does, engage in a 'quest for the historical Jesus', to the extent that he distinguished between the sources for the life of Jesus and identifies the extraneous influences to which the tradition was subjected in the course of time. But the objection to the quest as it was pursued by some liberal Protestants is that it effected a covert substitution of a Jesus, controversially reconstructed from the sources, for 'the mystery itself'. Against this Barth was surely right to protest. For quite apart from the reductive character of the method by which such a figure was 'discovered' behind the sources, it was absurd to suppose that theological professors were in a position to redirect the life and worship of the Church with each new advance in scholarship.

But it is apparent that the problem of Barth's attitude to New Testament Christology is rooted in his attitude towards 'the mystery itself'. To speak of John 1:14 ('The Word was made flesh') as 'the central New Testament statement' (*CD* I/2, 132), was to make a theological, not a historical judgement. Another statement, with a different background and set of implications, might have been chosen—for example, Acts 2:22 ('I speak of Jesus of Nazareth, a man singled out by God and made known to you through miracles, portents, and signs, which God worked among you through him'). If one asks why the Johannine statement has been chosen rather than the latter, the answer has nothing to do with historical priority. Even thorough discussion of the meaning of the text for John does not exhaust the meaning accorded to it in the context of a theological judgement. One can conceive only two conditions of a purely historical kind necessitating the revision of such a judgement, the proof of textual error, and the discovery of its thoroughly secondary character in the New Testament (e.g. the proof that the Prologue of John was written by the Gnostic, Valentinus). Other arguments, for example that of Käsemann, that the Christology of John is itself far on the road to 'docetism' depend so heavily upon alternative theological judgements that their historical force is correspondingly diminished.

But this last observation merely serves to accentuate Barth's problem. Even if it be granted that historical inquiry has only a minor role to play in the demolition of such theological judgements as Barth is making, what is to be said about theological judgements which are different from Barth's? It is notorious that Christian theologians, working upon the New Testament documents also as historians and exegetes, arrive at different conclusions. Why is there no unanimity of judgement? If the alternative views are mistaken, how has the mistake arisen and is it serious? We have already noted how seriously Barth views the error of 'modern Christology' in transmuting the mystery of the revelation of God into something devoid of mystery (*CD* I/2, 131f.). 'In doing so it has been guilty of an unpardonable error, an error which renders impossible any understanding, in fact in the long run any discussion at all, between itself and a Christology which refuses to commit this error.' (*CD* I/2, 132.) The reason for these strong words is manifestly the coincidence of Barth's epistemology and his Christology. Alternative Christologies can only be built upon, and relate to, alternative epistemologies; that is why understanding and discussion becomes impossible.

Although one shrinks instinctively from the dismal picture of mutual incomprehension to which such a position seems to point, the Christologies of Schleiermacher, Ritschl, Harnack, and Troeltsch furnish examples of the connection between a developed, or implicit epistemology and the content of the doctrine of the person and work of Christ. In all these cases the understanding of man characteristic of post-Enlightenment theology has been allowed to influence (one might argue in more than one of these instances, to determine) the presentation of the content of theology. For Barth this is not just a weakness; it is a fundamental failure to observe the rationality peculiar to the object. It implies, in the strict sense, theological irrationality. In the terms of his discussion of Anselm, it is made to seem as though there might be an alternative knowledge of the object of faith. The noetic necessity, on which Barth insists, is denied; the result can only be irrationality.

There is, however, another way of viewing the matter. In order to validate itself, this view is obliged to challenge Barth precisely on the doctrine of noetic necessity, the grounds for which, it must be said, are very difficult to make out. Freed from this constraint, one is in a position to give a very different account of the diversity of the New Testament witness to Christ. The mystery of Christ provokes this diversity and does not require that any theological statement regarding what is central should gird itself with the cloak of epistemological unchallengeability. Theological judgements about what is central and what peripheral have to be made, as Barth has shown, in full consciousness of the epistemological presuppositions and implications; indeed it is to Barth that modern theology is principally indebted for the discovery of the radicality of the decisions made in the area. But there are many arguments, not just one argument, which can be deployed to establish the claim of a doctrine of Incarnation to a position of centrality in the structure of dogmatics.

The alternative view which is beginning to be sketched out implies dissent from Barth at one other point, namely his attempt to avoid placing a doctrine, whether of the Atonement or of the Word of God, at the centre of theology. This point, which, as we have seen, is made repeatedly, coheres closely with Barth's understanding of God's being and his act and with his highly original and realistic appraisal of biblical narrative. But even granted these contentions, the question still has to be asked why there may not be a conceptual discipline, corresponding to, but in no way replacing, the actuality of God's revelation, which seeks to render conceptually what is there enacted really. Repeatedly Barth emphasizes the danger that by so doing the theologian will come to 'control' the object of theology. 'Dogmatics has a basis, foundation and centre. But—and we must remember this point when we are thinking of the autonomy of dogmatics—this centre is not something under our control, but something which exercises control over us.'[37] Although, as the

---

[37] *CD* I/2, 866. Similarly 'the choice of the dogmatic method cannot in any circumstances be made with the intention of procuring for the dogmatician an assured platform from which he can survey and control it.' p. 867.)

history of recent theology has shown, this danger is a perfectly real one, it is not to be avoided in the way Barth proposes to avoid it, namely by invoking the implications of the metaphor of the 'opening' in the centre of a wheel. To speak of the freedom of the Word of God to decide its own fundamentals, and of the requisite openness of the theologian to receive new truth, is a piece of unconvincing rhetoric designed to disguise (alas, from Barth himself!) the actual centrality of a particular Christological doctrine. I do not regard Barth's choice as a dogmatician as fundamentally mistaken; but the description of the method involved in the process of giving coherence to his theology is, in this respect (and it may be in others also) unhelpful.

If we ask why it is that Barth is not ready to affirm that his dogmatics has been systematized around a particular doctrine, the answer, it seems to me, has to do with the Romantic 'principle of the centre', which he invoked as an explanation for Schleiermacher's method. But whereas Barth understands this 'principle of the centre' to consist in Schleiermacher's inclination towards a point of reconciliation between two opposites, and in his repeated praise of peace as *the* theological virtue *par excellence*, in his own case the 'principle of the centre' consists in an essentially Romantic aversion to abstract clarity. In this revolt he is at one not merely with Kierkegaard, but also with Schleiermacher himself, whose quarrel with rationalist orthodoxy is hardly less profound than Barth's himself. Still more is he like Yeats in his determination to save Scripture from the exegetical activities of the grey old pedants who

> edit and annotate the lines
> that young men, tossing on their beds,
> rhyme out in love's despair
> to flatter beauty's ignorant ear.

But why, if we grant that theology is not itself living faith, any more than a commentary on a poem is the poetic insight, should we suppose that, for certain purposes, the Church needs as much abstract clarity as it can muster in its articulation of its conceptual furniture? The answer to this question seems to be that in Barth's ecclesiastical tradition the discipline of theology is brought into much closer proximity to its object than it need be in a tradition in which greater weight is placed on liturgy or on the sacraments. What takes place, in other words, is a radical elevation of theology in its association with preaching. Not that Barth can be accused of ignoring liturgy or the prayer of the community (cf. *CD* IV/3, 2, 865ff. and 882ff.). It is merely the fact that, from the moment when he emphasized, in an article on 'The Need and Promise of Christian Preaching' (1922), that the *verbum visibile*, the objectively clarified preaching of the Word, is the only sacrament left to the Reformation Church (*WW*, 97), he announced a consistently pursued ecclesiastical identity, whose implications cannot but have left their imprint on his theology. It has done so, I believe, in the following form: it has at once made of dogmatic theology a discipline vital to the life of the Church, as the testing-ground of the fidelity of its proclamation of the Gospel, and also, by investing it with the power and objectivity of its very capacity to serve the contemporary act of the Word of God, denied the theologian the right to clarify his meaning out of fear that he thereby presumes to 'control' his object.

The modesty of Barth's depiction of his dogmatics as a *consilium* is, of course, highly attractive. Indeed, a dogmatics which claimed more would be absurdly presumptuous. But even as counsel, the importance of dogmatics in the context of Reformed ecclesiology is greatly heightened by the relatively less important position accorded to the liturgical and sacramental tradition. If one comments on this as an Anglican, one does so conscious both of the fundamental contribution of the dogmatics of the Reformation to the reform of the Anglican liturgy and of the scandalous contemporary poverty of Anglican constructive theology. I do not propose to effect at this stage any such covert substitution of piety for theology as that against which Sir Edwyn Hoskyns rightly warned the Church of England.[38] A Church, however, which attempts to pray as Israel and the Christian Church have done over the centuries has already one powerful context in which the pursuit of theological clarity can be tested. The relationship between theology and Church proclamation in such a Church is slower

---

[38] 'Ein Brief aus England', in *Theologische Aufsätze. Festschrift K. Barth zum 50. Geburtstag* (Munich, 1936), p. 528.

and more indirect. If the preaching of the ministers can closely reflect contemporary theological movements, its liturgy can only change more slowly. The making of mature theological judgements, even those which are the fruit of a lifetime of dedicated study and reflection, are only one element in the service of the contemporary Word of God. Where Barth rightly emphasizes prayer, it would be right to add 'the prayer of the Church', meaning precisely the words and liturgical acts which have provided the matrix of the development of Christian character over the centuries and which are powerfully redolent of the presence of Christ.[39]

Where such other signs are given of the contemporary act of the Word, dogmatic theology is freed from the necessity of proclaiming for itself a protected status. It may be less inhibitedly and more openly hospitable towards a succession of alternative systems, without thereby losing that fierce respect for theological truth and impatience with banality which this century has every reason to learn from the work of Barth. Again if one is to speak as an Anglican one must protect oneself from the misunderstanding that one is defending the easy toleration of theological mediocrity which has been dignified by the title of the 'comprehensiveness of the Church', and to which Barth himself refers with evident scepticism (the Anglican's 'rather dubious boast about its special mission and capacity to combine all and sundry under its roof, however opposed their standpoints' *CD* I/2, 833). The clarification of theological argument, and the weighing of its force, is a slow process, necessarily involving the 'prayer of the Church'; hence, in the process, a plurality of theological systems are not merely conceivable, but inevitable, and not merely inevitable, but desirable. For in their very plurality is guaranteed the fact that theologians will not be thought to control their object, rather than in any personal disclaimers they may make. Where the discipline of theology is conceived as having a different, and more restricted, role in the life of the

[39] In a letter to his sons, Barth humorously complains about the length and repetitiveness of Evening Prayer, experienced at a preparatory meeting of the WCC (Busch, p. 399). But there is other evidence, chiefly in respect of his hostility towards a revised concern for liturgy amongst German Lutherans after the Second World War, which suggests a certain blindness to the constructive possibilities in a liturgical tradition (Busch, p. 328f.).

Church, it is freed to be as systematic and strictly conceptual as it may be.

What has been offered above by way of assessment of Barth's writing on the 'centre of theology' amounts to a proposal for an adjustment in his account, radical in relation to the very radicality of Barth's epistemological stance, but modest in relation to his identification of the centre of theological content. But as Schleiermacher's work impressed itself on Barth, as ineradicable except by corresponding counter-achievement, so Barth's impresses itself on me; what, therefore, I feel able to claim for the essay is no more than a way of reading Barth, which explains the roots of his methodology in relation to influential writing of his predecessors, which which adjusts (I do not say domesticates!) its claims to the context of a different ecclesiastical tradition.

3

Barth's Interpretation of the Bible

D. F. FORD

University of Birmingham

A student had prepared a paper on a christological issue he felt is evoked by a section of the *Church Dogmatics*. The first question was addressed to him by a peer. As frequently happens, it was in reality not a question but a charge, that he had seriously misconstrued the issue because he had misunderstood Barth's method.

The debate that ensued was as convoluted as spirited. It moved from one complex methodological issue to two others. It continued in white heat for a polarizing hour. Throughout the hour Barth peered over his spectacles (and his glasses), stroked and smoked his outsized pipe, sipped his Rhenish wine, and spoke not one word.

As the debate was beginning to move into a second hour, it suddenly occurred to one of the students that there was, as we say, a 'resource person' present, who might possibly be able to throw light on the issues and adjudicate the dispute. He turned and ricocheted the previous question to Barth.

After a full minute of heavy silence, Barth raised his head and above the welter of complex formal issues that had been strewn on the table:
'If I understand what I am trying to do in the *Church Dogmatics*, it is to listen to what Scripture is saying and tell you what I hear.'

What can be made of this simplistic, obviously heuristic ploy? I wish to suggest that it be taken seriously.[1]

To TAKE seriously that statement and the many similar ones made by Barth in the course of his life is to take a way that

[1] R. C. Johnson, 'The Legacy of Karl Barth', in *Reflection*, vol. 66, No. 4, (May 1969, New Haven, Conn.), p. 4.

leads through the whole of his theology and offers the opportunity for fruitful insights into its strengths and weaknesses. There are many other ways of understanding his work, especially the *Church Dogmatics*, as a unity, ranging from a straightforward following of Barth's own progress through the doctrines of the Word of God, God, creation, and reconciliation, to taking the standpoint of his doctrine of the Trinity,[2] or of grace,[3] or of justification,[4] or of Christ,[5] or of the Holy Spirit.[6] There has also been an attempt to see Barth's political biography as the key to his theology and method,[7] and Richard Roberts in this volume suggests Barth's understanding of time as another pervasive and unifying theme of the *Church Dogmatics*. Such diversity is necessary to illuminate Barth's rich thought, and my approach is more a supplement to others than a competitor. Yet it does have the advantage of engaging Barth over the one documentary authority which he accepted as a primary source and criterion of theology. I will try, while doing justice to his ways of arguing from Scripture to theological statements, to clarify the key points at which decisions for or against his method and conclusions need to be made.

Barth's exegesis covers the whole Bible and displays a great variety of hermeneutical skills and principles, but my thesis, to be supported by the rest of this essay, is that he uses one dominant approach which provides the structure of argument and much of the content of his whole theology. This is his interpretation of certain biblical narratives, notably the Gospels but also the creation stories and those Old Testament narratives to which he appeals in support of his doctrine of election. I shall trace this theme from his early works through

[2] e.g. E. Jüngel, *Gottes Sein ist im Werden* (Tübingen, 1966).

[3] e.g. G. C. Berkouwer, *The Triumph of Grace in the Theology of Karl Barth* (London, 1956).

[4] e.g. Hans Küng, *Justification. The Doctrine of Karl Barth and a Catholic reflection. With a letter by Karl Barth* (London, 1964).

[5] e.g. Hans Urs von Balthasar, *Karl Barth. Darstellüng und Deutung seiner Theologie* (Cologne, 1962). (*The Theology of Karl Barth* (New York, 1972) is an abridged trans. of 1962 German edn.)

[6] e.g. P. J. Rosato, 'Karl Barth's Theology of the Holy Spirit. God's noetic realization of the ontological relationship between Jesus Christ and all men', unpublished doctoral dissertation (Tübingen University, 1975).

[7] F.-W. Marquardt, *Theologie und Sozialismus. Das Beispiel Karl Barths* (Munich, 1972 (2nd edn.).

the main doctrines of the *Church Dogmatics*, and I will then suggest that his procedure has much in common with literary criticism of the genre of realistic narrative. This parallel is appropriate because it throws light on Barth's distinctive insights, and helps to explain both the nature of his appeal to Scripture and his virtual lack of theological concern about historical criticism. Finally, I will raise critical questions about Barth's method.

I

Late in his life, in a rare piece of spiritual autobiography, Barth ascribed to the hymns of Abel Burckhardt, which he was taught as a child and which simply retold Gospel stories in local dialect, a naïvety in which

> there lay the deepest wisdom and the greatest power, so that once grasped it was calculated to carry one relatively unscathed—although not, of course, untempted or unassailed—through all the serried ranks of historicism and anti-historicism, mysticism and rationalism, orthodoxy, liberalism and existentialism, and to bring one back some day to the matter itself. (*CD* IV/2, 113.)

Although Barth did little extensive interpretation of biblical narratives before writing the *Dogmatics*, this does suggest a thread worth searching for in his earlier work.

Barth's reaction against liberal theology during his pastorate in Safenwil was expressed through his new way of interpreting the Bible. His 1916 lecture 'Die neue Welt der Bibel'[8] set the tone for what was to follow, with its direct acceptance of the world of the biblical events as the revelation of God, and its insistence that the Bible interprets itself. There followed his exegesis of the Epistle to the Romans, in which this attempt to identify a hermeneutical circle within the Bible itself was focused on the two central events of the Gospel, the crucifixion and resurrection. This is true of the first[9] and second[10] editions of his *Epistle to the Romans*, though with the major difference that in the first the emphasis is on the resurrection, whereas in the second (influenced by Overbeck, Dostoyevsky, and Kierkegaard) the paradoxical relation

[8] Eng. Trans. in *The Word of God and the Word of Man* (New York, 1957).
[9] Bern, 1919.
[10] Munich, 1922.

between the two events is stressed and 'dialectical theology' proper is born.[11] Barth's dialectical thought-form has the relation between the crucifixion and resurrection as its main exegetical basis. The crucifixion is a negation which is so radical in its judgement on everything human that time itself cannot contain the Yes of the resurrection. Between them the two events enclose the meaning of reality, the hermeneutical circle being between God's posing of the ultimate problem through the crucifixion and answering it himself in the resurrection.[12] The logic of this radical concentration on one story is carried through in the second edition's sustained attack on 'religion'. The main effect of this polemic is to make the very use of the word 'God' depend on that story. God is no longer someone Christians can assume they have in common with other religious people, even (or especially) within the Church. Since the crucifixion is seen to have an epistemological role in rebutting all claims to knowing God except paradoxically through itself and the resurrection, there is no longer any positive connection between the Gospel and religion or natural theology.

In the period between the second edition of the *Epistle to the Romans* and the first volume of the *Church Dogmatics* Barth's development in relation to my theme can be summed up under two headings. First, there was a move away from the expressionist style of the *Epistle to the Romans*, with its preference for non-mimetic, often mathematical imagery, towards a sober doctrine of the Word of God which more easily allows for faithful reflection (*Nachdenken*—thinking through in correspondence with what is given) of biblical narratives. This included a lessened emphasis on the 'infinite qualitative distinction' between God and man and more on their *relationship* through God's Word. This shift is clearly seen in the *Prolegomena zur Christlichen Dogmatik* of 1927,[13] where Barth offers a positive doctrine of God as Trinity whose Word is God himself (*Dei loquentis persona*) communicated in a historical

---

[11] For three meanings of 'dialectic' in Barth's thought at this time see H. Bouillard, *Karl Barth*, vol. I, *Genèse et Évolution de la Théologie Dialectique* (Paris, 1957), pp. 73f.

[12] W. Lindemann, *Karl Barth und die kritische Schriftauslegung* (Hamburg—Bergstedt, 1973) is perceptive on this, esp. p. 30.

[13] Munich.

event (*geschichtliches Ereignis—Chr D*, 230ff.), which is understood as revelation only through the biblical account.[14] This retreat from the paradoxes of the second edition of *Romans* led increasingly to the resurrection tone of the first edition becoming characteristic of his whole theology.

The second development was an intensification of the second edition's polemic against religion and natural theology. Barth parted company with his chief colleagues of the 'dialectical theology' group, and each break can be symbolized by an emotion-laden concept—the 'pre-understanding' (*Vorverständnis*) of Bultmann, the 'orders of creation' (*Schöpfungsordnungen*) of Gogarten, and the 'point of contact' (*Anknüpfungspunkt*) of Brunner. In each case the issue might be subsumed under the heading of natural theology, which Barth's developing doctrine of the Word of God was increasingly rigorous in excluding. The culmination of his attempts to find an autonomous basis for theology was his study of Anselm's ontological argument for God's existence. In *Fides Quaerens Intellectum, Anselms Beweis der Existenz Gottes*[15] Barth interpreted Anselm as offering an *a posteriori* proof of God from his revelation.[16] This insight became the basis for Barth's exegesis which denied any vantage point outside the hermeneutical circle: God has given the proof of his own existence in his self-expression in history as told in the Bible, and so it is only the biblical stories which render his identity authoritatively.

II

Barth's doctrine of the Word of God in Volume I of the *Dogmatics* is less helpful in understanding his hermeneutics than might be expected. He engages there at great length in conceptual clarification and related polemics, with a strong emphasis on the divinity of the Word (an aspect discussed by Dr Williams below). This must, however, still be followed in each succeeding volume by exegesis which proves his doc-

[14] 'Die Offenbarung steht, nein sie geschieht in der Schrift, nicht hinter ihr.' (p. 344.)

[15] Munich, 1931. Eng. trans., London, 1960.

[16] See C. E. Gunton's illuminating comparison of Barth's and Hartshorne's interpretations of Anselm in *Becoming and Being, The Doctrine of God in Charles Hartshorne and Karl Barth* (Oxford, 1978).

trines anew from Scripture, so it is in those later volumes that he shows how he handles narratives in practice. From the point of view of hermeneutics, the two parts of the *Church Dogmatics* I are perhaps best read in retrospect when one can appreciate, for example, what Barth means by God's language being his act, how he supports his claims for the incomparability and universality of the biblical accounts, how he carries out his three operations for interpreting Scripture (observation, reflection, appropriation—see *CD* I/2, 719ff.), and, above all, the pervasive significance of his insistence that the form of revelation is inseparable from its content (e.g. *CD* I/1, 285), and that 'when the Bible speaks of revelation it does so in the form of narrating a story or series of stories.' (*CD* I/1, 362.)

Yet for an understanding of Barth's habitual use of Scripture his prolegomena do give one important indication: his doctrine of the Trinity. E. Jüngel[17] has given a masterful and concise account of the way in which Barth's hermeneutics and ontology coincide in this doctrine. My concern, which Jüngel's study supports, is to point to the crucial fact that Barth describes the Trinity as an order in God expressed in the interrelation of crucifixion, resurrection, and Pentecost. The doctrine of the Trinity, says Barth, is a 'self-enclosed circle' (*CD* I/1, 436), and the Trinitarian God's characteristic proofs in the N.T. are indicated by Good Friday, Easter and Pentecost, and accordingly His name indicated as that of the Father, the Son and the Holy Spirit' (*CD* I/1, 437. cf. 380, 382, 430). This story is not simply seen as an indicator, however, for Barth insists repeatedly on identifying God in himself (*Deus in se*) with God in his revelation (*Deus revelatus*), e.g.: 'Revelation is of course the predicate of God, but in such a way that the predicate coincides exactly with God Himself.' (*CD* I/1, 343. Cf. especially, 380.) This point is most comprehensively made by his understanding of the Trinity in terms of the *repetition* of the nature of God in three different ways. Since these ways are exclusively revealed in the events of Jesus Christ's existence (the Old Testament, as I show below, being included by typology), this inevitably gives a strong Christocentric bias to his doctrine of God.

[17] Op. cit.

The concentration of such immense significance in one story is an extreme case of what has been called the 'scandal of particularity' in Christian theology. In other theologians it is often softened by various forms of natural theology, but Barth devotes a section of his doctrine of the Trinity (*CD* I/1, 383ff.) to denying all claims to insight into the Trinitarian nature of God other than those appealing to 'the form which God Himself in His revelation has assumed in our language, world and humanity' (*CD* I/1, 399). So the main argument for the truth of the 'scandal' is the claim that as a matter of fact God chose to reveal himself in this unexpected but effective way. God's freedom to express himself in a particular way is therefore fundamental to Barth's conception of God. God is not primarily to be described in terms of general attributes such as omnipotence, omnipresence, justice, etc., but these attributes have their content determined by the way in which God has in fact determined himself, as told in the Bible.

The demand that all statements about the nature of God be 'cashed' in biblical terms, and expecially in terms of the Gospel's climactic events, dominates Barth's doctrine of God in the *Church Dogmatics* II/1. He says there that 'God is the One whose being can be investigated only in the form of a continuous question as to His action' (*CD* II/1, 61), and he champions the 'only' in another polemic against natural theology. Then in his account of the qualities (or perfections) of God the basic description of God as 'the One who loves in freedom' is consistently given its decisive content by reference to the story of Jesus, where the love of God is seen in what happened and the freedom of God is seen in God's own choice that it should happen in this way. As Barth says about God's omnipotence: 'we must recognize His capacity, His *potentia absoluta*, only in the capacity chosen by Him, in His *potentia ordinata*. We no longer need to reckon with the possibility that He could have acted differently.' (*CD* II/1, 541.) For Barth what is greatest is what God actually does, and so God's will, for example, is not infinite, for it 'fixes a sphere which it does not overstep . . . There is no outside this sphere.' (*CD* II/1, 555f.) This sphere is for Barth articulated primarily by the biblical stories, which is why his exegesis and his theological statements are so tightly locked together.

Such a concentration of course threatens to 'objectify' God in history, and so Barth needs the all-pervasive affirmation of God's freedom and grace. In hermeneutical terms the function of God's freedom in his theology is to enable the biblical stories to be the all-embracing world of meaning. This is clearest in the doctrine of election, according to which God freely decides that a certain stretch of history will determine all other history by containing his own temporal self-repetition. There God's freedom answers the problem of the scandal of particularity in relation to eternity. It plays a similar role in relation to men, for in the Holy Spirit God chooses to address all men through one particular man, and to do this using the biblical accounts. Barth's most general expression of this freedom of God with men is his concept of the *analogia fidei*. His objection to natural theology and the *analogia entis* is that they try to see God's relationship to the world as structurally fixed and discernible apart from God choosing to speak. The *analogia fidei* points in contrast to the fact that God is always a free personal presence, who is there to be invoked and who uses particular analogies to give knowledge of himself in ever new events (knowledge for which the *analogia entis* searches in the nature of the analogies themselves).[18] In relation to my theme it is important that Barth insists that his use of the term 'analogy' is 'not . . . a systematic but an exegetical decision' (*CD* II/1, 227). The exegesis concerned focuses yet again on the crucifixion and resurrection. The reason why there can be no calculation of the degrees of similarity and dissimilarity of God *vis-à-vis* the world is that God freely both veils and unveils himself in his revelation, and in neither case is it a matter of quantity. Rather, it is a matter of two events, the crucifixion and resurrection[19] which take place in an 'ordered dialectic' (*CD* II/1, 236) and definitively indicate the nature of God. So Barth concludes the section in which he deals with analogy with an explicit concentration of 'the limits and the veracity of our knowledge of God' on the crucifixion and resurrection of Jesus Christ (*CD* II/1, 254). Thus his doctrine of analogy is

[18] Cf. E. Jüngel, 'Die Möglichkeit theologischer Anthropologie auf dem Grunde der Analogie, Eine Untersuchung zur Analogieverständnis Karl Barths', in *Evangelische Theologie*, no. 10 (Oct. 1962).

[19] On the identification of veiling and unveiling, cf. *CD* I/1, 380.

tailored to fit this one story, and so of course repudiates more general theories; and his own generalizing is by means of the freedom of God—his fatherly freedom to express himself completely through a particular man's history, and his further freedom to offer to men through the Holy Spirit the knowledge of this all-embracing reality.

III

What Barth offers in his doctrine of God can therefore be seen from my viewpoint as a 'metaphysics of the Gospel story', a thoroughgoing attempt to understand the eternal God through a temporal history. This makes his understanding of time and of the relation of time to eternity crucial for the whole of his theology (especially the perennially central theological problem of immanence and transcendence), and Richard Roberts deals with this below. My concern now is to draw on selected volumes of the *Church Dogmatics* to illustrate in what ways Barth's three main doctrines of God, creation, and reconciliation are dependent on his use of biblical narratives.

My first example is the doctrine of election in the *Church Dogmatics* II/2, which is part of his doctrine of God and has been called the heartbeat of his theology.[20] His main point is that Jesus Christ is to be identified on the one hand with the God who elects and rejects and on the other hand with men who are elected or rejected by God. The place where this unity is decisively demonstrated is the history of Jesus Christ. Right at the beginning of his exposition Barth confirms the account I have already given above by seeing Scripture as rendering the history which 'plays out' (*abspielen*) in time the 'primal history' (*Urgeschichte*) in God himself (*CD* II/2, 8ff.). The doctrine which follows shows how Barth embraces within the Christian story both the Old Testament and all other history. The basic contention is that God has expressed himself fully and frankly in Jesus Christ. This means that there is no fear of God having any side to his nature which conflicts with what can be seen in Jesus Christ, nor is there a need to search anywhere else for a key to the character of God and of history: what God has actually decided is absolute, and is 'the principle and essence

---

[20] Von Balthasar, op. cit., Eng. trans., p. 145.

of all happening everywhere . . . a work which still takes place in all its fullness today' (*CD* II/2, 183). Hence Barth's insistence that a general idea of providence or world order be subordinated to that of this particular election, for God orders all things with this in mind. Hence too his qualified argument in favour of Supralapsarianism over Infralapsarianism, in the course of which he makes an uncompromising statement of his counter-intuitive claim about the biblical narrative world:

According to the Bible, the framework and basis of all temporal occurrence is the history of the covenant between God and man, from Adam to Noah and Abraham, from Abraham and Jacob to David, from David to Jesus Christ and believers in Him. It is within this framework that the whole history of nature and the universe plays its specific role, and not the reverse, although logically and empirically the course of things ought to have been the reverse. (*CD* II/2, 136.)

This appreciation of God's freedom to surprise us by expressing universal truth in a personal and particular way is at the root of Barth's rejection of most post-Enlightenment worldviews (cf. *CD* II/2, 144). The latter insisted on finding more general frames of reference (whether universal hisory, man's individual, social, religious, or political development, or some other frame) into which the biblical history was either fitted or not, whereas Barth sees God's acts as the context in which all other events are to be understood. The whole *Church Dogmatics* can be seen as an attempt to think through the implications of this for Christian faith, knowledge, and practice[21] in all areas of life.

Barth rarely tries in the *Church Dogmatics* to relate extra-biblical events systematically to his over-all framework, although of course he makes many references to such events. It is usually the Old Testament which stands as his representative of world history, and his method of relating it to the New Testament is generally that of typology. In traditional Christian exegesis typology has been described as 'at once a literary and a historical procedure, an interpretation of stories and their meanings by weaving them together into a common

---

[21] Barth's ethics have aptly been labelled 'theological contextualism', (G. Outka, *Agape. An Ethical Analysis* (New Haven, 1972), pp. 229ff.) but are usually considered without appreciation of their distinctive hermeneutical context.

narrative referring to a single history and its meaning.'[22]
Typology stands between, on the one hand, allegory (understood as the description of one reality under the guise of some
other which has suitable similarities) and, on the other hand,
the description of earthly, personal existence in such a way
that it does not 'mean' anything else—it just is what it is. The
mark of typology is that the literal meaning or historical
reality *both* is itself *and* at the same time points to another event
or person of fuller meaning. In biblical exegesis its fundamental presupposition is the providence of God: that God does
have a design, that the correspondences between various
stages of the biblical history are not random but providential,
and that God has the freedom to use the account of one event
or person or history to point to the meaning of another.

Barth sharpens this belief in providence into a doctrine of
election inclusive of providence. In exegesis this means that
Barth, even more than the traditional typological exegetes (as
my discussion of his doctrine of creation, below, shows) relates
all Old Testament history to Jesus Christ. In the second part
of the second volume of the *Dogmatics* his chief way of doing
this is to do a literary analysis of stories which give instances
of God's election and rejection (such as Cain and Abel, Jacob
and Esau, Saul and David, Judas and Paul), and to interpret
the elected and rejected as being in a binary opposition
throughout Israel's history until this is resolved in Jesus
Christ, who is the reality prefigured by both the elected and
rejected. Jesus' crucifixion is understood as the only rejection
in the full sense, and his resurrection shows God's election of
this rejected man. Therefore all other rejection and election is
relativized by Jesus Christ: both before and since him others
can exemplify either state only as imperfect types. Barth's
efforts to bring this structure to light in the Old Testament
result in some remarkable pieces of exegesis, in particular on
the sacrifices in Leviticus 14 and 16 (*CD* II/2, 357ff.), on Saul
and David (*CD* II/2, 366ff.), and on 1 Kings 13 (*CD* II/2,
393ff.). Noteworthy in his method is the deliberate lack of any
systematic connection between the exegetical assessment and
the judgement of faith that it is in fact Jesus Christ who is

[22] Hans W. Frei, *The Eclipse of Biblical Narrative. A study in eighteenth and nineteenth century hermeneutics* (New Haven and London, 1974), p. 2.

prefigured. The exegesis only claims to show the *possibility* of a Christological interpretation (e.g. *CD* II/2, 364). Here, as elsewhere in the *Church Dogmatics*, literary analysis fulfils a role similar to that in some other systems of natural theology or apologetics as a *praeparatio evangelica*: it is a way of posing an enigma which faith in the Gospel answers. This is not surprising, since Barth has ruled out extra-biblical 'natural theology', and so his own version of it must be one appropriate to a literary authority. Yet, as it is only in faith that one can pass from discerning a correspondence to belief that here God prefigured his later action, this is not a natural theology which falls under Barth's own criticisms—that is, it does not infringe the freedom of God's self-revelation.

The climax of Barth's typological exegesis in his doctrine of election is reached in his section 'The Determination of the Rejected' (*CD* II/2, 449ff.). Here the concentration of all decisive meaning into the story of Jesus Christ is at its most intense. Barth's doctrine is that the determination of the rejected is 'that from being a reluctant and indirect witness he should become a willing and direct witness to the election of Jesus Christ and His community.' (*CD* II/2, 458.) What determines this is Jesus Christ as the rejected on Golgotha representing all others and making their ultimate rejection inconceivable: 'With Jesus Christ the rejected can only *have been* rejected. He cannot be rejected any more. Between him and an independent existence as the rejected, there stands the death which Jesus Christ has suffered in his place, and the resurrection by which Jesus Christ has opened up for him His own place as elect.' (*CD* II/2, 453.) In supporting these conclusions the only exegetical evidence Barth offers is an interpretation of Judas' role in the Gospel story: 'There can be no doubt that here at the very heart of the New Testament we are confronted by the problem of the rejected . . . And we meet this question at the same central place where the New Testament raises and answers the question of the elect.' (*CD* II/2, 471.) This way of posing the question at once limits the argument to the meaning and logic of the Gospel story. Barth sees Judas and Jesus standing opposite each other at the pivotal point of the story. Judas sums up the sin of the apostles, of Israel, of the world (*CD* II/2, 472), in his handing over (παραδοῦναι) of Jesus. Yet this sinful action coincides with Jesus' own will to be handed over for the sake of others, which is in turn identical with the Father's handing over of his Son in the Incarnation. Therefore in the one action of Judas the pattern of handing over represents the convergence of the intentions of Judas (and through him of all sinful men), of Jesus and of the Father (cf. especially *CD* II/2, 502f.). This is the ultimate confrontation of God with evil, and what happens is that, through Jesus' obedience, the literal meaning of the event (sin) is given a new meaning (righteousness). The literal meaning still remains, but can now be seen to be no longer the final meaning: the story of Jesus' passion, death, and resurrection is now the all-embracing context in which to understand that sin has been taken up by God and the new resurrection life given in exchange. Barth demonstrates this only by employing typology which, by the discernment of patterns and types, can focus this universal meaning in particular events. He carries this method yet further in what follows, for he even sees grounds of hope for Judas' salvation not only in Jesus' substitutionary death and resurrection but also, as a result of that, in Paul's transition from being one who handed over Christians to punishment (this being a type of Judas) to being one who instead, after experiencing the resurrected Jesus, hands over the Gospel to others (*CD* II/2, 478ff.).

It is clear, therefore, that the main hermeneutical support for his doctrine of election that Barth offers is a literary analysis of certain biblical stories in such a way as to find the will of God making sense of the interweaving of good and evil by creating the master pattern, Jesus' death and resurrection, in which the relation of evil to good is finally defined.

IV

The creation story of Genesis was in the traditional Christian scheme the beginning of the overarching story and accepted as an accurate account of what happened. With the growth of modern biblical scholarship and of sciences such as geology and biology this world-view became untenable for many people, and there resulted not only a crisis over how to understand Genesis 1 and 2 and how to conceive creation, but also a deep disorientation as regards the place of man in time and history. To Barth, a theologian who wished to avoid natural theology and apologetics, this situation posed a special problem in his doctrine of creation. He discusses it in his introduction to the first part of volume three and says that, after some perplexity, 'the relevant task of dogmatics at this point has been found exclusively in repeating the "saga" (i.e. of Gen. 1 and 2), and I have found this task far finer and far more rewarding than all the dilettante entanglements in which I might otherwise have found myself.' (*CD* III/1, x.)

Barth's definition of saga, in distinction from history and myth, is that it is 'an intuitive and poetic picture of a prehistorical reality of history which is enacted once and for all within the confines of time and space' (*CD* III/1, 81). It is part of the larger category of biblical narrative, and Barth says: 'It does not merely use narrative as an accepted form. It is itself narrative through and through. It has no philosophical system as an accompanying *alter ego* whose language can express abstractly what it says concretely. What it says can be said only in the form of its own narrative and what follows.' (*CD* III/1, 87.) The definition therefore tries to cover both the fact that there was a creation and the fact that it was an event of such a nature that only an imaginative story could convey its meaning. It is an idiosyncratic definition whose main purpose seems to be to avoid the term 'myth', which Barth reserves for imaginative stories conveying some abstract truth. Yet clearly many definitions of myth would include Barth's 'saga' without prejudging the issue of the occurrence of creation.

What status does this lead Barth to give to the details of Genesis 1 and 2? At the simplest level he takes the details seriously and reflects on them theologically, a favourite method being to connect what Genesis says (e.g. on water, on man and woman) with what is said elsewhere in the Bible. But this is by no means the most important procedure for his theological conclusions, for he has two main further strategies. The first is to interpret the sagas as having their chief meaning not in any information about creation (for it is an imaginative story) but in the sort of God they portray—their 'only content is God the Creator' (*CD* III/1, 78). It is this that lets Barth affirm the authority of the sagas, for they evoke a sphere outside which we cannot go to find a vantage point (*CD* III/1, 65), one which 'has a genuine horizon which cannot be transcended . . . (which is the divine will and utterance and activity)'. By construing the details of the sagas as pointing to the identity of their chief character, God, Barth is engaging in an essentially literary exercise. This is underlined by his insistence on the indispensability of the right use of one's imagination in order to gain knowledge from the sagas. He strongly attacks 'a ridiculous and middle class habit of the modern Western mind which is supremely phantastic in its chronic lack of imaginative phantasy' (*CD* III/1, 81), and says that 'Imagination, too, belongs no less legitimately to the human possibility of knowing. A man without an imagination is more of an invalid than one who lacks a leg.' (*CD* III/1, 91.) So here too there is the suggestion of literary appreciation as a *praeparatio evangelica*. Nor is the attack on the modern Western mind incidental, for it is by his concentration on the self of God that Barth opposes the Cartesian stress on the thinking self of man (Cf. *CD* III/1, 360ff.). The reversal of the post-Enlightenment philosophical orthodoxy is here too closely tied to Barth's method of exegesis, for it is only by knowledge of God, the self who is truly central (knowledge gained through biblical accounts), that anthropocentric distortions can be avoided.

Barth's second strategy is to interpret the sagas typologically. He sets them on the lowest level of a typological hierarchy: the sagas point to the history of the covenant of God with Israel which itself prefigures Jesus Christ. In all of this the final test of 'reality' is the story of Jesus Christ (e.g. *CD* III/1, 275f.). Thus, by this strategy too, little theological weight need be placed on the 'concreteness' of the saga: its function, besides helping in a minor way to render a picture of God (which needs the evidence of other parts of the Bible as well), is to provide material for a typological scheme in which it is the later parts of the Bible that are decisive.

This twofold strategy represents a considerable modification of the traditional position of creation in the overarching story. Traditionally the 'sense of a beginning' about creation was strong. Barth by stressing not anything intrinsic to the sagas but rather their double correspondence with God's will and with the history of Jesus Christ, has relocated the sense of a beginning. It is now firmly in God's will (the doctrine of election) on the one hand, and in its historical expression, the Incarnation, on the other.[23] The first of these points to the beginning in the author of the story, the second to the beginning of the one story in which all other stories have their figural place. Since, as we have seen, Barth's doctrine of election is strongly Christocentric, this innovation in the traditional framework means placing immense weight on the interpretation of the Gospel, to which I now turn.

V

It may seem strange that the problem of the historical accuracy of the Bible has not arisen so far, despite Barth's great reliance on biblical stories. My discussions of God, election, and creation give part of the answer: Barth is more concerned with the sort of God portrayed than with the verifiability of details in the stories. More important still, God's freedom is clearly such that if he chooses he may speak through the Bible despite any errors in it, just as he is able to take up and transform Judas' sin. Yet such general principles do not do justice to Barth's position on the role of historical verification. His whole theology pivots around two events in one man's life-story, the crucifixion and resurrection, and it is chiefly in relation to these that his attitude to history must be examined. Further, since few question the factuality of the crucifixion, the resurrection will emerge as the main issue as I now discuss some of the *Church Dogmatics* IV/1, where Barth presents the first part of his doctrine of reconciliation.

In this section of the *Dogmatics* Barth is clear about the importance of the historical factuality of the Gospels: 'It is a matter of history. Everything depends upon the fact that this turning as it comes from God for us men is not simply imagined and presented as a true teaching of pious and thoughtful people, but that it happened in this way, in the space and time which are those of all men.' (*CD* IV/1, 247.) Yet this history also has peculiar features:

There is no question of appealing to His remembered form as it had necessarily appeared to His disciples before the verdict of the Holy

---

[23] Cf. his statements on the Virgin Birth in *CD* I/2, esp. pp. 182ff.

Spirit was pronounced on His life and death, abstracted from the verdict of the Holy Spirit. In the editing and composition of the Evangelical narratives the interest and art and rules of the historian do not matter. What matters is His living existence in the community and therefore in the world. What matters is His history as it has indeed happened but as it is present and not past. (*CD* IV/1, 320.)

Within this history there is also a distinction: 'The death of Jesus Christ can certainly be thought of as history in the modern sense, but not the resurrection.' (*CD* IV/1, 336.)

The crucifixion and resurrection are central to the very structure of this part. Sections 57, 58 stress in an introductory way the importance of the history of Jesus Christ for reconciliation; Section 59.1 prepares for the next two sections of Section 59 on the crucifixion and resurrection; and Sections 60 to 63 build on the basis of what has been laid out in Section 59. In Section 59,2 the most revealing indication of how Barth interprets the Gospel story is an excursus, (*CD* IV/1, 224ff.), which offers a literary analysis of the story from the beginning of Jesus' ministry to his resurrection. Barth's main point is that the pattern of the synoptic Gospels represents the pattern of Atonement. In his ministry Jesus emerges as alone and superior to his disciples and other men, who are judged by his presence and by their reaction to him. Then comes the contrast of the passion story in which the roles are reversed. Now Jesus is the object of what happens, he suffers rather than acts, and instead of judgement falling on other men it falls on him. This pattern of exchange is shown best by the Barabbas episode. Finally the third part of the story, the Easter narratives, tell that the same person, the judge who was judged, was acknowledged by God, was with his disciples again, and is still alive. Because his identity is known in his history, one must know that history in order to know him now. In all of this Barth makes no attempt at historical criticism or even at redaction criticism. The nearest he comes to the latter is in pre-empting it by noting that the events of the passion narrative are substantially the same in all the Evangelists. Therefore what count as historical facts for theological reflection are the events as described in the Gospels. Barth does not try critically to distinguish the history likeness of the Gospels from their reference to verifiable events. In other words he does not try to distinguish the story from a novel by historical methods.

Yet Barth does not think the Gospels are fiction, and so the most crucial question in relation to his whole method is raised: granted that the events of this story are not to be verified by referring them to whatever historical critics can reconstruct, does Barth suggest an alternative referent? He does: Jesus Christ alive now. Until we reach the third part of the story, the resurrection (*CD* IV/1, 227), there is nothing to suggest that the Gospel is not a novel or fictional short story. A novel too can render a character, and it might be impossible and unnecessary to be able to draw the line between fact and fiction in order to understand the character's identity and the story's general relevance. But in this story as it is told, the referent is not just a historical or imagined character but one who is alive now as the same person.

The question at once arises how this affects the historical status of the story. Barth's answer is that it makes the history 'significant in and by itself' (*CD* IV/1, 227), for now the story is simply the means of knowing someone who is present himself to speak through it: 'He speaks for Himself whenever He is spoken of and His story is told and heard.' (*CD* IV/1, 227.) Barth, by making the identity of Jesus Christ the referent, has created a closed circle of the accounts and the presence of Christ, in which any turning aside to check historical details is theologically superfluous. This is Barth's Christocentric sharpening of God's freedom to speak through the biblical text as it stands. No amount of historical reconstruction can make Jesus Christ any more willing to speak than he is already. Later, Barth states the same circle in its subjective aspect (*CD* IV/1, 314ff.). He answers the question of how to experience and prove this reality by saying that prayer is the way. This prayer is through Jesus Christ as portrayed in the Gospels, and again there is no room for any turning aside to assess the reliability of those accounts. The argument amounts to an assertion that this is in fact how the story 'works', or, in Barth's terms, to the affirmation of Jesus Christ's self-authentication by speaking for himself.

We can now see how fundamental for his hermeneutics Barth's conception of the resurrection is. It not only expresses the Father's affirmative verdict on Jesus' life and death but it also justifies two positions essential to Barth's whole theology. The first, as has already been suggested, is his taking of the Gospel narratives straightforwardly as his data for theological reflection. This means that the most appropriate handmaid for theology is literary reflection, especially of the sort that understands a character's identity through his words and actions and the encounters and events in which he took part. David Kelsey, in a pregnant half-chapter on Barth's use of Scripture, has well illustrated this in relation to Barth's interpretation of parts of the Gospel in the *Church Dogmatics* IV/2.[24] The climax of the first part of the doctrine of reconciliation in the *Dogmatics* IV/1 can also be seen as intensive literary discussion, first on the meaning of the passion and crucifixion in Section 59,2 (with the excursus on Gethsemane, *CD* IV/1, 238ff., parallel to that on Judas, *CD* II/2, in its assessment of the convergence of the intentions of Satan, Jesus, and the Father), and then Section 59,3 on the complex continuity and discontinuity between the crucifixion and resurrection as together they express the natures of the Father and of the Son as a differentiated unity.

The second position that the resurrection makes possible is that of an inclusive Christology, one which embraces all men and all history in the meaning of this event. In the three part-volumes of the *Dogmatics* IV the resurrection explicitly plays this transitional role in moving from the one man Jesus to his universal significance. Barth describes the result of the resurrection as follows:

But the fact that He is risen to die no more, to be taken from the dominion of death (Roms. 6:9), carries with it the fact that His then living and speaking and acting, His being on the way from Jordan to Golgotha, His being as the One who suffered and died, became and is as such His eternal being and therefore His present-day being every day of our time. (*CD* IV/1, 313.)

What this means for the 'hermeneutical gap' between the first and twentieth centuries is that he can call it a 'technical' issue (CD IV/1, 287ff.) which is not serious in theology because the

---

[24] *The Uses of Scripture in Recent Theology* (Philadelphia, 1975), Ch. 3, pp. 39ff. Note Kelsey's embracing of Barth's interpretation of other parts of the Gospels besides the passion, death, and resurrection in a theory similar to mine.

situation has been revolutionized by answering positively the question: 'Supposing our contemporaneity with the Word of God made flesh, with the Judge judged in our place, is already an event?' (*CD* IV/1, 241.) This reverses the commonly understood position: no longer is the interpreter autonomously standing in judgement over the records of past history, but instead the interpreter is himself being questioned by the living Christ, and the vital matter is not what status the interpreter will allow Christ, but 'How will it stand with us when we are alongside Jesus Christ and follow Him, when we are in His environment and time and space?' (*CD* IV/1, 293.) This universalizing of a particular person and the events of his life is the ultimate expression of God's freedom to communicate himself in a way appropriate to himself and to men.

Barth's own label in the *Church Dogmatics* IV/2 for what he has contributed to the doctrine of the Incarnation is 'actualization', which (as *CD* IV/2, 150ff. best explains) turns out to mean the sort of concentration of the event, or history, of Jesus Christ that I have described. How does this help him with the main traditional doctrine of the humanity and divinity of Christ? The brief answer is that both natures are defined from within the Gospel story, but interpreting it from different angles. Thus IV/1 uses the story to identify Jesus as the Son of God, seeing it as a description of the free self-humiliation by God for the sake of men, while IV/2 identifies Jesus as the Son of Man in whom humanity is raised to unity with God. Barth therefore does not want to talk about two natures in the sense of separate definitions of what is divine and what is human which then must somehow be reconciled in relation to Jesus Christ. Rather he holds that the primary datum is the involvement of God with men as told in this one story, that this story is God's own way of defining the two natures, and that therefore the story (and not any outside definition) must be allowed to dictate what true humanity and true divinity are. In other words, we have here another aspect of Barth's insistence that there is no higher viewpoint on God and man than this story. Expressed through traditional terminology, the *communicatio idiomatum* is seen as the whole event of Jesus' life from birth to resurrection (IV/2, 75); a definition of divinity in itself is ruled out by rejecting the idea of a λόγος ἄσαρκος (IV/2, 33 ff.—i.e. the humanity of Christ is integral to the eternal nature of God through the act of election); and the only sure guide to what true human nature is is to be found in Jesus Christ, where it is of course in union with the nature of God, above all in the *communicatio operationum* (*CD* IV/2, 104 ff.)

In all of this the resurrection again plays a vital role, for Jesus' obviously human history is recognized as an act of God only in the light of the resurrection (e.g. *CD* IV/2, 100, 107, 250, 299, 310), and the Gospels themselves are rightly understood only when they are seen to 'breathe the resurrection' (*CD* IV/2, 132). In an earlier volume Barth expressed the role of the resurrection in relation to the two natures most succinctly:

What implications has it for the being of Jesus in time that He was in time in this way too, as the Resurrected? . . . The answer is that the particular content of the particular recollection of this particular time of the apostolic community consisted in the fact that in this time the *man* Jesus was manifested among them in the mode of *God*. (*CD* III/2, 447f.)

In the same section Barth suggests a new temporal concept as the mediator between time and eternity: the time of Jesus' resurrection appearances (*CD* III/2, 449; cf. *CD* II/1, 19f., *CD* IV/1, 301). It seems to me that Dr Roberts is right when he finds no clear conceptual resolution of the relation of time to eternity in the *Church Dogmatics*, but I interpret Barth as suggesting that there can be no such resolution. Instead, there are stories of a man risen from the dead and in this person participating in and uniting time and eternity—something of such novelty that it can only be stutteringly indicated by a variety of unharmonized stories.[25]

---

[25] Barth's use of the time of the resurrection appearances to signify the concord between time and eternity is strikingly like Frank Kermode's literary critical use of Aquinas's concept of *aevum*, which is likewise used to resolve the dissonance: 'The concept of *aevum* provides a way of talking about this unusual variety of duration—neither temporal nor eternal, but, as Aquinas said, participating in both the temporal and the eternal.' (*The Sense of an Ending. Studies in the Theory of Fiction*, London, 1966, p. 72.) Kermode sees such a concept expressed today largely in novels or poems, and his comments on their imaginative and narrative resolutions of the problem are relevant to the way Barth understands the resurrection narratives to function in the Gospels.

How Barth, with this understanding, goes about describing the *distinction* between humanity and divinity in detail cannot be discussed here, but his main procedure should be noted. It is to see man as truly human when he is freely responding to God, reflecting back the freedom and love of God himself. The dominant pattern is therefore that of correspondence or reflection, an ordered relationship in which the initiative rests with God, expressed in his grace, and man's fulfilment is to be found in ever new responses of gratitude. In Jesus this subordination in love is shown to be part of God's own nature and so man has the privilege of being a participant in God through Jesus Christ. As regards hermeneutics the correspondence means that the sort of intensive discussion of the Bible's crucial paradigmatic events as offered by the *Church Dogmatics*, is essential as a guide to appropriate forms of response.

VI

In the above analysis of some of Barth's hermeneutical principles in key parts of the *Church Dogmatics* I referred several times to the literary critical nature of Barth's approach. The literary genre that seems to be most fruitful as a comparative model is that of the realistic novel. Erich Auerbach's classic, *Mimesis, or the Representation of Reality in Western Literature*[26] has already set parts of the Bible in a long tradition of realism in literature on which, he claims, they had a powerful influence. In England Dame Helen Gardner has endorsed Auerbach's insights into the New Testament in her criticism of Austin Farrer's exegesis of St. Mark's Gospel—his method, she says,

does nothing to illuminate, and indeed evaporates, St Mark's sense of what we mean by historical reality, the 'Here and Now' of our daily experience, the 'Then and There' of memory, by which I do not mean detailed precision of testimony, but the deep sense of 'happening' . . . which has struck, and strikes, reader after reader[27]

Besides, Hans Frei has recently made out a strong case that eighteenth- and nineteenth-century biblical hermeneutics failed to appreciate the Gospel's realistic form.[28] There were

---

[26] Princeton, 1969. First published, Bern, 1946.
[27] 'The Poetry of St Mark,' in *The Business of Criticism* (Oxford 1959), p. 118.
[28] Op. cit.

two main reasons for this. The first was that their 'history-likeness' (literal meaning) was confused with ostensive reference, the former was reduced to an aspect of the latter, and realistic reading of the text came to mean reading with a view to critical reconstruction of the events referred to. The second was the attempt to find the essential meaning of the stories either in the ideas they illustrated, or in the subjectivity of their narrators or readers. This too led to ignoring what the stories said in irreducibly narrative form. Frei's suggestion that Barth is one of the few modern interpreters not to have this blindspot is the seed from which the ensuing interpretation has grown.

My simplest contention, therefore, is that Barth is one of the readers who sees in the Bible what Auerbach, Dame Helen, and Frei see, and that therefore the sort of literary criticism the latter explicitly engage in might illuminate Barth's implicit principles. The realistic novel is, of course, the subject of many conflicting interpretations and theories, but as further support for the following necessarily condensed reflections I would propose *On Realism* by Peter Stern,[29] a work that both develops Auerbach's insights in a more theoretical way and also gives independently a sensitive account of the main problems and issues that I discern in Barth.

Barth, as I have shown, recognized that it is chiefly through stories that the Bible conveys its understanding of reality. He went further in insisting that this way of rendering reality is one in which form and content are inseparable. The portrayal of complexity, individuality, and particularity as they unfold in a sequence of characters and events in interaction is not something that can be understood except by following the sequence attentively. The meaning is built up cumulatively and in an irreducibly temporal form, and amounts to a rich reality to which abstractions and generalizations cannot do full justice. This way of writing is what I mean by 'realism', and it is found in many novels and biblical narratives which render a world of meaning in terms of its characters and particularities, presenting it as they go along.[30] One problem

---

[29] London, 1973.

[30] Indeed a case can be made for the plurality of worlds offered by novels being the successors in Western culture to the one overarching biblical story; see C. A. Patrides, *The Grand Design of God. The Literary Form of the Christian View of History* (London, 1972).

which this parallel raises in the relation between fact and fiction, but before dealing with that it is neccessary to draw some more exact comparisons between Barth's method and that of literary realism.

The major thing in common is appreciation of what Stern calls the 'middle distance' perspective of realism. This is a perspective which is suited to the description of people in interaction, of 'individual lives informed by what in any one age is agreed to constitute a certain integrity and coherence' (op. cit., p. 121). Barth does not see the Gospels as biographies of Jesus, but their portrayal of him by his words, acts, and sufferings and by the reaction of others to him is of great importance for his theology, and it is just these elements which in the first century were accepted forms of character-portrayal.[31] Furthermore, much of Barth's polemics can be interpreted as aimed at preserving the form of accuracy appropriate to a perspective which tries to describe people and events in the way the Gospels do. On the one hand he is suspicious of any 'generalizing' which gets so far away from the story as to blur its particularities. He attacks any perspective which fails to take the distinctive interrelationships, sequences, and identity-descriptions of the Gospels as the primary data for theological reflection—any meaning which can be formulated apart from the story's content and structure is ruled out. On the other hand he sees much historical criticism as having a perspective that misses the wood for the trees by coming too close. He is quite happy with contradictions and alternative accounts of the same events, but without a certain 'middle distance' agreement and reliability (above all in the sequence of crucifixion and resurrection) most of his theology would be baseless. The most dangerous enemy of the middle distance that Barth sees is, however, a third perspective, one which takes its stand in the Christian's subjectivity. Here the decisive meaning of the narrative is located not in a sequence of events that happened to Jesus (the point being primarily a rendering of the identity of Jesus by telling his story) but in the consciousness of the believer who has had his self-understanding illuminated. Barth does not deny the

---

[31] See e.g. Graham Stanton, *Jesus of Nazareth in New Testament Preaching* (Cambridge, 1974), esp. Ch. 5, pp. 117ff.

change in self-understanding, but he insists that it is secondary, and that to focus on it is to miss the meaning of the narrative and to change the primary object of Christian theology from Jesus Christ to the believer. His concern is for the correct ordering of the Christian in relation to Christ. He sees the hermeneutics of Schleiermacher and Bultmann as his chief opponents here, but his criticisms go well beyond them to strike at what he saw as the post-Enlightenment tendency to let the self of the individual usurp the central place reserved for Jesus Christ. He also makes parallel criticisms of Roman Catholic theology for its Church-centred version of the same error.[32]

In this context too the resurrection is the key event. The resurrection appearance stories have a middle distance perspective on Jesus, and the resurrection itself is also, as would be agreed by most New Testament scholars, the main determinant of the Gospel writers' own perspective on their whole story. The purpose of the whole is to lead up to this news. For Barth the resurrection is also the place where God's own perspective is expressed—it is 'the verdict of the Father' on Jesus' life and death. So here in the resurrection we are given a God-guaranteed point of view which we must share if we wish to understand Jesus correctly. Barth is here claiming an insight into the structure of the Gospel story, into the way it is shaped so as to convey its message. There is a parallel with his way of supporting the doctrine of election by showing how God's verdict on the elect and rejected is expressed in the course events took. This is an important further accord with the insights of literary critics into realism. For literary realism is not just a matter of a certain sort of description, but it also involves realistic structures and assessments—literature that is not realistic can be produced (as by Kafka) by subjecting a realistic description to a non-realistic or fantastic assessment, as Stern shows (op. cit., pp. 129ff.). Furthermore, as Stern says, 'The structures which display moral and legal assessments translate more readily from one language to another and one era to another than do the textures of descriptive passages.' (Op. cit., p. 131.) They therefore offer an irreducible minimum of realism which is least vulnerable to the

---

[32] Cf. Stern, op. cit., p. 150.

problems of the hermeneutical gap, and Barth's use of them
takes advantage of this. But as regards the resurrection, the
main issue is whether that event can offer a realistic perspective on Jesus. Many readers, of course, see it as offering rather
an unusual and fantastic one, and they, if they wish to attach
decisive significance to him, often on the one hand interpret
the resurrection as an event whose significance is not for Jesus
himself but for his disciples (i.e. it was some sort of subjective
event which does not let us say anything about the present
state of Jesus), and on the other hand relocate the ending of
Jesus' own story at the crucifixion (finding his primary
significance either there or in his teaching or example or in
some combination of these). Barth, however, sides with the
mainstream Christian tradition in seeing the resurrection as
the verdict which is the ultimate in realistic assessment
because it is so not only in a literary sense but also through its
being God's act in raising Jesus so that he can still be present
as himself.[33]

This brings us again to the problem of fact and fiction. How
can Barth both claim the resurrection as a historical fact
(albeit only describable indirectly, through saga-like realistic
stories) and also refuse to base his conclusion on ordinary
historical investigation? There have been many analyses of
Barth's position on the historicity of the resurrection (which
changed between the *Epistle to the Romans* and the *Church
Dogmatics*). One of the most acute on the validity of his
arguments is that by Van A. Harvey.[34] Harvey's conclusions
seem to me sound in so far as they show that Barth's
arguments (*CD* III/2, 437ff.) do not succeed in establishing
the resurrection to an ordinary historian's satisfaction. Yet
Harvey is open to the objections that he has neither taken
seriously enough the 'imaginative-poetic' status of the saga of
the resurrection appearances in the *Church Dogmatics*, nor
tackled Barth's claim for the uniqueness of the resurrection.

The first objection raises the whole problem of the relation
of truth to fact and to fiction. This has been hotly debated,
especially since the post-Renaissance rise of historical critical

---

[33] Cf. here Stern's Ch. 3 about the expression of the transcedent in realism, and his
remarks about the realism of assessment of pp. 140f.

[34] *The Historian and the Believer* (London, 1967), pp. 153ff.

method.[35] The core of the problem is that there seems to be an inevitable imaginative element in reconstruction of events which tries to do justice to their many-faceted richness, and this can even lead to a historical novel expressing the truth of a person or period better than conventional history. Brian Wicker, commenting on our understanding of the Gospels, makes the same point: 'Perhaps it is only now, as a result of our long experience of reading novels, that is, narratives which once again combine the empirical and the fictional in a mode of narration more complex than either of these can be by itself, are we able to recover the true nature of narratives written before the split occurred.'[36] Any simple separation of fact from fiction is especially difficult when it is a matter of conveying a vivid character. How important is the verification of details when they are being used as part of a complex synthesis to portray an individual? Given that the rendering does not contradict known facts, but embraces them, of what might falsification consist, short of giving an alternative portrayal which would raise the same problem? Barth is well aware of the complex amalgam offered by biblical narratives and is committed to reflecting theologically on the whole synthesis, taking it in its integrity as literary work. As regards the Gospels, he recognizes that, since we have four versions, the authors and their traditions are engaging in creative reconstruction to some degree. But he also insists that they offer quite enough to identify Jesus unequivocally, and he centres his understanding of Jesus on the passion, death, and resurrection, where the agreement of the Gospels on the 'bare facts' is greatest. One thing that the fixing of the canon could be seen as saying is that we may trust that the rendering of Jesus given in these stories is the best available and so we may confidently begin our theological reflection from them. It seems to be the practical function of Barth's doctrine of Scripture to support such a view, enabling him to get on with the business of *Nachdenken*.

It seems to me therefore that Barth's principle is to trust

[35] For an account of its origins, with a look forward to its continuation in discussions of the novel, see William Nelson, *Fact or Fiction. The Dilemma of the Renaissance Storyteller* (Cambridge, Mass., 1973).

[36] *The Story-shaped World. Fiction and Metaphysics: Some Variations on Theme* (London, 1975), p. 105.

that the Gospels do have a 'middle distance' reliability which is sufficient for theological truth and that when there is a choice between the Gospels and any other (inevitably partly imaginative) reconstruction he will always choose the former. He is willing to accept that the accounts of the resurrection appearances are in saga (imaginative but realistic) form, but he holds that they unanimously point to the continuity of Jesus' identity through death and that any reconstruction which denies this is contradicting all the sources and engaging in imaginative storytelling on its own account.

The second objection possible to Harvey's criticisms is that he does not explore Barth's distinctive claim for the uniqueness of the resurrection. It is here that Barth goes beyond any parallel in fiction or history, for, as I have already described, he is saying that the main character of this story is alive to confirm it. In other words, the identity of this person is defined by events which include one that allows him to be present now. I have shown how Barth supports this by elucidating the logic of the Gospels: they are told in a way which poses for the reader the problem of the present status of Jesus, and they offer a solution in the telling. This sets a unique epistemological problem, which can be stated as follows: the Evangelists *both* inescapably raise the question: Did the resurrection actually happen? *and* describe what is claimed to have happened in a way which makes verification inseparable from faith in the presence of Jesus.[37] Therefore the logic of the story converges uniquely with the necessity for faith; and Barth's theology includes here at its heart his literary insight.

VII

Having described what I consider the essence of Barth's hermeneutics of biblical narrative and offered a possible rationale for it, I now come to the task of criticizing it. The issues raised have been so vast that an adequate assessment would require at least a book, so for the most part I will be content with identifying the points at which important deci-

[37] See esp. his remarks in *CD* IV/2, 478f., and R. Smend's lengthy comment on its significance for Barth's whole theology in an article that is one of the best on Barth's hermeneutics, 'Nachkritische Schriftauslegung' in *Parrhesia, Karl Barth zum 80. Geburtstag*, (Zürich, 1966), pp. 215–37.

sions for or against Barth may be made, and I will go into somewhat more detail only about the criticisms that spring from my literary parallel.

One central question on which Barth is conscious of being opposed to most contemporary thought is that of the overarching story, or plot of history, whose author and chief character is God. There are many points at which one may diverge from him on this. Does Barth's God exist? Is Barth's combination of literal and typological exegesis the right way to understand the Bible? Is it also the right way to understand God's purposes in history? Even if one accepts affirmative answers to these three questions, one might still ask whether Barth's Christocentric concentration of the story is convincing. Can he do justice to world history, to other religions, to the importance of history since the resurrection? Or is his 'scandal of particularity' sharpened polemically beyond anything intended by the Bible?

Implied by some of these questions is the problem of Barth's rejection of natural theology. Might it not at the very least be desirable to combine his understanding of God through biblical stories with the granting of some theological weight to factors such as the natural and human sciences, historical criticism, and other religions? Two ways of posing this sort of question in Barth's own terms would be: Is he limiting too dogmatically God's freedom to speak in various ways? and: Granted that the Genesis sagas used the cosmology of their time in understanding creation, might it not similarly be the task of a modern doctrine of creation to use contemporary cosmology and sciences rather than simply to reflect on Genesis?

Historical criticism is an area where damning attacks on Barth have become usual. I have tried to moderate this by showing the coherence and plausibility of Barth's achievement. He grasped better than most exegetes in recent centuries the significance of realistic narrative form in the Bible. He then concentrated his reflection of this feature, shared by novels and historical writing. This raises a range of issues which his critics must not bypass, such as the relation of truth to fact and fiction, the role of imagination in knowing, the possibility that realistic narrative is the highest form of religious language about a God who acts in history, the way in which works of literature cross the hermeneutical gap, and the freedom of the Holy Spirit. Above all, by taking the resurrection as his main methodological principle he draws attention to its claim to uniqueness and to the decisiveness for the identity of Christianity of the question of the presence of the living Christ. None of this can be ignored simply because one finds that his statements about the historicity of the resurrection or of other events fall short of one's norms of historical proof. Yet on the other hand one must ask whether at the very least he ought to admit a criterion of historical falsification into his theology, and whether at the most he should accept that God is free to make historical reconstructions or the results of redaction criticism into data for theological reflection. Such a position would make his theology more complex (as would an admission of natural theology) but perhaps that would be the right result of trying to reflect a complex reality.

Barth's sustained attempt to avoid such complexity is in the interests of his powerful appeal to the centrality of the resurrected Jesus Christ. He is undoubtedly right that if his understanding of the crucifixion and resurrection is correct then this necessitates a revolution in our knowledge and existence. The characteristic 'tone' of his whole theology is a blend of astonishment and thanks: 'The statement "God reveals himself" must be a statement of utter thankfulness, a statement of pure amazement, in which is repeated the amazement of the disciples at meeting the risen One.' (*CD* I/2, 65.)

We are here facing the fundamental challenge of Barth's theology, his assertion that there is this extraordinary reality, the risen Christ, whose presence is endlessly rich and fruitful for understanding and for all of life. Barth's main concern is to state this clearly and to work out its implications, and this involves his distinctive theological method centred on biblical narratives. The critical question of the complexity of reality arises as Barth claims that the presence of Christ carries with it a complete world of meaning defined, in the way I have described, by stories. I suspect that it is in wrestling with the problems of presence and completion that one faces the deepest theological problems in the *Dogmatics*. They arise in his anthropology (*CD* III/2) where biblical the material must be squeezed hard to produce a universal definition of man traceable to Jesus Christ. They arise in his orientation of all world history to the one history of Jesus Christ, and in the accompanying doctrines of election and creation which use typology to create an unprecedented totality of correspondences. They arise in the questioning of commentators such as W. Pannenberg, J. Moltmann, and R. Jenson about whether Barth attaches proper importance to history since the resurrection or whether the resurrection for him marks history's essential completion.[38] They have arisen in other forms too in this article, and their common factor is that in my terms they suggest a weakness in Barth which is closely related to his strength.

What I refer to is Barth's tendency to load the story of Jesus Christ with significance in such a way that it twists under the strain on its main character. A good example is his treatment of Judas in II/2, referred to above. In his eagerness to see all rejection enclosed in Jesus' death and overcome in his resurrection, Barth presses the typology of Judas with Paul so as to support the possibility of an ultimately favourable verdict on Judas. Yet the two grim New Testament versions of Judas' death clearly make no attempt to remove in this way the sting of finality from Judas' fate. Barth is intent on enveloping Judas in salvation whatever his crime (e.g. Judas is 'wholly elect', *CD* II/2, 104) and in doing so not only tries to know more of God's purposes than can be elicited from the story but also does violence to its realism, which does not let any general understanding of salvation gloss over Judas' final responsibility for his action. The literary analogy of Barth's approach here is a genre which has been dominant in German fiction and which Stern contrasts with the realistic novel. This is the *Entwicklungsroman* or *Bildungsroman*, which is centred on one person's development and of which Stern says that in it the hero eats up the background—the whole world yields before him and is organized around him (*CD* II/2, 104). One can appreciate Barth's great temptation to this sort of interpretation, for he does believe that all creation is ordered

---

[38] Note that Barth can say that the resurrection, Pentecost, and the *Parousia* are only different forms of the one event (*CD* IV/3, 293).

around Jesus Christ. Yet the Gospels do not reflect this in the manner of an *Entwicklungsroman*, but are stubbornly realistic. So Barth's tendency is to interpret them as more Christocentric than they are and so upset the realistic 'ecology' of responsible and free agents in interaction.[39] It is no accident that such a flaw should appear in the doctrine of election which integrates so much of Barth's theology. He is straining to put in place the keystone of his structure, the Christocentric interpretation of election which will let it retain the importance it had for Calvin while avoiding the objectionable aspects of 'double predestination'. But the story will not quite fit, and so he uses typology in a way that obscures the literal, realistic sense.

Barth's tendency, here as elsewhere, is to try to peep over God's shoulder, to claim an overview which is not in keeping with the humble *Nachdenken* of the story. His danger is that in his astonished gratitude for God's self-expression through one set of events, he will absolutize them and play down the possibility of God using different and new combinations. This leads to a clear statement of what he considers essential, but risks impoverishment at other levels. Søren Kierkegaard wrote:

If one does not maintain strictly the relation between philosophy (the purely human view of the world, the *human* standpoint) and Christianity, but begins straight away, without special penetrating investigations of this relation, to speculate about dogma, one can easily achieve apparently rich and satisfying results. But things can also turn out as with marl at one time, when, without having investigated it and the soil, people used it on any sort of land—and got excellent results for a few years, but afterwards found that the soil was exhausted.[40]

I have used realistic novels as a purely human standpoint and given some examples of their value in explaining what Barth is doing. That has had the effect of making the logic of Barth's theology more comprehensible and more amenable to discussion and criticism. It also suggests ways in which Barth's

---

[39] Another suggestive instance is his interpretation of ἐσπλαγχνίσθη in *CD* IV/2, 184ff., where the reality of other people's suffering becomes 'secondary' in relation to that of Jesus.

[40] *Journals and Papers*, III (London, 1970), p. 3253.

theology needs to be more open and comprehensive. This is not at the level of the rendering of Jesus Christ, but at the level of general conclusions drawn from this. Above all, there is the question as to whether story-language should have the virtual monopoly Barth gives it, or whether Barth's way of concentrating on it, for all its value, also overloads it, and is restrictive.

Yet already one can imagine Barth's self-defence, asking us to consider whether gratitude might not be the continuation appropriate to a perfectly complete event. Might it not be, he asks, that one event, one person, is so astonishingly rich that the significance of all subsequent history might consist in becoming more and more thankful for it in thought, speech, and action?

4

Karl Barth's Doctrine of Time: Its Nature and Implications

R. H. ROBERTS

University of Durham

I

In this essay Karl Barth's conception of time (and its correlate eternity) is presented as follows. After some introductory remarks Barth's theological method is set in the context of German idealism in the first section. In section two Barth's own development is outlined from the 'theology of crisis' to the emergence of the first half-volume of the *Church Dogmatics*. Following this, in section three, the temporal vacuum of the eternal 'Now' moment inherited from the dialectic of idealism and *The Epistle to the Romans* is seen to become the vehicle of the time of revelation itself. In sections four, five, and six the fundamental concept of 'contingent contemporaneity' is seen to undergird the doctrines of God, Christ, and creation, respectively. The so-called 'inner logic' of the *Church Dogmatics* is the axis of eternity and time unfolded through the motif of the 'analogy of faith'. Thus in the concluding section it becomes apparent that despite Barth's efforts to posit a resurrection of Jesus Christ in time in its 'simple meaning' he nevertheless provides a theology whose total structure remains enclosed within its own temporal envelope. The consequences of this are twofold: first, severe ambiguity of thought occurs whenever this structure encounters commonplace reality; second, the whole structure is a paradoxical combination of concrete assertion and unreality *in toto*.

Before proceeding in the directions outlined above, certain preliminary remarks must be made upon the general nature of Barth's theological endeavours in the *Church Dogmatics*. Barth makes a decisive and profound reassertion of the being of God in Jesus Christ. The act of God in Jesus Christ may be understood in a number of ways. Dr Ford has addressed himself to what I regard as the exegetical norm of the 'story'. I direct my attentions to the ontological norm of God's being in act, understood in its significant persistence and continuity through the category of time. Indeed epigrammatically it might well be said that, for Barth, time is a surrogate for substance in general.[1] The relation of God's being in eternity to his being in time is understood in a mutual actualism in such a way that ontology and temporality are deeply enmeshed. It is my contention that having demonstrated and analysed the profound involution and convolution of these categories it is then possible to map out the structure of being in the *Church Dogmatics* by tracing the application of temporal conceptions. In this way questions may be put to Barth's work that are normally pre-empted and repudiated by his method of deriving all theological explanation from the posited 'reality' of revelation, a reality that demands conformity and submission rather than critical investigation.

In his posthumous Warfield Lectures, Ronald Gregor Smith[2] made the following comment upon the *Church Dogmatics*, from which emerges an important question:

In Barth we have the last, and possibly the greatest, certainly an awe-inspiring, effort on the part of traditional metaphysical theology to overcome the difficulty of relating 'God in his being for himself' with 'God for the world in Christ'. But if you begin with 'being', is there any way to the world of time and movement, the historical world where faith takes its rise?

It is precisely this ontological 'way' from the being of God to the world of time and movement that is to lie at the centre of attention in this essay. The very scale of Barth's achievement means that many issues can only be alluded to in an essay of these dimensions: they remain, as it were, unlit corridors leading away from the primary passage being explored. It is my intention to unravel something of what

---

[1] I have analysed this equation of time and substantial being and its consequences for the doctrine of analogy in 'The Ideal and the Real in the Theology of Karl Barth', S. W. Sykes and J. D. Holmes (eds.), *New Studies in Theology* (London, 1980).

[2] R. Gregor Smith, *The Doctrine of God* (London, 1970), p. 91.

T. F. Torrance has called the 'inner logic' of this theology in such a way as to show that the autonomy of theology as conceived by Barth inevitably leads into a tortuous ontological double-bind, an all-pervasive theological ambiguity and unreality. In consequence it will become apparent that the profound and legitimate mystery of Christ must not become (albeit unwittingly) the cloak for mystification and the infringement of the bounds of theological sense.

I

The most relevant factor in the immediate historical context of Barth's early development and his later, mature work concerns the treatment of the axis of eternity and time, understood as categories of infinite and finite existence, in both the evolution of idealist thought in Germany and in its later dissolution in the face of hostile philosophical criticism. Such a growth and subsequent declension in European thought is, in the first instance, 'philosophical' by nature, but its ultimate origins, nature, and its renewed criticism had undeniable and important theological dimensions. Again such a context is relevant because Barth's over-all theological stance bears many signs of operating within parameters laid down and dictated by the late German Enlightenment as well as idealism. It is, however, necessary to consider both these conditioning factors as well as general but fundamental features of his theological method. Thus whilst Kant, Hegel, and Kierkegaard have had their effect, their influence must be understood in conjunction with the truly constitutive role of *analogia fidei*, the 'analogy of faith' in the work itself. Whereas the former thinkers (all intimately connected with the idealist tradition) conditioned the theological possibilities open to him, it is Barth's massive adherence to the principle of analogy of faith which comes to motivate the interrelation of eternity and time and provides the rationale for the dominance of the former over the latter.

In the light of these remarks it may be seen that whilst Karl Barth was not a philosopher, his comments upon the idealist philosophers Kant and Hegel (made at some length in his *Protestant Theology in the Nineteenth Century*) constantly reveal his understanding of the theological significance of their work.

Thus Barth sees an irony in the fact that Kant's segregation of philosophical and theological activity allowed for an emancipation of constructive theology outside the framework of the latter's own critical undertaking. This insight is that the 'biblical theologian proves that God exists by means of the fact that He has spoken in the Bible' (*PT*, 311–12). Indeed for Barth the problem to be solved was of how and where God had spoken once the Kantian emancipation of faith into its own discrete sphere had been accomplished.

According to Barth[3] there is thus a scientific living-space for theology in relation to its proper object and some indication as to the nature of this 'proper object' is apparent when an examination is made of the notable study of Anselm[4] originally published in 1931. In this he argued that theology should recognize the point of departure for its method in revelation and thus stand on its own feet in relation to philosophy. More specifically, Barth argued that Anselm provides 'a vital key, if not the key, to an understanding of that whole process of thought that has impressed me as the only one proper to theology' (*FQI*, 11). At the very core of this process of thought is Anselm's recognition of a '*ratio* peculiar to the object of faith' a '*ratio* of God', that is, a 'Word . . . not divine as word but because it is begotten of the Father—spoken by Him' (*FQI*, 45–6). Truth is thus the consequence of God's own action, not an attempt to produce or evince truth from autonomous human ratiocination. The 'analogy of faith' is, therefore, a grace-given correspondence between theological language and its object. Such a correspondence is not predictable or static in the manner characteristic of Roman Catholic analogy of being (against which Barth polemicizes) but given in the event of God's own self-revelation in his Word in Jesus Christ.[5] The very possibility of theo-logy is intrinsically conditioned by God's own act

---

[3] We cannot concern ourselves with the adequacy of Barth's argument for the use of this presupposition but with its consequences.

[4] *Anselm: Fides Quaerens Intellectum* (London, 1960). See the further discussion in Professor Sykes's paper, pp. 36ff.

[5] Barth defines the analogy of faith as follows: 'The correspondence of the thing known with the knowing of the object with the thought, of the Word of God with the word of man in thought and speech even as it distinguishes true Christian prophecy taking place in faith from all that is untrue' (*CD* I/1, 279).

and does not depend upon any persistent, given affinity between the being of God and the being of other entities.

The link between Barth's comments upon Kant and his analysis of Anselm's *Proslogion* is of major importance because it indicates in the barest outline the nature and the limitations of his understanding of the range of theology, and with it, the basis of his doctrine of time. The theological foundation of the first volume of the *Church Dogmatics* was laid therefore in Barth's study of Anselm in an identity of knowing and being, as 'It is in the Truth and by the Truth, in God and by God that the basis is a basis and that rationality possesses rationality.' (*FQI*, 51.)

In more specific terms it is necessary to see how the movement of idealist thought in respect of the antitheses of eternity and time, finite and infinite, brought about developments in Barth's own thought relevant to our argument. It must be remembered that Barth made no simple theological obeisance to Kant, but he quite clearly regarded the distinctions found most lucidly expressed in *Religion Within the Limits of Reason Alone*[6] between the rightful spheres of philosophy and theology, as in a certain relevant sense correct. Thus, far from *inhibiting* theological endeavour, Kant's work served to *free* it for its proper task, an unqualified adherence to the Word of God. This was but one aspect of Kant's influence upon Barth, for another crucial element concerned the basic assumptions concerning the relation of the categories of finite and infinite existence.

In the *Critique of Pure Reason* Kant argued that the antinomy of finite and infinite space and time, part of the traditional diet of metaphysical thought, was irresolvable and formed an aspect of those problems imposed upon the human mind by the nature of reason itself. The 'dialectical play of cosmological ideas' is something to which reason is subject whenever it attempts speculation in the 'endeavour to free from all conditions and apprehend in its unconditioned totality that which according to the rules of experience can never be determined save as conditioned'.[7] The attempt to think the 'unconditioned', that which lies beyond the 'universal laws of

---

[6] Trans. T. M. Greene and H. H. Hudson, *Religion within the Limits of Reason Alone* (New York, 1960).

[7] Trans. N. Kemp Smith, *The Critique of Pure Reason* (London, 1968), p. 422.

nature' is implicit in the illicit and futile strivings of metaphysical thought. The deep metaphysical agnosticism that resulted from Kant's 'limitation' of reason found its corresponding expression in his conceptions of the religion of 'revelation' and 'biblical theology' in *Religion Within the Limits of Pure Reason Alone*. Any identity between speculative metaphysics and theology was abrogated and a 'religion of reason' replaced the pretensions of metaphysical theology.

The metaphysical agnosticism of Kant contrasts with Hegel's positing of absolute knowledge. Here the implications of the latter's thought for that of Barth can be initially traced in *Protestant Theology* where the wealth of references to Hegel's *Lectures on the Philosophy of Religion* is apparent. What is equally remarkable is the dearth of reference to Hegel in the *Church Dogmatics* itself, but this should not mislead the reader, for the implicit response of Barth is nevertheless pervasive. Indeed Hegel's virtual rediscovery of the doctrine of the Trinity subsisting in the divine act and of his concept of synthesis are clearly highly significant for Barth (*PT*, 413–17) and for his understanding of time.

The importance of Hegel's response to Kant as regards the problem of time is to be seen in the transformation of the antithesis of finite and infinite existence (conceived in theological terms as the contrast of time and eternity). In the dialectic Hegel subsumed all aspects of reality, including those in a state of apparent contradiction, such as time and eternity, into a single, over-all process of noetic realization, that is in absolute thought. This ran counter to Kant's circumscription of possible human knowledge, for in the Hegelian dialectic thought and being enter into identity as the being of God and the being of man become one through the coming to self-consciousness of God through human self-consciousness. The very similarity between Barth's Christological synthesis and that of Hegel might raise certain difficulties, but at least Barth's intentions are clear when he contrasts the 'Hegelian concept of synthesis' and the 'incomprehensible synthesis of God' (*PT*, 417). The latter can only be understood upon its own terms, that it is as related to its 'proper object' given in revelation.

It is precisely Barth's disagreement with Hegel over the

nature of the 'proper object' of synthesis that indicates the
nature and direction of his work and the context in which his
emergent doctrine of time must be understood. Barth
approved of Hegel's 'discovery' that 'Life itself is not a unity
resting in itself, but a perpetual $a = non-a$, in despite of the
whole of western logic' (*PT*, 413), but indicates that 'in
making the dialectical method of logic the essential nature of
God' Hegel made impossible the 'knowledge of the actual
dialectic of grace, which has its foundation in the freedom of
God' (*PT*, 420; cf. *CD* II/1, 270). Barth's theological synthesis
is of Hegelian proportions and involves the comprehensive
embrace of diverse categories within a complex whole. Just as
with Hegel the danger of reduction constantly threatened such
a synthesis on the level of pure thought, so with Barth there is
a threat of reduction of the diverse totality of being into the
realm of the divine being in act.

As regards time itself, Hegel's conceptions bear a strong
resemblance to those Barth adopts in his major work. In the
Philosophy of Nature Hegel asserted that,

In the positive sense of time one can therefore say that only the
Present is, while what is before and after is not. The concrete Present
is however, the result of the Past, and is pregnant with the Future.
The true Present is therefore pregnant with eternity.[8]

The exploitation of eternity as the true indweller of the
transient temporal present in the *Church Dogmatics* owes much
to Hegel but is given its dynamic impulse by the principle of
analogia fidei as Barth attempts to propound the nature of
God's revelation in Jesus Christ. Barth's own response to the
actual dialectic of the antitheses follows the breakdown of the
idealist synthesis at the hands of Trendelenburg[9] and, following him, Kierkegaard. Out of this criticism arose essential
elements in the so-called 'theology of crisis' or 'dialectical
theology', in which Barth played a leading part in the years
following the end of the First World War. It is most important
to follow this development in some detail because its resolu-

---

[8] *The Philosophy of Nature* (Eng. trans. London, 1970), p. 86.
[9] Notably in *Logische Untersuchungen* (Leipzig, 1870). The only English translation
of Trendelenburg's work appears to be 'The Logical Question in Hegel's System',
trans. T. Davidson, *Journal of Speculative Philosophy*, V (1871), 349–59; VI (1872),
82–93, 163–75, 350–61.

tion raises questions which must be borne in mind in examin-
ing Barth's *magnum opus* and its doctrine of time. Trendelenburg's critique of Hegel's use of Aristotelian categories was
the product of the former's philological expertise and fidelity
to the text of Aristotle. The synthesis of apparently incompatible categories was exposed as the radical confusion of such
categories, real and logical. This exposure of the impossibility
of a total identification of thought and that which existed was
developed by Kierkegaard in a theological polemic. Using the
logical tools forged by Trendelenburg, Kierkegaard forced
apart the false and illusory categorical homogeneity of
Hegelian idealism.[10] In specific terms this attack was concentrated upon Hegel's misuse of the Aristotelian concept of
κίνησις in indicating the movement from possibility to actuality. This, according to Kierkegaard, cannot be expressed or
understood in the language of abstraction, for, in the sphere of
the abstract, movement cannot have assigned to it either time
or space, its essential presuppositions.[11]

The noetic goal of identity in the Hegelian dialectic,
achieved through the overcoming (*Aufhebung*) of contradiction, was supplanted in Kierkegaard's *Postscript* by an existential dialectic, in which the temporal is confronted by the
eternal, in the 'either-or' experienced in the striving of the
becoming subject (*CUP*, 270–1). The Hegelian stance, *sub
specie aeterni*, is an illusion for it presupposes an abstraction
from the inevitable and actual existential pathos of the
individual. Whereas for Hegel 'The systematic Idea is the
identity of thought and being', Kierkegaard argued that
'Existence, on the other hand is their separation.' (*CUP*, 112.)
In consequence the most pressing problem is how it is possible
for 'eternal truth . . . to be understood in determinations of
time by one who as existing is himself in time' (*CUP*, 172).
Kierkegaard pointed to the theological implications of this
reassertion of the ‾ *diastasis* (a radical disjunction) of the

[10] Accounts of this critique may be found in H. Diem, *Kierkegaard's Dialectic of
Existence*, trans. H. Knight (Edinburgh, 1959), and J. Collins, *The Mind of Kierkegaard*
(Chicago, 1965).
[11] See *Concluding Unscientific Postscript*, trans. D. F. Swenson and W. Lowrie
(Princeton, 1941), p. 306 and *The Concept of Dread*, trans. W. Lowrie (Princeton,
1957), p. 43, 'In logic no movement can come about for logic is and everything else
logical simply is.'

temporal and the eternal, in that 'the paradoxical nature of Christianity consists in its constant use of time and the historical in relation to the eternal' (*CUP*, 88). He asserted an existential paradox of encounter over against the Hegelian possibility of abstract synthesis:

The eternal and essential truth, the truth which has an essential relationship to an existing individual because it pertains essentially to existence . . . is a paradox. But the eternal essential truth is by no means in itself a paradox; but it becomes paradoxical by virtue of its relationship to an existing individual. (*CUP*, 183.)

Such an existential paradox shifts the focus of difference from an abstract contrast of being to an encounter of finite consciousness with an infinite Wholly Other God. The consequences of this new perspective for Christology and the doctrine of creation were completely realized by Barth in the theology of crisis, and in so doing he exploited anew with extreme destructive power the dialectic of eternity and time. This was quintessentially expressed in the epochal second edition of the *Commentary on the Epistle to the Romans*. The existential dialectic of the temporal and the eternal found in Kierkegaard, in which the existing individual '*in time* comes into relation with the eternal *in time*' (*CUP*, 506), becomes in Barth an eschatological crisis, a confrontation of the temporal by a consuming eternity. The underlying Christological equilibrium maintained by Kierkegaard was shattered in an eschatological annihilation of time by eternity.[12] Whereas we shall see that Barth perceived and rectified the Christological difficulties in his later work (and he must be given full credit for his remarkable capacity for self-correction), it is in his understanding of creation (and time as its basic form) that problems will emerge that are unresolved and even unacknowledged.

II

Having seen how certain important and influential factors condition the emergence of Barth's own theological theory of time we are now in a position to examine the actual develop-

---

[12] See J. Heywood Thomas, 'Kierkegaard's View of Time', *Journal of the British Society for Phenomenology*, 4, No. 1 (Jan. 1973), 33–40 and 'The Christology of S. Kierkegaard and Karl Barth', *Hibbert Journal* (1954–5), 281ff.

ment of his thought from the dialectical theology of the period immediately following the First World War up until the appearance of the Prolegomena to the *Church Dogmatics* proper.

In the decisive edition of *The Epistle to the Romans* which appeared in 1922 Barth stated in well-known words that if he had a 'System' then it was 'limited to a recognition of what Kierkegaard called the "infinite qualitative distinction between time and eternity"—"God is in heaven and thou art on earth"' and that 'The relation between such a God and such a man, and the relation between such a man and such a God, is for me the theme of the Bible and the essence of philosophy.' (*ER*, 10.) Barth carried his theme further, for 'Philosophers name this KRISIS of human perception—The Prime Cause; the Bible beholds at the same crossroads—the figure of Jesus Christ.' (*ER*, 10.). So Barth conceives of a theological triumph over what is regarded philosophically as *Krisis*. By a powerful conjunction of eschatology (inspired by its so-called 'rediscovery' by Schweitzer and Weiss) and the principle of justification on the basis of God's grace alone (a return to a radical Lutheran insight) Barth was able to pass beyond the dialectic of finite and infinite categories, that is, time and eternity. In the dialectical phase of Barth's development this overcoming of the antithesis was by the annihilation of time by eternity and in his later dogmatic work a renewed Christological synthesis was asserted. Demolition had to precede reconstruction and the development we are to examine has only the appearance of dramatic discontinuity. In reality there is a progression in which Barth brilliantly utilizes an extraordinary wealth and diversity of insights drawn from the Christian tradition. The *Church Dogmatics* embodies his own response to this dilemma: a massive effort of self-correction that has been aptly classified as a movement from dialectic to analogy, a transformation that has elements of both continuity and discontinuity. The temporal dialectic of *Romans* clears the ground for a theologically generated theory of time strictly analogous to the general structure of the *Church Dogmatics*. We must turn once more to *The Epistle to the Romans* in order to appreciate the sheer power and consistency of his theological transformation and positing of a new beginning.

The eschatological extinction of the fragile equilibrium of Kierkegaard's Christology of paradox in Barth's *Romans* is precipitated by an absolute and unmediated dichotomy between time and eternity, juxtaposed as a dialectical divine 'Yes' and 'No', for, in a mutual annihilation, 'time is nothing when measured by the standard of eternity.' (*ER*, 43.) In the *Krisis* of revelation a tangential intersection is posited in 'Moments' linked together in the 'crimson line' of points of intervention. Unlike Kierkegaard, for whom 'To believe is to believe the divine and human together in Jesus Christ',[13] Barth allows the consistent impulse of the dialectical tension of time and eternity to run freely against the merely asserted relation of the divinity and the humanity of Christ, which is thereby overwhelmed. The ontological *diastasis*, the drawing-apart into antithesis of time and eternity (representing the categories of finite and infinite existence), becomes the real locus of theological power. The antithesis is empowered by realized eschatology understood as the judging and the justifying act of God. The eschatological crisis blasts away any reliance upon a liberal Christology focused upon the life of Jesus or an orthodox Christology of a risen, triumphant Christ.

The combination of this radical disjunction with the principle of divine justification means that eternity purges time and any 'magnificent temporality of this world that can justify man before God' (*ER*, 56). The Pauline extinction of human boasting apart from God's justifying act in Jesus Christ is interpreted in the temporal categories of the dialectic. The philosophical antithesis of the idealist tradition becomes the vehicle of radical theological insight. So Barth commenting on Romans asserts that, 'They knew the judgement of God to be *according to the standard of truth*; and if men are measured by the standard of the truth of God, who can withstand it? Can stability be attained anywhere or at any time?' (*ER*, 58.) This demolition of human security includes Barth's own standpoint in time which has become highly problematic. His only recourse is to begin from outside of both speculative idealism and the passionate subjectivity characteristic of the existentialist alternative. In brief, Barth was to attempt to pass

---

[13] J. Heywood Thomas, 'Kierkegaard's View of Time', p. 36, referring to the *Papirer* IX, A101.

beyond the horns of a dilemma into what he came to understand and propound as the 'God-given'. In the years between the second edition of *The Epistle to the Romans* (1922) and the first volume (the Prolegomena) of the *Church Dogmatics* (1932) proper, he explored such ways of escape from the inevitable outcome of the theology of crisis.

According to Barth's interpretation of St. Paul in *Romans*, 'No road to the eternal meaning of the created world has ever existed, save the road of negation' (*ER*, 87) for the 'redemption that is in Christ Jesus' is 'the dissolution of history in history, the destruction of the structure of events within their own structure, the end of time in the order of time' (*ER*, 103). The disclosure of the 'timeless, necessary reality in the longitude of time' (*ER*, 116) is an exposure of the hidden victory of election over rejection, of life over death in a temporal dialectic. Barth's 'greedy dialectic of time and eternity' (*ER*, 530) is characterized as follows: 'Between the past and the future—between the times—there is a "Moment" that is no moment in time. This "Moment" is the eternal Moment—the *Now*—when the past and the future stand still, when the former ceases its going and the latter its coming.' (*ER*, 497.) Eternity is understood as the intrusion of a timeless 'Moment' 'between' the successive stages in the temporal order. As such it is the formal basis of the eschatological crisis, but offers little to a Christology that must not only mediate the encounter of judgement and justifying grace by divine *fiat*, but must also be related to creation and to the life and work of Christ and his salvation.

At this point a comparison may once more be drawn between the content of this essay and that of Dr Ford. Given the empty 'Now' of the 'eternal Moment', Barth has provided a theological receptacle at the centre of his renewed dialectic. Dr Ford's approach to Barth explores the method implied by the introduction of biblical narrative. R. W. Jenson's insight[14] that if the intersection of time and eternity were replaced with 'the story narrated by the second article of the Apostles' Creed, he would obtain the theology of the *Church Dogmatics*' is amply justified by Ford's analysis. It is my contention that

---

[14] *God after God: The God of the Future and the God of the Past seen in the Theology of Karl Barth* (Indianapolis, 1969).

such a substitution is fraught with difficulties exposed by analysis of the nature of time as it is exploited in Barth's new synthesis.

Barth's intermediate work between *Romans* and the first volume of the *Church Dogmatics* was extensive and much may be learnt, in particular, from his articles in *Zwischen den Zeiten* concerning his changing understanding of the nature of the theological task. In *The Resurrection of the Dead*[15] and the abandoned *Christliche Dogmatik* of 1927 Barth demonstrates a growing appreciation of the shortcomings of the post-*Romans* theological situation and of the difficulties of rebuilding theology. In the former, St. Paul is said to be speaking not only of the end of history and of time but also of a 'reality so radically superior to all happening and temporality, that in speaking of the finiteness of history and the finiteness of time, he is also speaking of that upon which all time and all happening is based' (*RD*, 110). Barth criticizes, moreover, the 'annihilation' of time by eternity, for 'real eternity' is that which 'marks' time as infinite. Eternity as the timeless crisis of tangential intersection is ontologically inadequate, it provides no 'base', and is merely subversive of time, adding nothing to it at all. Above all, Barth argues, the insight that 'God's eternity sets a limit to the endlessness of the world, time, things and men must be made fruitful.' (*RD*, 112.) The change from a negative to a positive appreciation of the importance of the concept of eternity in relation to time is one gauge of the degree of transformation in Barth's theological thought. In the abortive *Christliche Dogmatik* Barth made his first statement of an allegedly emancipated theology, that is, one free from the extraneous philosophical and non-biblical allusion so characteristic of *Romans*. But the 'existentialism' of the *Christliche Dogmatik* was heavily criticized[16] and Barth recommenced in earnest in the Prolegomena of the *Church Dogmatics* proper, working within the limits and upon the theological foundations outlined in the opening paragraphs of this paper. It was, according to Professor T. F. Torrance, a way forward that

---

[15] Trans. H. J. Stenny (London, 1933).

[16] See J. D. Smart, *The Divided Mind of Modern Theology* (Philadelphia, 1967), Ch.10.

must come from a concentration upon Christology, upon the Word made flesh, for therein there opened up the possibility of a dogmatics genuinely bound with a form taken from the Word rather than from contemporary and temporal philosophies ... With the concentration upon the Incarnation of the Word, upon Jesus Christ, God and Man in one Person, dialectical thinking had to fall away and positive Christological thinking had to take its place.[17]

We may agree with Torrance that this change took place, but its consequences remain unclear and merit sustained analysis.

Thus it is the precise nature and implications of this 'positive thinking' as it bears upon the problem of time that lies at the centre of interest in this essay. The profoundly 'negative' understanding of eternity over against time is evident in the early thought of Barth. This is both as regards its theological impulse, which is governed by the eschatological motif, and its actual temporal content, a conception of apparently 'timeless' eternity inhabiting momentary interstices in the temporal order. The changing theological demands made by the progress of Barth's thought as outlined above, calls for a corresponding transformation not merely in the theological framework of the encounter of eternity and time but also in the actual content of his temporal conceptions. This latter transformation is of crucial importance and an assessment of it leads the reader into the labyrinthine depths of the *Church Dogmatics*. The universality of the category of time entails a corresponding breadth of theological response, and it is such a response that is to be found in Barth's *magnum opus*.

In the foregoing sections the context and the development of Barth's thought have been set out briefly so as to allow a systematic examination of the doctrine of time and eternity in the *Church Dogmatics* to take place. Here can be found an extended and complex doctrine of time, which, whilst uniting many features of Barth's theological thought, is nevertheless built upon deep problems inherited from the idealist tradition and, beyond that, from the recurrent Platonizing tendency of Christian theology. The range and profundity of Barth's work demand a comprehensive response; and the following sections

---

[17] *Karl Barth, An Introduction to his Early Theology 1910–1931* (London, 1962), pp. 106–7.

attempt to achieve this comprehensive stance by means of a brief paraphrase of the *Church Dogmatics* from the standpoint of time, showing how certain fundamental conceptions form an indispensable aspect of the 'inner logic' of theology.

III

The theological integrity of Barth's thought allows of no simple distinction between conceptual bones and theological flesh. Thus it is only in the context of theological exposition that an analysis of the doctrine of time and of the conceptions employed can be made. Barth uses within a vast, variegated, but ultimately unified vision certain fundamental conceptions. If these are to be examined and criticized their function in this scheme must be understood. The passage, 'Man in his Time' (*CD* III/2 para. 37) (often regarded as most significant with regard to the problem of time) is but the culmination and anthropological application of a set of conceptions which operate throughout the whole structure of the *Church Dogmatics*. Because of this the following extended statement contains an outline of the theology of the *Church Dogmatics* as informed by the temporal and closely allied ontological ideas that form part of that basic structure. In this way the architectonic nature of the doctrine of time may be understood, as well as its consequences and particular applications.

The shift in Barth's method evident in the differences between the *Christliche Dogmatik* of 1927 and the first volume of the *Kirchliche Dogmatik* is expressed in the titles. The former retains the possibility of a subjective emphasis, the latter indicates *in nuce* the starting-point that Barth adopts, the given reality of the 'essence of the Church', Jesus Christ. In the *Church Dogmatics* the task of dogmatic theology 'presupposes the ascertainability by man of the proper content of Christian language about God' and, according to Barth, 'Language about God has the proper content, when it conforms to the essence of the Church, Jesus Christ'.[18] The Church has been and is constituted by the figure to which the New Testament

---

[18] *Church Dogmatics* I/1, 11. In the following pages both translations of the first half-volume have been used. The version quoted is considered the most apposite translation and is indicated by the translators' names, G. T. Thomson and G. W. Bromiley, respectively.

narrative witnesses. The theological exposition whilst related to such narrative, relies upon and exploits a conceptual structure which allows the 'Now-moment' to undergo extension in time. It is this structure which must be perceived as it underlies and informs Barth's exposition.

It is on the basis of the 'free personal presence of Jesus Christ' that theology may take place, but dogmatics as such seeks an explanation of this 'presence' which is indispensable and original, 'the uncontrollable presence of its ontic and noetic basis' (*CD*, I/1, 22, Bromiley). It is out of the 'reality' of this recurrent presence that the 'possibility' of theological explanation may be generated, resting upon what Barth terms 'the fundamental transcendence of all human possibilities' (*CD*, I/1, 44, Thomson) which takes place not as some inherent essence in the Church, but as '*actus purus*, divine action beginning with itself . . . free action, not a continuously present relation; grace is an event of personal approach.' (*CD* I/1, 43, Thomson.) The presence of God in proclamation, that is the realization of the Word of God, correspondingly occurs as 'man's language about God on the basis of an indication by God Himself fundamentally transcending all human causation, and so devoid of all human basis, merely occurring as a fact and requiring to be acknowledged' (*CD* I/1, 101, Thomson). The uniqueness of the divine presence in the self-objectification of God (*Selbstvergegenständlichung Gottes*) is secured by the unpredictable divine condescension, not by any immanent means of continuity. This emphasis upon the transcendent root of the occurrent divine presence gave rise to J. Hâmer's mistaken charge of an 'occasionalism' directed at the early volumes of the *Church Dogmatics*.[19] It is towards the basis of the divine presence in Church proclamation that Barth turns, postulating no timeless foundation, 'temporarily hidden but peacefully abiding' (*CD* I/1, 112, Thomson). This is not open to a Neoplatonic recollection or *anamnesis*, but, on the contrary, asserts a dynamic duality of immanence and transcendence which is experienced as a *fulfilment*, not a *negation* of time.

In a passage of importance, Barth sums up the temporal

---

[19] J. Hâmer, *Karl Barth* (London, 1962), pp. 33–5. It is precisely Barth's doctrine of God's temporal being that ostensibly overrides such a misconception as Hâmer's.

dimensions of the 'fulfilled time' (*die erfüllte Zeit*) in terms not incompatible with the early conception of the 'eternal Moment—the Now', cited earlier from *The Epistle to the Romans*, in which 'the past and the future stand still, when the former ceases its going and the latter its coming' (*ER*, 497). Thus, the 'God with us' has happened 'in human history and as part of human history', yet, according to Barth, 'it has not happened as other parts of this history usually happen' for it is self-sufficient and 'self-moved being in the stream of becoming (*Strom des Werdens*)', a 'completed event, fulfilled time, in the sea of the incomplete and changeable and self-changing' (*CD* I/1, 116, Bromiley). Barth is to derive not only 'eternity' or 'fulfilled time' from the '*Deus dixit*, to which there are no analogies', but also time itself, through the so-called 'true time' given in the revelation of God in Jesus Christ. In what follows the doctrine of time Barth provides has both function theologically and also to provide a concrete account of time as it is experienced and understood outside the purlieu of theology. Without such an actual fulfilment the threat of unreality will loom over his efforts.

The actual explication of the temporal continuity of revelation, the so-called gracious divine presence, is made in terms of the doctrine of the Word of God as the direct sign and correlate of the doctrine of the Trinity, for the 'Word needs no supplementing by the act. The Word of God is itself the act of God.' (*CD* I/1, 163, Thomson.) The 'natural and corporeal' realities of preaching, the man Jesus Christ, the Church, and the Word of God written are the vehicle of the 'fulfilled reality' which is underlaid and sustained by the 'contingent contemporaneousness' (*kontingente Gleichzeitigkeit*) of God's act. By this term Barth conveys to the reader (albeit inadvertently) the ambiguity of his conception of time in relation to revelation, for, as will become apparent, he is at pains to posit contingency of the basis of revelation, not upon the basis of what are normally considered historical acts. The derivation of the ultimate reality of all realities from revelation (given the validity of the eschatological purge entailed by Barth's conception of justification expounded in *Romans*) makes quite inevitable a persistent and often uncomfortable synthesis of conflicting attributes and categories, not least in the temporal dimension. This will become increasingly apparent as analysis of the theological basis of the early volumes of the *Church Dogmatics* proceeds below.

The initial presupposition in Barth's argument is that, 'God's word is God's act means first its contingent contemporaneousness.' (*CD* I/1, 164, Thomson.) Barth's meaning is conveyed by the etymology of 'con-temporaneousness', that is a kind of 'temporal togetherness'. By means of this conception Barth argues that the 'times' of prophecy, apostolate, and Church, and so on, are at one with the 'direct, original utterance of God Himself in His revelation, the time of Jesus Christ' (*CD* I/1, 164, Thomson). Quite literally for Barth these times are 'together which Christ' by virtue of the fact that the 'Word of God is itself God's act' (*CD* I/1, 168). Such a temporal grasp by means of the actuality of the divine Word should not be taken as a sure and certain sign of a radical disregard for history on Barth's part. On the contrary it is his unending struggle to do justice to *both* temporal and historical diversity as well as to a final unity which informs his doctrine of time and eternity throughout the *Church Dogmatics*. If, however, Barth's understanding of history and time is not to fall back into a quasi-idealist de-temporalization of the biblical witness or Church history then he is bound to resist the tendency towards a negative atemporal conception of eternity that was characteristic of his thought in *The Epistle to the Romans* and is indeed still evident in the early parts of volume I/1 of the *Church Dogmatics*. It is by the positing of the 'act' of God as a dynamic, living basis of the unity of the Word of God that Barth strives to escape the constant threat of a Platonic dissolution of time into eternity.

The notion of the 'act of God' is therefore of decisive importance for it underlies the apparently distinct theological concepts of election, revelation, calling, new birth, and so on. This 'act' 'shatters the immanence of the historical connection from within', thus allowing, so Barth asserts, the time of Christ to be contemporary with the time of the prophets and the Church 'without removal of the difference' between them (*CD* I/1, 168, Thomson). The divine 'Now' to which the whole of biblical history and Church history relates is not a simple unity *per se*, but the ostensibly dynamic ground of the act of

God. It is thus exclusively by reference to Jesus Christ (who is, as will be seen, the 'reality' of God's act) and to the Trinity, that the trans-temporal unity and thus the hermeneutical interconnection of the proclaimed, written, and revealed God is achieved.

What is the 'possibility' that can be deduced from the 'reality' that Barth posits? How is this 'act' to be understood? Answers to these questions will reveal a considerable amount about the nature and function of the concept of time in the *Church Dogmatics*. In congruity with Barth's epistemological principles[20] the 'reality' of revelation leads through analysis into an account of the Trinity as its 'possibility'. Correspondingly the temporal structure of the inner possibility of the statement, 'God reveals Himself' is the Trinitarian foundation of the 'presence of the Word of God between the Times' (*CD* I/1, 334, Thomson). Barth adheres exclusively to the doctrine of the Trinity as the basis of the knowledge of God (*CD* I/1, 349–383, Thomson) and it is *within* these parameters that the doctrine of time must consequently be understood. The doctrine of the Trinity as an 'explanatory confirmation' of the revealed name Yahweh–Kyrios is the explication of 'a unique entity, of a single unique Willer and Doer, whom Scripture designates as God' (*CD* I/1, 400, Thomson). By such an identification Barth introduces the conceptions of being and act, entity and agent *in unity*, and thus he claims to build a bridge between the ontological thinking of the Greek Fathers and the revealing God of the Bible. The unhestitating equation that is made here between the biblical concept of revelation and the lordship of God, on the one hand, and on the other the language of essence and substance, characteristic of patristic theology, presages an integration of 'being' and 'act' of great significance and this has a consistently important influence upon the conception of time in the *Church Dogmatics*.[21]

The relative worth of Barth's doctrine of the Trinity developed in the latter parts of volume I/1 of the *Church Dogmatics* is not of prime importance here, save to note that it

---

[20] See *CD* I/1, (Thomson), 214, 236–7 for an account of knowledge as 'acknowledgement'.

[21] Such an integration is not of course unique to Barth.

is above all the unity of the Godhead that he seeks to confirm. This is to be expected, as Barth must at all costs preserve the unity of the divine act, for 'all God's operation, as we are bound to conceive it on the basis of this revelation, is a single act, occurring simultaneously and unitedly in all His three modes of existence' and consequently it must be said 'Of creation, past revelation and reconciliation, to the redemption to come it holds good that He who acts here is the Father and the Son and the Spirit.' (*CD* I/1, 430, Thomson.) The unity of Barth's whole theological scheme can only be preserved if the unity of the divine act is sustained, because the doctrine of God's being-in-act is the ontological *fundamentum* of the *Church Dogmatics*, and the axis of eternity and time the medium through which this ontology is diffused throughout the theological structure of his work. So it is that the pattern of antecedence and consequence and the corresponding method of *analogia fidei* informing the *Church Dogmatics* take on an urgent importance in the context of the doctrine of time. Here the derivation of the fullest and truest reality from the divine arm of these dualities gives immense theological power to the doctrine of time, yet, simultaneously, this raises not inconsiderable problems.

Given the axis of antecedence and consequence, the Fatherhood of God is derived from his Fatherhood of Jesus Christ. As the functional reciprocity of Father, Son, and the Holy Spirit is realized in the life, death, and resurrection of Jesus Christ, so God the Father is revealed as Creator. It is from within the 'self-enclosed circle' of the doctrine of the Trinity that God the Creator is known (*CD* I/1, 436, Thomson). The status of this assertion is a factor of great importance because the whole *catena* of temporal conceptions must be understood in relation to the central revelatory events in which the Trinitarian life-in-act of God is realized. Indeed the ontology of human existence is likewise bound up with the 'Lordship' of God for 'our existence is held by him, and only by him, over the abyss of non-existence . . . It is real so far as He wills and posits it a real existence.' (*CD* I/1, 446, Thomson.) Human existence, and thus time which is 'real so far as He wills and posits it a real existence' raises a difficulty inherent in the *Church Dogmatics* as a whole: How does this 'real existence' relate to that existence experienced by the human subject as a mere percipient being? This problem is acute with regard to time, as will become apparent in the exposition of *Man in his Time* (*CD* III/2, para. 37). Suffice it to note here that as Barth derives the Fatherhood of God from his antecedent, eternal Fatherhood of Jesus Christ, so, likewise, must time be derived from within the 'self-enclosed circle'. Furthermore, in the light of this antecedence and the centrality of the divine 'act' as the content of the 'presence' of Jesus Christ, the 'essence of the Church' in revelation, so it is not time, *per se*, upon which attention must be concentrated, but eternity as the temporal *plenum* from which time takes its reality.

IV

Having made an initial examination of the relation of time to the divine act in Jesus Christ and observed that this act is spelt out in Trinitarian terms it is now possible to proceed to a more detailed presentation of Barth's understanding of the nature and relation of eternity and time. This is most clearly expressed as regards eternity in the account of the divine perfections in volume II/1 of the *Church Dogmatics*. Here the 'act' of volume I/1 becomes the 'perfection' of God's eternity.

'Eternity' first emerges as an important theme in the exposition of the Niceno–Constantinopolitan Creed that concludes volume I/1 of the *Church Dogmatics*. Here it denotes the status 'before all time' of the Persons of the Trinity and it is at this point that the transformation of the temporal conceptions is once more apparent. The phrase 'before all time' indicates the mysterious inclusion of the time of revelation and that of the sinful creature (*CD* I/1, 425, Bromiley). The πρo πàντων αἰώνων (before all worlds) of the Creed does not grant a 'temporal definition' but, according to Barth, gives an indication of 'genuine and eternal transcendence' (*CD* I/1 427, Bromiley). Despite this proviso, there is here the initial presentation of a conception that has ordinary temporal implications. The theological conditioning must not, however, shroud the logic of the concept of eternity and time being developed. In *Romans* there was the eternal ' "Moment" that is no moment in time', a '*Now*—when the past and the future stand still' which becomes the 'unborn secret of revelation' qualifying the moments of common time (*ER*, 497). In the first volume of the *Church Dogmatics* the basis of such qualification is indicated, for once more the 'absolutely marked (i.e. distinguished) events in time' (*schlechterdings ausgezeichnete Ereignisse*) (*CD* I/1, 488, Thomson) are moments in which the eternal encounters time; but now, by contrast, the reader is initiated theologically into the 'unborn secret of revelation' (*ER*, 497).

What has happened is that the dialectic of antitheses in *The Epistle to the Romans* has given way to a dialectic informed by a new conjunction of transcendence and immanence, that is a creative 'inclusion' of time by eternity. The simple 'annihilation' of time has apparently been superseded. The distinction between the temporal concepts of *Romans* and those of the first half-volume of the *Church Dogmatics* deserves qualified statement, for there remains both continuity and new development. The decisive temporal source (the 'Now' moment of *Romans*) is given temporal and historical extension as it becomes identified with God's act in Jesus Christ as propounded in volume I/1.

Much now depends upon whether the actual content of the temporal conceptions can bear the positive (as opposed to the destructive) weight now laid upon them. The dialectic of *Romans* made highly effective use of the Platonizing dissolution of time into eternity through the eschatological annihilation of human (and therefore temporally bound) assertion in the *Krisis* of divine judgement. Whether the remnants of such temporal conceptions can function as adequately in the context of a positive theological exposition, such as Barth attempts in the *Church Dogmatics*, remains to be seen. In volume I/1 the beginnings of such a transmutation are evident, but the ambiguity of Barth's efforts are equally apparent given the incipient tension between theological intention, and the conceptual tools to be employed in the theology of eternity and time *per se*.

The ambiguity of affirming time and its reality through the 'analogical' use of eternity stems from the problematic 'temporal' nature of the latter. The weight placed upon the antecedent and essential concept of the divine act extended in 'contingent contemporaneity' is markedly increased by

Barth's corresponding denial of natural theology. Once more we need not enter into the rationale of Barth's adoption of this stance, save to point out that it is entirely congruent with his uncompromising and consistent advocacy of the principle of justification by God's grace alone. It is the consequences of such a rejection that concern us, for, as we shall become aware, the denial of natural theology comes dangerously close to a repudiation of natural reality itself.

In the context of the uncompromising rejection of the pretensions of natural theology and of the analogy of being (which is to be understood in the light of the exclusive source of the knowledge of God, and God's identity with knowledge of himself, *CD* II/1, 10–16) man is consequently denied 'independent existence' for 'the vitality of natural theology is the vitality of man as such' (*CD* II/1, 165). Once more the purge of human self-assertion is sustained with consistency, but a new element has appeared for 'Man exists in Jesus Christ and in Him alone.' Indeed, Barth asserts, 'The being and nature of men in and for themselves as independent bearers of an independent predicate, have, by the revelation of Jesus Christ, become an abstraction which can be destined only to disappear.' (*CD* II/1, 149.) This denial and Christ-ologically inspired affirmation must be stressed because it is in direct parallel with the assertion of humanity in Christ that temporality is likewise to be understood. These affirmations of man in Christ are the realization and correlates of the divine act in being, of the God 'who is in His act of revelation' (*CD* II/1, 262).

This 'act' is explicated in paragraph 28 of volume II/1, 'The Being of God in Act', where Barth asserts the divine being apart from, and over against, any doctrine of being *qua* being. The first declaration, 'that in God's revelation, which is the content of this Word we have to do with His act' is followed by an exposition which exploits and develops the temporal 'inclusiveness' advanced in the latter stages of volume I/1 and outlined in the preceding section of this essay. The being-in-act of God has immediate temporal implications, as might be expected if it is to contain within its 'simplicity' the total time-scale envisaged. The event is in the past yet it also happens now and will happen in the future, for the birth, death, and resurrection of Jesus are temporally unlimited. This because if the event is the act of God whose being as 'event' or 'act' is final, then there can be no further penetration, only the explanation (in effect the *exegesis*) of what is posited in his act. The theological spade turns upon the bedrock of the utterly surpassing actuality of the divine Word[22]—it is ultimate reality.

God's act, his *actus purus et singularis*, exists in revelation in 'dialectical transcendence', that is, it is self-distinguished from 'general happening' within which the 'definite happening' (*bestimmtes Geschehen*) of revelation takes place (*CD* II/1, 264). The particularity and specific freedom of God's act, event, and life is by way of the concrete existence of Israel, the birth of Jesus Christ, his resurrection, and so on, which are the indispensable correlates of the divine act. In the briefest terms, 'the whole content of the happening consists in the fact that the Word of God became flesh and that His Holy Spirit is poured out on all flesh.' (*CD* II/1, 267.) Barth's integration of the *Deus in se* and the *Deus revelatus* in his active freedom is expressed in a doctrine of the divine perfections which extrapolates and integrates his emphasis upon the dynamic and the actual. The activity of God understood as the fulfilment of the statement that 'Jesus Christ is the same yesterday and today and forever' (Heb. 13:8) is explicated in terms which stress the positive attributes expressing that activity, rather than as metaphysical statements and limitations. Against what he conceives of as a Hegelian depersonalized doctrine of Absolute Spirit, Barth stresses the 'particularity of the divine event in the particularity of the being of a person' (*CD* II/1, 267–71). This being does not subsist in holy isolation, but love and grace overflow, they take place in 'the whole intervention of the divine action and being' (*CD* II/1, 281). In the equation '"God is " means "God loves"', act, being, love, and person are unified in Jesus Christ. By locating his synthesis of categories in the divine act and by identifying this act with the person of Jesus Christ, Barth putatively escapes the reductive comprehensiveness of the Hegelian dialectic. The pattern of antecedence and consequence struc-

---

[22] Close study of pp. 262–4 of *CD* II/1 is essential for a full understanding of Barth's argument at this point.

turing in dynamic terms the divine act is realized in the concrete historical man Jesus Christ, in his time and in his person. In the account of the divine perfections the idea of eternity is developed, but it remains subordinate to Christology and the Father–Son axis which constantly informs Barth's exposition.

In the context of this framework there follows an account of the divine perfections in which the attributes of God are expounded as a positive doctrine of the 'Biblical idea of God' (*CD* II/1, 302). Included among these 'perfections', eternity is developed in the context of the discrete originality of the divine being, which is 'itself perfection and so the standard of all perfection' (*CD* II/1, 322). The perfections of God (as the Persons of the Trinity) are dynamically coexistent and consubstantial, as this doctrine is the 'development and confirmation of the doctrine of His being' (*CD* II/1, 327). The scholastic appearance of Barth's exposition is belied by his consistent attempts to avoid the pitfalls of the traditional arguments concerning attribution, which he sees as providing grounds for a rejection of metaphysical theology parallel to that of Kant. The being of God is not a speculative entity, but is one with his revelation, and thus the exegesis of the simplicity of God, as the foundation upon which constancy, eternity, omnipresence, omnipotence, and glory are built, is conducted in such a way as to avoid logical reduction. Again it is impossible to convey in outline the richness of Barth's exposition, as the very essence of his argument consists not in an extended or connected logic in which each proposition follows from the former, but in a 'vertical' logic whereby the validity of the cohering assertions is given by the quality of purported witness each makes to the divine being. For Barth the very uniqueness of God would logically demand such an approach. Following the exposition of God's unity and simplicity, and his omnipresence and spatiality (all understood in the context of their utter prototypical superiority in God's active and dynamic being), comes the first extended consideration of eternity *per se*.

Having denied the participation of eternity in the finite-infinite dialectic (*CD* II/1, 188–9) and based his conception upon purely theological postulates, Barth contends that eternity, in itself and as such is to be understood as a determination of the divine freedom. Like the unity and constancy of God, it primarily denotes the absolute sovereignty and majesty of God in itself and as such, as demonstrated in the inward and outward activity of His divine being and operative in His love as the eternal love. God's love requires and possesses eternity both inwards and outwards for the sake of its divinity, its freedom. Correspondingly it requires, creates and therefore possesses in its outward relations what we call time. Time is the form of creation in virtue of which it is definitely fitted to be a theatre for the acts of divine freedom. (*CD* II/1, 464–5.)

Eternity and time are defined in terms of their functional roles in the doctrine of God as Revealer and thus any conceptions of omnipresence and eternity based upon an understanding of God as 'the supreme principle of existence and the universal' embracing space and time are ruled out. The latter stem from the 'problems of a created existence and a created world' and such fail to relate to the God of Christian revelation. Infinity as such can form no adequate basis for a concept of eternity, for 'It speaks of the non-finiteness, the non-limitedness or non-limitableness, and therefore the time-lessness and non-spatiality of God.' (*CD* II/1, 465.) The ensuing criticism of a timeless eternity as an adjunct of the immanent antithesis of finite and infinite and 'the general concept of tradition' is made on the basis of its 'insufficiency' in describing what God is in relation to space and time. God's 'infinity' involves no contradiction with finitude, for his 'whole action posits beginning and end, measure and limit, space and time'.

It is now apparent that Barth's argument is double-edged at the very least. On the one hand he denies the involvement of true eternity with the dialectic of finite and infinite categories; on the other he affirms eternity as the total time-positing action of God. This position can only be consistently maintained if the temporal categories asserted by the latter at no point identify with the finite-infinite dialectic. This means that the vast and complex temporal system that emerges in the *Church Dogmatics* must never coincide with non-theological temporal categories in identity, only in the so-called dialectic of transcendence. Can, however, the 'time' that emerges be the time of the world of experience and the cosmos if it is systematically at one remove from it, as what Barth will term the 'true time' of revelation? If this 'time' is not so correlated then what consequences will there be? Can the most powerful theological assertions be made about the shared realities of human existence, if such theologically posited realities are absolutely undetectable outside the peculiar theological mode of their positing and perception? Indeed can such an entirely self-consistent system escape from a certain triviality or even logical circularity? More specifically, can the concept of time reside entirely within the 'theological circle' that Barth expands, without what may be called a logical implosion into timelessness, once the relationship and identity of this concept with the shared time of human and cosmic existence is systematically excluded? The doubts raised here must remain in mind as continuing examination is made of the concept of eternity and its temporal correlates.

On the basis of the foregoing exposition of the theological factors informing Barth's doctrine of eternity the passage 'The Eternity and Glory of God' (*CD* II/1, 608–77) can be seen to contain a new aspect of the synthesis between the systematic and the biblical in Christian theology. In this passage of Boethian conception, *Aeternitas est interminabilis vitae tota simul et perfecta possessio*, (eternity is the complete and perfect possession of unending life) receives, according to Barth its 'proper exploitation' as the legitimate fulfilment of both biblical and systematic insight. In a passage concrete, yet rhapsodic in style, the ambiguity of Barth's thought is perceived in that it progresses towards the apparent, yet ostensibly resolvable contradiction of deriving time from eternity.

God's eternity, as an expression of the divine freedom, is 'pure duration' (*reine Dauer*). 'Pure duration' denotes the divine simultaneity (*Gleichzeitigkeit*) in which beginning, middle, and end are not three, but one, not separate as on three occasions, but one simultaneous occasion. Time, on the other hand, has beginning, middle, and end which are distinct and even opposed as past, present, and future. In consequence, Barth argues, eternity is 'just that duration which is lacking to time'. In that eternity is simultaneity, so it is said to provide the duration lacking in time.

God, as the 'prototype and foreordination of all being, and

therefore the prototype and foreordination of time' (*CD* II/1, 611), does not negate time because eternity as 'pure duration', the 'pure present', is only properly exploited when it 'includes' time. Time pre-exists in God's eternity, his endurance, 'duration itself', does not prevent him being 'origin, movement and goal' (*Ursprung, Bewegung und Ziel*). What distinguishes eternity from time is that 'origin, movement and goal', past, present, and future, 'not yet', 'now', and 'no more', rest and movement, potentiallity and actuality, and so on, are all held in God's being, his eternity in a pure present. In eternity, therefore, these distinctions exist, but purportedly without the fleeting nature of the present, the separation between before and after.[23] Eternity is not the negation of time, an 'abstract non-temporality' in any simple sense, although it is 'certainly the negation of created time in so far as it has no part in the problematical and questionable nature of our possession of time', that is, 'to the extent that it is first and foremost God's time and therefore real time (*wirkliche Zeit*)' (*CD* II/1, 613).

With the introduction of the notion of 'God's time' and 'real time' on the basis of a positive 'proper exploitation' of the Boethian concept of eternity, Barth has carried his synthesis a stage further. The apparent contradiction of deriving the many from the one has now become explicit: 'God does not first create multiplicity and movement, but He is one and simple, He is constant, in such a way that all multiplicity and movement have their prototype and pre-existence in Himself.' (*CD* II/1, 612.) God, in his true being, in the begetting of the Son and the procession of the Spirit, exemplifies an order and succession in which 'unity is in movement' and in which there is a 'before and after' (*CD* II/1, 615). 'God's time' is 'the form of the divine being in its trinity' in which beginning and ending do not imply and limitation (*Begrenzung*) of God nor does this inner juxtaposition (*Nacheinander*) mean that there is any exclusion (*Auseinander*). So Barth develops his exposition of 'pure duration' upon an explicitly Trinitarian basis of prototypical interaction and reciprocity without division. The relationship between the Trinitarian and the temporal doc-

[23] There is an affinity here with the arguments advanced concerning the time orders of 'before' and 'after' and 'past, present and future' in J. M. E. McTaggart's *The Nature of Existence* (Cambridge, 1927), vol. II, Bk. V, Ch. 33.

trines is enhanced by similar terminology used by Barth in both contexts, thereby implying a continuity of argument.

It would be possible at this stage in the exploration of the doctrine of time to turn to Barth's antecedents and compare his conception of eternity with those inherited from Parmenides, Plato, Plotinus, St. Augustine, and Boethius, and presented in systematic form in, for example, the *Summa Theologica* of St. Thomas Aquinas.[24] The importance of Barth's argument lies in its synthetic impulse and therefore in this essay attention must remain focused upon his goal of renewal and integration. The 'pure-duration' which stems from the informing of the Boethian *totum simul* by the Trinitarian impulse is then applied to the biblical context. The 'from everlasting to everlasting' of Ps. 90:2 which is 'so common in both Old and New Testaments . . . can be taken to mean from duration to duration, that is, in pure duration' (*CD* II/1, 609). The phrase, 'can be taken to mean' indicates in fact a substantial and methodological identity between the dogmatic conceptions that Barth has appropriated and developed and the biblical insights hinted at in Isa. 43; Ps. 90; 2 Pet. 3: 8; Ps. 102, and so on. Barth's positive appropriation of the Boethian notion of a divine simultaneity, which is reasserted upon a Trinitarian basis developed in the first half-volume of the *Church Dogmatics* and now identified with biblical insight, is ready to be applied and exploited. Eternity, 'pure duration', is God's 'real time' and so now all God's revelatory activity in history, supremely (indeed in a sense, exclusively) in Jesus Christ can be conditioned by this positive theological conception of eternity.

In strictly temporal terms the *nunc stans*, 'the "now", the total and simultaneous present' which is the '*possessio vitae*, the total, simultaneous possession of unlimited life' is opposed to the merely negative 'now', the 'fluid fleeting present, which can be understood only as a mathematical point'. The theological elements underlying the former allow it to 'heal' the latter, as its 'duration' encounters the 'division' of mere

[24] Consultation of F. H. Brabant's Bampton Lectures, *Time and Eternity in Christian Thought* (1936), and relevant chapters in E. Bevan's Gifford Lectures, *Symbolism and Belief* (1933–4), provide initial guidance. More recent discussion may be found in W. Kneale, 'Time and Eternity in Theology', *Proceedings of the Aristotelian Society*, vol. LXI, (1961), 87–108.

(human) time. This juxtaposition is of course interpreted in positive theological terms and in correspondence with the initial exposition of the 'fulness of time which is identical with Jesus Christ' (*CD* I/1, 131, Thompson). As the Word became flesh, so eternity (without ceasing to be eternity) became time. In Jesus Christ it is not, Barth argues, merely that God has given us time, 'our created time, as the form of our own existence and world', but that 'God takes time to Himself, that He Himself, the eternal One, becomes temporal' and so, in consequence he not merely 'embraces' but 'submits' to it (*CD* II/1, 616).

v

We have at this point accumulated the essential elements which allow us to proceed to review the systematic application of the basic equation of the divine being in act (with all its temporal implications) with the person of Jesus Christ. Eternity as the pure act of the divine being is the ground of the temporal unity and comprehensiveness of Jesus Christ, the 'essence of the Church'. Enormous weight is consequently laid upon Christology if the God-man is to be man in any acceptable sense and not merely the supra-philosophical expression of the divine being and the resolution of antitheses.

So it is that the very nerve-centre of Barth's theology is reached, that Christological concentration in which is located the realization of the divine being, expounded in the Trinitarian and ontological treatises of volumes I/1 and II/1 of the *Church Dogmatics* respectively. Christology, *per se*, has a temporal structure in which may be perceived three interconnected 'moments', predestination (or as Barth prefers, 'election'), incarnation, and resurrection. All three elements have a unified application in theological anthropology, that is in 'Man in his Time' (*CD* III/2, para. 37).

(a) Election

'The election of grace is the sum of the Gospel.' (*CD* II/2, 13.) With these words Barth enters into his positive exposition of the doctrine of election and his dialogue with the Reformed tradition. The election of grace is 'the choice of God, which preceding all His other choices, is fulfilled in the eternal

willing of the man Jesus and of the people represented in Him'
(*CD* II/2, II, 25). Repudiating the classes of humanity, the
elect and the reprobate, Barth places all men in a similar
relationship to God in Christ, to the 'primal and basic act of
God'. There can be no probing beyond the eternal choice of
God already made in God's act, that is his own election of
Jesus Christ. The eternal decision to elect Jesus Christ and to
elect man in solidarity with him is realized in time. In
becoming man, a particular man who represents the whole
people, 'God Himself realized in time, and therefore as an
object of human perception, the self-giving of Himself as the
Covenant—partner of the people determined by Him from
and to all eternity' (*CD* II/2, 53).

The eternal decision of God made in 'primal history' is
realized in the concrete particularity and revelation of God in
the history of Israel and in the Incarnation itself.[25] In Jesus
Christ 'electing God' and 'elected man' are one, and it is upon
him *alone*, Barth argues, that attention must be focused and
not upon 'abstract presuppositions concerning God or man, or
of the abstract consequences of such abstract presuppositions'
(*CD* II/2, 59). Progress in understanding should only be made
in confirming and developing the presuppositions 'contained
in the name of Jesus Christ'. It would seem possible at this
point to draw out an invidious contrast between on the one
hand the eternal basis of election in the 'perfect presence' of
God in the pre–, supra–, and post-temporality of 'primal
history' (in which there is 'duration' without, Barth argues,
'division') and on the other the realization of revelation in
time in the life and death of Jesus Christ. In Barth's own
theological terms the tension does not exist, given the pre-
eminence of the divine contingent act in revelation from which
all history ostensibly derives its contingency. In more general
terms, however, it is possible to point to an incompatibility
between election in the 'perfect presence' (a presence of
'duration' without the 'division' of before and after) and the
contingent historical acts of salvation. If the latter are to be
significant acts, then they certainly must have a distinct before
and after. Without such 'division' nothing could have been

---

[25] H. Küng's excursus, 'The Redeemer in God's Eternity', pp. 272–88 of *Justification* (London, 1964), is relevant for the following exposition.

achieved by the death of Christ, or indeed his resurrection precisely because nothing could be said to have *happened* in a significant sense. The reality of what takes place is sapped by Barth's argument at this and other points.

The mutuality of electing God and elected man in the doctrine of predestination is the basis upon which a fully integrated Christology and soteriology is to be developed. The Johannine elements in Barth's thought now become apparent: the Word from the beginning is the Word which becomes flesh. This is to be expressed in a doctrine of the two natures from which all soteriological possibilities flow. In so far as God's works are done 'in time they rest upon the eternal decision of God by which time is founded and governed' (*CD* II/2, 99). Thus it is that grace precedes creation, for prior to the establishment of any reality distinct from God, 'God anticipated and determined within Himself . . . that the goal and meaning of all His dealings with the as yet non-existent universe should be the fact that in His Son He would be gracious towards man, uniting Himself with him.' (*CD* II/2, 101.) Creation and covenant as the consequence of the resolve of the triune God are derived from their central point in Jesus Christ. Without the unity of predestination and Christology eternal work and temporal event would fall apart. The very comprehensiveness and unity of Barth's vision, whilst entirely corresponding with the extensive dogmatic basis outlined here, is not without its dangers in that the distinction between the area of divine antecedence and that of temporal consequence, between the transcendent and the immanent, becomes blurred and ambiguous.

In the election and rejection of Jesus Christ sin is overcome and, therefore, 'In Jesus Christ we can see and know this sphere of evil as something which has already been overcome . . . which has been destroyed by the positive will of God's overflowing glory.' (*CD* II/2, 172.) 'Sin' must here be understood in the light of Barth's doctrine of 'nothingness' (*Nichtigkeit*) as the 'impossible possibility', that which exists in despite of the divine will. The overcoming of sin in Jesus Christ is the overcoming of 'nothingness' or non-being and its replacement or 'fulfilment' by the reality of revelation. The assertions also cohere with Barth's polemic against natural theology and compound the difficulty of his position. Inevitably 'sin' is in danger of being identified with the natural order as such which only becomes positively real as it is realized in the sphere of the analogy of faith. The relatively static and distinct categories of traditional theology (grace and nature, transcendent and immanent, and so on) are reinterpreted in the context of revelation and the analogy of faith in such a way that they appear as mere functions within a larger, dominant equation concerning the nature of the divine being.

The particular consequence of Barth's compression of election and rejection into the elected and rejected Jesus Christ is to shift the fulcrum of the divine action from Jesus Christ's act in history to God's act in him in eternity or the 'perfect presence'. A consequence of the surpassing completeness of the redemptive activity of God in his act in Christ is to make the path to salvation a merely noetic realization such that the 'godless man' comes to know that his choice is 'void' and that he is elected in Jesus Christ. The 'new creation' has taken place in Jesus Christ and the hearers and believers realize in their affirmation the completedness of the election of man made in Jesus Christ. Such a conception of election in its concentration upon the exclusive centrality in Jesus Christ is once more congruent with the utter self-sufficiency of the divine act as expounded temporally in the doctrine of eternity.

The problem is that given this exclusiveness, the temporal dimension of salvation becomes questionable, and what Barth calls the 'consummation' of the Reformation insight into the work of Christ and God's justifying act comes dangerously close to a *reductio ad absurdum*. The election of men in Christ 'transcending their own being, . . . also transcends the being of everything which God has created and which is distinct from Himself, with the exception of one man, Jesus of Nazareth'; as the 'eternal basis' of the existence of those who live as the elect this election is something which 'happened *to* and not *in* their human nature and its possibilities, *to* and not *in* their human history and its development' (*CD* II/2, 321). Correspondingly men's 'special calling simply discloses and confirms the fact that they are already the elected' (*CD* II/2, 341) and that the 'rejected man' only exists as the 'object of the divine non-willing' (*CD* II/2, 450), that is, as sinners.

In over-all outline Barth's doctrine of election is a reworking of the Protestant tradition in such a way as to integrate the Reformed emphasis upon the primacy of divine grace with the Lutheran concentration upon the utter exclusivity of the revelation of God in Christ alone. As noted above, the completeness of the election of man in Christ is congruent with the dogmatic ontology of the act of God, the *actus purus et singularis*, outlined in this essay. If, however, the act of God in Christ is not to remain unrelated to the human condition and to the sin-ridden complexity of individual human lives, then it must be expressed in adequate temporal terms, not only in relation to the shared human temporality of ordinary life, but also to the actual death and resurrection of the man Jesus Christ. Such as identity and involvement cannot remain frozen within eternal election, albeit an election in the eternal act of God (which contains within itself the pre–, supra–, and post–temporality of the divine being), but must truly enter time as it does in the 'story' of the Gospels.

Barth is aware in his own way of this danger of unrelatedness, which he sees as an adjunct of the traditional legalistic conception of election in an eternal decree dividing humanity into elect and reprobate. According to the traditional view, 'God was', for 'in time he predestinates no longer' (*CD* II/2, 182); the election exhibits a Deistic pattern, in which the divine decision is, once made, worked out without further reference to God. Such inadequacy may be countered, Barth argues, by exploitation of the full doctrine of eternity and its application to the doctrine of election. In his understanding of election, predestination ceases to be an *apologia* for God's absence, but becomes the means of his presence in time for the 'predestination of God is unchanged and unchangeably God's activity' (*CD* II/2, 183). So God's ontology of act conditions the doctrine of election, as it does all doctrines, for the pre–, supra–, and post–temporality of God in his eternity is the reality underlying election. The tension between eternal work and temporal realization is still problematic, however, so long as all the interpretative categories are grounded in and derived from the divine and eternal being of God. Thus a great deal depends upon the adequacy of Barth's conceptual distinction of, and relation between, eternity and time, as well as upon the purely theological exposition which is to reach its temporal consummation in the death and resurrection of Jesus Christ.

(b) Incarnation and Christology

Karl Barth's doctrine of the Incarnation is determined by the pattern of thought expounded in his book on Anselm, according to which fact precedes interpretation, and so the 'simple reality of God' (*CD* I/2, 11) is revealed in 'God's time'. This simple reality is not a 'repeated or general event, like that of an event formulated in a law of causality', but a 'definite, temporally limited unrepeated and quite unrepeatable event' which has happened once for all, but which at the same time acts as the 'midpoint of time' (*die Mitte der Zeit*). The midpoint of time is the fulfilment of time with which are identical both the 'real temporal pre-existence of Jesus Christ in prophecy and his real temporal post-existence in witness' (*CD* I/2, 12). Cullmann's understanding of the 'midpoint of time' differs quite decisively from Barth's in that the latter is not contrasting eternity and time as mere finite (limited) and infinite (unlimited) duration but is once more asserting a temporal transcendence. The danger that we encounter in Barth's account is not merely that of an alien remnant of philosophy (Cullmann's charge)[26] but whether the 'mid-point' really is truly temporal, whether it does in fact determine human time or remains a purely theological construction, in danger of being what H. Bouillard terms a 'dream'.[27]

Barth proceeds to develop his doctrine of the Incarnation along classical Christological lines, 'the becoming flesh of the Word that remains the Word' (*CD* I/2, 38). In 'God's Time and our Time', the theme of the Incarnation is developed in specific and detailed temporal terms laying down the pattern of thought applied in the remaining two sections of paragraph 14, 'The Time of Revelation'. Barth's exposition is influenced by that of St. Augustine in the *De Trinitate*[28] but the former's work must remain at the forefront of attention. The statement 'God reveals Himself' is equivalent to the assertion that 'God

---

[26] See *Christ and Time* (rev. edn., London, 1962).
[27] *The Knowledge of God* (London, 1969), p. 61.
[28] See Bk. IV, Ch. 19 and the *Confessions*, Bk. XI, esp. Chs. 16 and 39.

has time for us'; this is 'the time that is real in this revelation' and this time-concept is determinative. No time-concept apart from that of revelation itself maybe used, 'we must let ourselves be told what time is by revelation itself' (*CD* I/2, 45) and it is this principle that is applied with absolute consistency.

The completeness of Barth's account becomes even more obvious, but its problematic nature no less so. The difficulty concerns the relative spheres of natural and revealed knowledge in Barth's thought. According to T. F. Torrance, 'Barth's understanding of the Incarnation as the truth of God incarnate in space and time, encountering us in space and time, encountering us objectively in Jesus Christ, had the unavoidable effect of calling into question any idea that the truth about God arises within us.'[29] This is only half the truth for in his advocacy of 'the special concept of this special time' (*CD* I/2, 45) Barth is effectually calling into question not merely anthropocentric sources of revealed knowledge of God but natural knowledge of the natural world. The demand that the Incarnation be 'real', yet its reality lie in its own sphere and temporal reality, creates an unresolved tension and contradiction between it and the time experienced by extra-theological humanity. Such humanity cannot legitimately exist in terms of Barth's strict presuppositions: it exists only in so far as it affirms its reality in the elected and saving humanity of Jesus Christ.

The structure of human existence is temporality (for as Barth asserts: 'Humanity is temporality') and time thus has a corresponding position of 'unreality' outside the realm of revelation. In view of this juxtaposition does the knowledge and correlative reality experienced in God's grace actually effect a confirmation and fulfilment of nature or its annihilation? The relation between the epistemological demands of faith and the ontological reality of the object of faith entails an inescapable contradiction, not merely between contrasting theological realities, but between reality as the purveyor of revelation and all reality apart from revelation. This contradiction necessitates a complete reconstruction of reality on

[29] 'The Problem of Natural Theology in the Thought of Karl Barth', *Religious Studies*, vol. 6, (1970), 24.

theological foundations which strives towards completeness, but, in so far as it remains dialectically transcendent, stays systematically at one remove from the texture of reality as normally experienced. An ontology and epistemology of the world are produced in direct correlation with those of faith and its object, Jesus Christ. Nature as such becomes wholly problematic in the face of this revelation.

Under the influence of St. Augustine, for whom in the Eternal, 'the whole is present' (*Confessions*, XI, 13), Barth rejects the former's 'subjectivism' and implicitly endorses his doctrine of eternity, giving it, as with Boethius' conception, a 'proper exploitation'. The positive elaboration of the temporal aspects of the Incarnation is matched by a correspondingly negative attitude towards extra-theological time. Barth begins to develop the logical content and fulfil the demands of a position which opposes theological and extra-theologically based time, for, as indicated above, there can be no peace between the two spheres of reality. There begins to emerge a positive theological development of the negative influence of eternity in the dialectic of *The Epistle to the Romans*. Eternity still annihilates time, but now instead of explosive demolition, a vast and 'unnatural' theological growth chokes and smothers the natural order and its reality, for grace consumes nature in putative, but merely apparent recreation. We are faced with a synthesis of reduction hidden in the folds of a theological cloak cast over the perennial dialectic of Western thought.

The power of Barth's doctrine of the Incarnation and his Christology is not an unambiguous triumph, but one under-laid by an epistemological and ontological repression, even, it becomes apparent, a repression of humanity precipitated by a profound confusion of theological and epistemological categories. Yet, here once more the reader is faced with the possibilities that Barth's thought may lead (as von Balthasar has said, doubtless without irony) to the true 'consummation of Protestantism', or, in reality, to the *reductio ad absurdum* of the principle of the Reformation, *sola fides, sola gratia*. Like some cancerous *Doppelgänger*, theological reality appears to inflate itself, drawing life from the reality it condemns, perfecting in exquisite form what could be seen as the most profound and systematically consistent theological alieniation of the natural order ever achieved.[30] The theological evidence for this interpretation, that is the exclusive and irresistible progress of revealed reality enshrined in the dogmas of God, the Trinity, and God's act in eternity, is clear and indubitable. The impulse from eternity ostensibly encounters time in the Incarnation, but, as outlined above, this Incarnation 'is' in its own 'time'. A very careful analysis of the impinging of eternity upon time must now take place, in order, finally, to determine whether the ontological and epistemological alienation of the natural order is stemmed by the logic of Barth's temporal notions, or if at this fundamental conceptual level, an analogous logical parasitism does not confirm our analysis.

On the basis of the given time of God, 'the time we know and possess, is and remains lost time, even when we believe that God is the creator of time.' (*CD* I/2, 47.) Knowing neither time as 'fallen' nor time as 'created' the third 'time', that of revelation, eclipses both and must be 'a different time, . . . created alongside our time and the time originally created by God' (loc. cit.). Barth supports the denigration of the natural knowledge of time as either created (and subsequently 'lost') or experienced by an appeal to the 'three great difficulties in the common concept of time' (*CD* I/2, 47). These are the problem of the ungraspable present, the antinomy of the finitude or infinitude of time, and the relation of time and eternity. Revelation is able to 'assert the reality of time in the face of and in spite of these difficulties without the desire or ability to set them aside' (*CD* I/2, 49).

The contradictory nature of Barth's assertions is demonstrated in that using (as he will again later) the products of philosophical scepticism against the knowledge of time he paradoxically asserts the reality of revelation time, but denies the latter's ability to offer grounds of affirmation against sceptical negation. Man may know the 'lostness' of his time,

---

[30] A certain affinity exists here between the logic of Barth's position and that of Hegel as criticized by Karl Marx in the 'Critique of the Hegelian Dialectic and Philosophy as a Whole' in *The Economic and Philosophical Manuscripts of 1844*. Marx's comment upon Luther in 'Private Property and Labour', that he 'recognised *religion—faith* as the substance of the external *world*' indicates the direction of this criticism. That is in general terms the substitution of a spiritual, inner reality for the wider fabric of a reality of scientific, social, and economic relations, and the generation thereby of a 'false consciousness'.

but the response postulated with great concreteness and ontological zeal in revelation 'time' is 'known' by the noetic acknowledgement of faith alone.

An uncomfortable tension is apparent here which is indicative of the ambiguity of revealed and natural knowledge in Barth's theology. This ambiguity once more emerges in the relationship of the revelation's time to 'our' time. 'God's revelation', according to Barth, 'is the event of Jesus Christ' and 'We do not understand it as God's revelation, if we do not state unreservedly that it took place in "our" time.' This sanguine note is immediately confounded, for 'conversely, if we understand it as God's revelation, we have to say that this revelation had its own time' (*CD* I/2, 49). The time of revelation, 'God's time', 'time for us' has a present with past and future and is 'fulfilled time', with the expectation and recollection of its fulfilment and it is 'therefore real time'. This ambiguity between 'our time' and 'real time' stems, as seen above, from the fundamental assertion that 'we can only *believe* in the creation of time by God, as we believe in the creation itself, but we cannot *know* it.' It is only possible to believe in creation by virtue of belief in Christ and therefore all 'knowledge' (including explicitly that of the the natural world and time) is consequent upon this prior 'belief'. The New Testament insight derived from Hebrews 11:3 has undergone an extraordinary universal interpretation, saved from absurdity by the mere assertion of the 'unreserved' happening of God's revelation in 'our' time. By faith, so argues the author of the Epistle to the Hebrews, we understand that the worlds have been framed by the Word of God. 'By faith' alone, Barth asserts, we may know the reality of creation itself. This is the consequence of his thoroughgoing subordination of cosmic and human reality to the epistemology (and the correlative ontology) of faith.

It is not possible to make a final judgement upon this crucial passage, for Barth makes extraordinary efforts to affirm the parallel between the Word's becoming flesh and its becoming time; but he remains ambiguous: 'It does not remain transcendent over time, it does not merely meet it at a point, but it *enters* time; nay it *assumes* times; nay, it *creates* time for itself.' (*CD* I/2, 50.) Aware of the dangers of his position

Barth immediately refers to *The Epistle to the Romans* knowing that the reader will not 'fail to appreciate that in it Jn. I, 14 does not have justice done to it'. The positive theological conditioning of Barth's thought is obvious, but is there not the serious danger of a distinct Docetism exposed in his doctrine of time? 'Revelation has its time, and only in and along with its time is it revelation. How otherwise can it be revelation to and for us who are ourselves temporal to the core?' How indeed, for as the event of Jesus Christ is 'genuinely temporal', so it is 'not to be confused with any other time' (*CD* I/2, 51).

The temporal structure strictly analogous to that of the Incarnation, Christology, and the resurrection is couched in theological terms of an entry into, assumption of, and creation or healing of time. As 'man's existence became something new and different altogether, because God's Son assumed it and took it ever into unity with his God-existence, . . . so time, by becoming the time of Jesus Christ, although it belonged to our time, the lost time, became a different, a new time.' (*CD* I/2, 51.) The presence of Jesus Christ as the fulfilment of time does not allow any position from which 'to see through and regard any part of this old time as new, fulfilled time' (*CD* I/2, 58). The Word raises time into God's own time, which is 'alone real, self-moved, self-dependent, self-sufficient' (*CD* I/2, 52).

The incarnational initiative of volume I/2 of the *Church Dogmatics* underlies the Christological synthesis of volume IV in which Christology and soteriology interact in a full integration. Failure to observe the 'necessary connexion of all theological statements with that of Jn. I, 14' is said to be prey to the 'devastating inrush of natural theology' (*CD* I/2, 123)—though one might add that the substitution of 'natural reality' for 'natural theology' would perhaps be more apt in indicating the truth of Barth's position. None the less it is of importance to note how Barth fully exploits the hypostatic union of patristic Christology and Protestant scholasticism and relates to it the categories of eternity and time. The 'assumption of grace' is central and thus the union of natures, (*unio naturarum*), is always regarded from the standpoint of the unity of person, (*unio personalis*). The supreme theological *locus* of the union of God and man in the Word become flesh subordinates all other categories. This union is propounded through the distinction of *an–* and *enhypostasis*, a Christological conception which presents its own difficulties, but which is, in this context, extremely important as an explanation of the basis upon which eternity and time are reconciled. Jesus Christ exists as man so far as he exists as God, and so in consequence his human nature does not exist apart from its divine mode of existence; it is ἀνυπόστατος. Positively the human nature acquires existence, that is subsistence, in the existence of God; it is ἐνυπόστατος. Christ's flesh has its existence 'through the Word and in the Word who is God Himself acting as Revealer and Reconciler' (*CD* I/2, 164). This unity of Godhood and manhood is no mere accidental co-location but is grounded upon the 'Eγὲνε το, 'the event of the incarnation of the Word'. God's being in the Incarnation is 'in becoming', thus 'being' (the 'person' of Christ) and 'act' (his 'works') are secured by reference once more to the ubiquitous divine act.

The corresponding and consequent relation of time and eternity is not simple but based upon the functional and unique co-location of God and man in the *unio hypostatica*. The temporal reality of the existence of Jesus Christ in which 'God is directly the Subject' is not only 'called forth, created, conditioned and supported by the eternal reality of God, but is identical with it' (*CD* I/2, 182). The problem of the identity of 'God's time', the time of revelation, with human time, is to be understood Christologically and its solution is directly analogous to that postulated in the doctrine of the hypostatic union. Such a development does, however, forge a further link in the theological chain of Barth's thought on time and renders the temporal sphere of revelation as problematic as the conception of the so-called 'impersonal humanity' of Christ. As the *vere Deus vere homo* of the Incarnation fulfils itself in the humanity of Christ (given its ontological ground in the Word of God's assumption of that flesh) so the 'temporal reality' of his humanity is likewise sustained. The 'self-enclosed circle' of the events of revelation bounded by the Virgin Birth and the empty tomb is constituted by the self-identification of God with man, and of eternity with time, in a unique collusion which provides the basis of the Christology-soteriology of volume IV of the *Church Dogmatics*.

(c) Soteriology

The doctrine of reconciliation (*Versöhnung*) is a soteriological elaboration of the primary Christological postulates and in Barth's own estimation he has 'actualised' the doctrine of the Incarnation. All the main traditional concepts are understood as concentrically related terms describing one and the same ongoing process. Barth's statement of the doctrine of the Incarnation is in the form of a 'denotation and description of a single event' (*CD* IV/2, 105). On this basis he expounds the covenant of grace which is ontologically 'already included and grounded in Jesus Christ, in the human form and content, which God willed to give His Word from all eternity' (*CD* IV/1, 45). Jesus Christ is likewise the 'basis of the whole project and actualisation of creation and the whole process of divine providence from which all created being and becoming derives' (*CD* IV/1, 48). The eternal Word *is* Jesus Christ, very God and very man, preceding the creative will and accomplishing the Atonement. The foundation of such assertion is the self-interpretative Word of God whose being lies in the 'inner basis and essence of God' (*CD* IV/1, 52). Jesus Christ is consequently the 'decision of God in time' and the 'decision . . . made from all eternity'. In a renewed and integrated Chalcedonianism, Barth makes this the ground of the functional and systematic movement of soteriology in 'The Way of the Son of God' and 'The Homecoming of the Son of Man'.

The ensuing argument presupposes the mutual but distinct contributions of the 'omnipresent, almighty, eternal and glorious One' and the one 'limited in time and space' (*CD* IV/1, 184), as God 'acts as Lord over this contradiction even as He subjects Himself to it' (*CD* IV/1, 185). Correspondingly the *forma servi* and *forma Dei* of Jesus Christ are matched by his submission to time: 'The eternity in which He Himself is true time and the Creator of all time is revealed in the fact that, although our time is that of sin and death, He can enter it and Himself be temporal in it, yet without ceasing to be eternal, able to be the Eternal in time.' (*CD* IV/1, 187–8.)

Once again when confronted with Barth's assertion and defence of the Christological basis of this interaction the theological spade strikes bedrock and can penetrate no further. The 'greedy dialectic' has been resolved by a comprehensive Christological synthesis of great power, cohesion, and consistency. There remain, nevertheless, profound doubts about the tenability of this position, given Barth's explanation of the logic of the reality of the divine being. In other words the Christological resolution asserts an identity of the eternal and the temporal, but the doctrine of *anhypostasis* and *enhypostasis* also provides a rationale for the circularity in speaking of a divine act realized within its own time and of a time posited on the basis of divinity (that is, temporally speaking, upon a basis of God's being in eternal act). The significant time of revelation remains within the theological realm whose bounds have been traced from their ultimate ontological source.

In the foregoing section of this essay we have examined the interlocking circles that find their point of integration in the *locus* of the divine act. This eternal act, realized in the Incarnation and the hypostatic mutuality of divine and human being in the Incarnation, Christology, and the doctrine of reconciliation also underlies and realizes Barth's conception of creation itself. The resurrection and the temporally decisive 'forty days of resurrection time' is the consummation of the Incarnation and Christology but it takes place within the bounds of creation. Thus in pursuit of our investigation and in conformity with the logic of Barth's thought we may ask if the problems we have outlined are finally overcome. Does Barth succeed in sustaining the reality of the time of creation through the happening within it of the resurrection, the all-determinative temporal event, or are we merely left with the conceptual ambiguity of eternity and time writ large in the theological rhetoric of revealed 'reality'?

VI

(d) Creation

The eternal act of God's being, realized in the Incarnation and the hypostatic mutuality of divine and human being in Christology and reconciliation, also sustains creation. Creation itself is the immediate context of theological anthropology and determines the application of the doctrine of time upon man. In the third volume of the *Church Dogmatics* the interaction of eternity and time is viewed in its closest relation to the existence and condition of common humanity and its shared and public world. It is in the spheres of creation and of 'Man in his Time' that the 'reality' and the logic of Barth's assertions may be tested, having explored the ontological substructure of his *magnum opus*. Whether the reader can emerge from this underworld into the light of experience and inter-subjective reality remains to be seen. The fabric of Barth's analogical recreation of temporal reality has been extended by Christology into the closest contiguity yet achieved with the 'fallen' and 'lost' world of man. The fabric of 'real' time has so far not been broken, however closely such a structure has moulded and conformed itself to the structure of what is commonly conceived as reality. In creation the temporal aspects of Barth's doctrine of man and the basic structure of his theological vision interact. Given such interaction it will prove possible to examine the conceptual interaction of eternity and time, the divine and extra-divine realms, and, in consequence to see how Barth's temporal 'negation of the negation', the supersession of time by 'God's time' (i.e., eternity) takes place in human existence itself, as manifested in the death and resurrection of Jesus Christ.

In this study, the pattern and impulse of Barth's thought has been followed. Now, in approaching the doctrine of creation additional complexity is encountered, but this dimension has yet once more to be approached in the light of the knowledge and the reality of faith. The priority of faith is both epistemological and ontological, for 'The insight that man owes his existence and form, together with all the reality distinct from God, to God's creation is achieved only in the reception and answer of the divine self-witness', and consequently this self-witness is 'in the knowledge of the unity of Creator and creature actualised in Him, and in the present mediated by Him, under the might and in the experience of the goodness of the Creator towards His creature' (*CD* III/1, 3).

Whether the distinction between Christ and creation is adequately sustained by Barth is a relevant question, especially in view of their close correlation, for creation is 'the external basis of the covenant', and the covenant 'the internal basis of creation'. This distinction is traditionally grounded upon a recognition of the eternal generation of the Logos and the temporal beginning of the creation. For Barth his all-pervasive actualism posits a single 'act' or 'event' of God that is unsurpassable (*CD* II/1, 263) and underlies both Christ and creation. Any distinction between God's 'essence' as it is in the Trinitarian relation of Father and Son and in the grounding of creation in the divine will ('externally' to the divine essence) is problematic in Barth's thought in the light of the exclusive power and function of God's benign act.

The God who self-posits himself 'in the Son by the Holy Spirit' determines that the eternal Father 'in the act of His free expression' and 'from within' is also the Creator. Only as 'Eternal Father' does God reveal himself as the Creator, that is for Barth, 'in Jesus Christ His Son by the Holy Ghost' (*CD* III/1, 11–12). In direct congruence with the consistent denial of natural theology there is an equally strict confinement of knowledge of the Creator to the Word and revelation. The logical structure of Barth's argument is again such as to call in question the status not merely of the act of creation but of the created order, the world, and the cosmos themselves, which enjoy a merely derivative and secondary status over against the self-authenticating reality and objectivity of revelation. Barth's point is that creation, as divinely originated reality, is known only by the 'real analogy' evident in the logic of the revealed reality of the inner begetting of the Son by the Father, and, therefore, 'not at all in the life of the creature'. According to Barth's theological epistemology, the knowledge of creation itself is derived from revelation. Failing a theory of knowledge of creation as mundane, empirical reality (and such knowledge is systematically excluded by the logic of Barth's stance so far) an extremely insecure position results for natural knowledge of the natural world, and for individual man's place in it.

According to Barth, the 'fact that God has regard to His Son—the Son of Man, the Word made flesh—is the true and genuine basis of creation' (*CD* III/1, 51). Because of this dependence the doctrine of creation becomes deeply enmeshed in Christology and soteriology and the *circulus veritatis* is forged into ever more complete inner self-consistency. Not only creation itself but

The insight that man owes his existence and form, together with all reality distinct from God, to God's creation, is achieved only in the reception and answer of the divine self-witness, that is, only in faith in Jesus Christ, i.e. in the knowledge of the unity of Creator and creature actualised in Him. (*CD* III/1, 3.)

Both creation and creature rest under the shadow of Christology and thus the temporal and dogmatic structures implicit in Barth's conception of Jesus Christ.

With regard to the specific problem of time Barth once more expounds the axis of eternal antecedence and temporal consequence in the light of the Christologically based creation. The covenant, the 'internal basis of creation', is the validation of the 'sphere of the creature' which God has determined from all eternity, and the history of this covenant is the sequence of events for which God 'gives time' (*CD* III/1, 59). Creation and history are thus made a function of the revealed purpose, and acquire their meaning and temporal 'fulfilment' from it. Indeed, here is found an echo of the statement of volume I/1, that history is the predicate of revelation, not revelation the predicate of history. It is in Christ that the 'fulfilment' takes place and once more in the context of creation Barth elaborates and 'properly exploits' the Boethian conception of eternity as the basis of this fulfilment in 'the organising centre of all God's acts', the reality of Jesus Christ. Predictably, eternity is 'supreme and absolute time, i.e. the immediate unity of present, past and future; of new, once and then; of the centre, beginning and end; of movement, origin and goal' which is the 'essence of God Himself' (*CD* III/1, 67). The supra-temporality of eternity is the active and creative being of God, expressing *ad extra* the inner convenantal decision and the reconciling purpose of God, thus constituting the possibility of creation. Only on the basis of the axis of eternity and time as unified in the Christological resolution of volumes I/2 and IV, can creation thus be the work of Christ, who, according to Barth, is the continuing reality of temporal fulfilment. So it is that the all-pervasiveness of the category of time becomes apparent again through its ontological and integrative role in the *Church Dogmatics*.

Only upon the foundation of the alleged 'temporality' and 'historicity' of God may Barth hold together and sustain his vision, for such derivation is absolutely essential, given the systematic exclusion, and therefore complete absence, of any immanent starting-point within his theological scheme. The involuted position to which this leads is demonstrated in such comments as 'Even the basis of creation in God's eternal decree is not a non-historical pre-truth, for this eternal pre-truth obviously has a historical character in the bosom of eternity.' Consequently, 'Not even the pure eternal being of God as such is non-historical pre-truth, for being triune it is not non-historical but historical even in its eternity.' (*CD* III/1, 66.) In other words, a complex logical and conceptual reconstruction of creation statements in Trinitarian and Christological terms takes place. As regards the problem of time expressed in the contrasting thrusts of eternity and time, what distinction can there be if the 'history' and 'time' of eternity are translated into the history and time of God's will and purposes in the covenant?

It is at this juncture that Barth allows the formal contrast between eternity and time to emerge once again in explicit, logical terms. Eternity as the 'source of Time' is 'supreme and absolute time', that is, 'the immediate unity of present, past and future' and so on, which is the 'essence of God Himself'. God's eternity is the prototype of time and God is 'simultaneously before time, above time, and after time'. By contrast 'our time . . . is the form of existence of the creature' and, in contradistinction to eternity, it is 'the one-way sequence and therefore the succession and division of past, present and future; of once, now and then; of the beginning, middle and end; of origin, movement and goal' (*CD* III/1, 67–8). The contrast between the 'duration' of the simultaneity of past, present, and future and the "succession and division of past, present and future' is the *only* logical or conceptual distinction between eternity and time. In 'healing' time, eternity implants its durational simultaneity into the succession and division of time. This is the distinction that arises in every context in which temporal categories are employed to sustain the structural unity of the doctrine of being in the *Church Dogmatics*. Correspondingly the same basic problems of the competing realities of the time of revelation and of the mundane temporal order recur and become extremely acute with regard to creation.

The complex nature of Barth's arguments concerning creation and Christ is matched by a corresponding analogical ambiguity in the explication of the creative interaction of eternity and time within the doctrine of creation. In a spate of double negations, Barth attempts to reconcile the positive creative aspect of 'God's time' with its not being 'fallen' time, that is the time of creation as it now is. God's eternal being as such, 'His pure, divine form of existence', is not in time, but even in this sense God is 'not non-historical and therefore non-temporal' because of the prototypical inner Trinitarian life. God is not 'non-temporal' because his eternity is 'not merely the negation of time, but an inner readiness to create time' (*CD* III/1, 68). God's supra-temporality, that is, his not being 'in time', but 'before, above and after all time' in such a way that 'time is really in Him', is the expression of his impulse towards the 'other', his creature. The theological impulse to create and sustain is explicated in terms of interacting conceptions of time, the nature of which are questionable at the very least. The distinctive feature of the time of the creature, its 'one way sequence, in that succession and separation, on the way from the once through the now to the then' (loc. cit.) is transformed by God's compassion and grace revealed in the act of his creation into 'His readiness for Time, as pre-temporal, supra-temporal (or co-temporal) and post-temporal and therefore as the source of time, of superior and absolute time' (*CD* III/1, 70).

Eternity and time are apparently distinct on the basis of the discrete theological entities to which they refer, but in strictly conceptual terms the ambiguity of Barth's argument stems from the illicit separation of the past, present, and future of time as 'simultaneous' and 'supra-temporal' from the 'succession' of 'before and after'. The 'real contrast' of eternity and time is temporally expressed solely in the contrast between 'contemporaneity' (in the full sense Barth intends) and 'division' and 'flux', respectively. Barth's equivocation regarding 'time' (that underlies the systematic and pervasive ambiguity of this concept in the *Church Dogmatics*) relies upon a conceptual distinction, the separation of a 'simultaneous' from a 'successive' time order in a contrast of 'duration' and 'division'. Is such a distinction not in fact a mere conceptual sleight of hand, in which two logically interdependent aspects of the idea of time, as used by Barth, are distinguished and subsequently hypostatized into deceptively distinct categories of reality? Whatever response may be made to this it is quite clear that the distinction is utterly pervasive and fundamental to the *Church Dogmatics*.

(e) Resurrection

In the passage 'Man in his Time', Barth applies the doctrines that have been developed elsewhere, to the human condition as he understands it. Above all, the time of revelation as consummated in the resurrection becomes the actual pro- totypical basis of human time. In theological anthropology man is the central object of the doctrine of creation as 'the creature whose relation to God is revealed to us in the Word of God', but this means that 'the man Jesus is Himself the revealing Word of God, He is the source of our knowledge of the nature of man as created by God.' (*CD* III/2, 3.) This circumscription of the area of the knowledge of the creation and the consequent exclusion of knowledge of creation as cosmic totality is in entire congruity with the structure that has constantly emerged in Barth's thought.

As expected, the doctrine of time is governed by the insight that 'in practice and doctrine of creation means anthropology' (*CD* III/1, 3) and that 'the Word of God does not contain any ontology of heaven and earth themselves (*CD* III/2, 6). Again using the principle of the analogy of faith, Barth asserts that in 'the disclosed relationship of God with man there is disclosed also His relationship with the Universe', and this is in congruity with Christological conditioning of the doctrine of creation. Human sin having made the understanding of human nature impossible, a new disclosure is necessary made in the one man Jesus, on which basis inquiry as to man in general may be made. The temporal structure of this 'disclos- ure' is what Barth explicates in 'Man in his Time'. It is inevitably preceded by a restatement of the eternity-time axis, that is, of simultaneity over against succession (*CD* III/2, 437–8), here designated by the terms of 'authentic' over against 'inauthentic' time.

According to Barth, man 'needs an inauthentic temporality

distinct from eternity' in which past, present, and future are in succession forming a sequence 'corresponding to his life-act as a whole and in detail' (*CD* III/2, 438). Jesus, 'like all other men' is 'in His time', but in this time he lives hypostatically in virtue of his unity with God. He lives with God and for God, with men and for them as Representative and Judge in a twofold representation which 'makes the barrier of this time on every side a gateway'. Leading this life 'in His time' and in consequence 'His time becomes for God, and therefore for all men' (*CD* III/2, 439). The application of hypostatic unity to Christ's life in time is the basis of 'likeness' of his time with men's time, it being derived from the divine time. The *apparent* historical and temporal identity is always by virtue of the hypostatic unity, which works towards a 'fulfilment' of time ostensibly needed by the inauthentic time of men, a time that men in fact already have, and must have, if they are to live lives at all.

In the first section of 'Man in his Time', subtitled 'Jesus, Lord of Time', it is Barth's aim to establish by means of the integration of Christology and creation the absolute priority of the life of Jesus, as the life whose time will be 'at once the centre and beginning and the end of all the lifetimes of all men' (*CD* III/2, 440). Thus it is that Jesus' time is all men's times in virtue of his supreme contemporaneity, his 'Lordship of time'. Jesus' time is the time of men in consequence of the hypostatic self-positing of God and not through any imma-nent, non-hypostatic identity. This hypostatic realization of time is consummated in the 'forty days of Easter-history and Easter-Time' subsequent to the resurrection. Barth asserts that in the resurrection an irreversible time-sequence is established (*CD* IV/1, 447) resulting in the 'forty days' of resurrection time, the end and goal of predestination. The culmination of Christology and creation in the resurrection is the fulfilment of time *par excellence*, and represents the applica-tion of the insight elaborated elsewhere, for example in volume IV/1, in the passage entitled 'The Verdict of the Father' (pp. 283 ff.). Here, 'the event of Easter Day and the resurrection appearances during the forty days were the mediation, the infallible mediation as unequivocally disclosed in a new act of God, of the perception that God was in Christ.'

(*CD* IV/1, 301.) In the context of the doctrine of creation the resurrection-conditioned time of the 'forty days' becomes the foundation of the phenomenological and schematic account of time, 'Given Time', and 'Allotted Time' respectively.

In the 'forty days' of resurrection time the hidden mystery of the being of Jesus Christ was exposed, for 'during these forty days the presence of God in the presence of the man Jesus was no longer a paradox . . . He had been veiled, but He was now wholly and equivocally and irrecoverably manifest.' (*CD* III/2, 449.) With relentless consistency the theological and temporal dimensions correspond, for Jesus declared and known to be Lord is exalted from the dead and 'He was then the concrete demonstration of the God who not only has authority over man's life and death, but also wills to deliver him from death.' In addition, 'He was the concrete demonstration of the God who has not only a different time from that of men, but whose will and resolve it is to give men a share in this time of His, in His eternity.' (*CD* III/2, 450–1.) In this act God's time overcomes the discontinuity of temporal bondage and manifests 'real' temporal continuity.

Barth unambiguously asserts the 'real and therefore physical' resurrection of Jesus and thereby repudiates Bultmann. Barth's assertion is perhaps inconsistent with the thrust of his over-all argument, for it has concentrated, certainly as regards time, upon the instantiation of the eternally real in time and the consequent tranformation of time. In a manner corresponding with this affirmation of a physical resurrection Barth affirms that 'It is the Creator of all reality distinct from Himself who, taking flesh of our flesh, also took time, at the heart of what we think we know as time.' (*CD* III/2, 455.) Because of the creative temporal condescension of God, the philosophical denial of the reality of time may be abandoned in the face of the fact that 'God Himself took time and thus treated it as something real.' (loc. cit.) This 'making real' is a fulfilment applicable to all time through the properties of 'eternal time'. Barth now makes his crucial claim for the reality of the time of Jesus and he recognizes the dangers of granting the force of his own 'analogical' derivation of all realities (including that of time) from the divine prototype. Without the identity of Jesus' time with our own he becomes a mere function of divinity, a gnostic figure vouchsafed to man in the seamless receptacle of his own time.

... the time of Jesus is also a time like all other times; that it occurred once and once for all; that it had beginning, duration and end; that it was contemporary for some, future for others, and for others again, e.g. for us, past. *Only a docetic attitude to Jesus can deny that His being in time also means what being in time means for us all.* [my emphasis] Our recognition of His true humanity depends on an acceptance of this proposition. Even the recognition of His true deity, implying as it does the identity between His time and God's, does not rule out this simple meaning of His being in time. On the contrary, it includes it. (*CD* III/2, 463.)

Barth has moved with utter consistency along the path of analogical derivation. The reality of the divine denies, subverts, and supersedes the reality of the mundane. Having thus severed all but a single thread connecting his theological system to the world of the commonplace Barth has now to retract and defend the reality of Jesus Christ. Can Barth give a positive answer to any of his implicit questions? Can Jesus' being in time mean what it means for us all? Barth's ambiguity is here quintessentially expressed, for his answer is affirmative, yet immediately qualified by the 'inclusion' of such time by the divine time. We are aware, however, that the divine time draws mundane fallen time into a synthesis of logically distinct temporal categories of dubious origin. The dialectic is resolved upwards in every context we have so far examined and Barth's defence of the resurrection time against the 'docetic' charge is groundless in view of his own arguments that we have examined at length. We must grant him the logic of his own theological position and allow the utter priority of the divine, and the analogical derivation therefrom. By this we allow ourselves insight into the dialectic of reality and unreality that suffuses the whole *Church Dogmatics* once the systematic completeness of the *circulus veritatis Dei* is unbroken by any arbitrary inconsistency on Barth's part.

The concluding passages of 'Jesus, Lord of Time' contain the application of the fulfilment of time posited in the life, death, and, above all, the resurrection of Jesus Christ. In this Barth presents an elaborate interpretation of the axis of eternity and time as the distinctive feature of time of Jesus in 'the removal of the limitations of its yesterday, to-day and tomorrow of its once, now and then' (*CD* III/2, 464). Above all, Barth attempts an exposition of Revelation I:8 in terms of the temporal transcendence he has elaborated (see *CD* III/2, 465). Jesus' time is always simultaneously present and therefore he is the Alpha and Omega, the beginning and the ending, and so on. After the attempted repudiation of ambiguity apparent in Barth's conception of the resurrection, the dialectic of eternity and time as a conceptual juxtaposition of duration and contemporaneity over against succession and division, becomes once more dominant. On the basis of the divine supra-temporality, the *parousia* and the resurrection, which are for us separate, are for Christ one. Having descended inconsistently to the single point of unambiguous identity of Christ's time with human time in the resurrection, Barth ascends once again into the structural logic of the *Church Dogmatics*, constituted by the dogma of God's being in act, that is, the dynamic 'Now' of the divine eternity.

On a schematic and structural level, having re-established this central affirmation of the divine simultaneity, Barth in exploring its more concrete application commences with a devastating return to the epistemological and ontological impossibility of any knowledge of time, apart from that posited in revelation. In an exposition strongly reminiscent of Augustine's critical reflections in the *Confessions* and the *Contra Academicos*, Barth rehearses the sceptical arguments concerning the ungraspability of the 'Now', that lies between future and past. The present is the time between the times that is 'no time at all, no duration, no series of moments, but only the boundary between past and future, . . . which is never stationary, but always shifts further ahead' (*CD* III/2, 514). Out of this flux of 'infinite succession of moments, or rather constant shiftings of the boundary' stem the attempts to gain the illusory knowledge of metaphysics and the creation in such poetic expression as that of Hölderlin. Over against this 'flight' the 'I am . . . which is, and which was, and which is to come, the Almighty presents itself' (*CD* III/1, 516). In the being of Jesus Christ a protest is made against the 'perverted and disturbed reality' of man. God has 'come to our rescue, and therefore to the defence of our true creaturely nature against the unnatural condition into which it had fallen' (*CD* III/2, 518).

It is well to recall at this point that Barth has previously affirmed the need for man to live in such a 'fallen' time and there is little evidence of an appreciation of the inconceivability of existence in the divine 'I am' of eternity as the basis of human experience and subjectivity, that is, of subjectivity in a present without the division of before and after. What would it mean for a man to experience the eternity in which God is said to subsist in Barth's exposition? Is the use of the axis of eternity and time, thus understood, an adequate or desirable ontological vehicle for the mediation of the divine-human relation in the broad sense in which it is employed by Barth? The peculiar objectivity of Barth's account and its shortcomings are demonstrated in his explicit denial, 'We do not know what time means for animals or plants, or for the rest of the universe.' (*CD* III/2, 521.) Only because man himself is in time may he 'conclude or suspect that time is the form of existence of everything created' (loc. cit.). The principle of knowing by analogy, exploited in the notion of *analogia fidei*, is thus applied in a more normal way to knowledge of the external world as a temporally conditioned world. Barth's denial of direct knowledge does little to lessen the danger of the intrinsically stultifying limitations of never moving beyond anthropology into discussion of cosmic realities. So it is that Barth closes any final gaps in his theory of time, through the full enclosure of human life within the limits of a time posited in the manifestation of God's revelation, Jesus Christ.

'Humanity is temporality. Temporality, as far as our observation and understanding go, is humanity.' (*CD* III/2, 522.) By the strict application of this equation, interpreted by the content of temporality (*Zeitlichkeit*), defined as 'that movement from the past through the present into the future', Barth eliminates any treatment of time outside what may be termed a structural phenomenological analysis. The denial of any correlation between human time and that conditioning the 'being of plants and animals in the rest of the universe' (*CD* III/2, 521), except by way of an inferred analogy, provides additional evidence for our analysis of the self-

enclosed nature of Barth's theology. The reasons for this, and
Barth's derivation of 'real' time prototypically from revelation
have been outlined in this essay. Ostensibly, as we have seen,
grace confirms, even establishes, nature. The fact that grace
cannot coexist with but destroys nature in the act of confirming it constitutes the ambiguity of the doctrine of time in the
Church Dogmatics. Does the time of Jesus Christ merely confirm
(by the removal of illusion and misconception) or does it
destroy and re-create time? Clearly in 'Man in his Time'
Barth asserts both, but both based upon, and sustained by,
the will of God and his purposes. Why, might a reader ask,
should the original time which is recovered from its lost
division and transitoriness be different from the 'time' posited
in revelation?

Barth does not answer this, but proceeds to an explanation
of 'sin' in temporal terms which now corresponds to the
existential 'ought' constituted by the paramount 'is' of God's
time. A 'pledge' of the 'reality' of time is given in God's time:
there is no material, metaphysical, or even phenomenological
change. The epistemology of faith is fulfilled in the presence of
God, 'The fact that the living God is present makes our
present not only real but weighty and therefore important',
and in this is enclosed 'the mystery of the grateful response we
now owe to Him and in consequence to our fellow men' (*CD*
III/2, 531). 'We are sinners who have forfeited our time': by
these words Barth places the reader once more before the
dilemma evident in the early work. Time and eternity conflict
and eternity confronts and overcomes time. Grace has con-
sumed nature and regurgitates it in the form of a natural
theology derived from revelation, but such reality as is
mediated through revelation remains the knowledge of faith.
The healing of time which comes by means of the ontological
and temporal structure of the object of faith is immediately
translated, at the moment of encounter, back into purely
theological terms of a 'pledge' and 'graceful presence'. The
theological circle is ultimately complete in that it subsumes a
legitimate and irreducible duality, that of Creator and Creation, into a unified epistemology and ontology of the divine
being, a Christology of hypostatic unity and noetic reception
and a subsequent realization through the 'acknowledgement'
of this dogmatic nexus.

At certain points an identity of revealed reality and natural reality is made (and only unambiguously so in the resurrection itself). Ultimately the only 'cashed-out' content of the fulfilment of time is 'a promise', 'For the eternal and gracious God, who is the boundary of our beginning, will surely guarantee the whole of our life, the span which we are given, and its final end.' (*CD* III/2, 570.) Everything *is* as it *was* except that now we are *sure* that it *is* on the basis of the divine promise. The futility of human temporal exertion is obvious, our yearning and striving in time give way to acceptance of the 'already accomplished and uninterrupted work' of the inner life of God given in 'content' and 'promise'. Contemplation of the theological circle in its perfection, complexity (and ambiguity) constitutes the true obedience of faith, the 'knowledge' gained in 'acknowledgement'.

The character of the doctrine of time in the *Church Dogmatics*, seen as the logic of the object of faith is confirmed in Barth's account of death (*CD* III/2, 589 ff.). Death happens to man and is 'extinction', but in Christ eternal life is promised in a manner corresponding with the entire vicariousness (and consequently, theological circularity) of Christ's activity. Death for mankind is, according to Barth, a 'sign' of the 'second death' suffered by Christ and so once more everything *appears* to change, but in reality remains as it is, except for the promise of the 'beyond' of Jesus Christ. Man is to live in hope in God for, 'the definitive prospect in which he rejoices is for him an authorisation and command to serve God in his allotted span with all the preliminary joy without which his joy in his end and new beginning with Him would be purely imaginary' (*CD* III/2, 640). Man is to affirm Jesus Christ as his 'beyond' in his life now, in the intentionality of faith. God's revelation, held for so long at one remove from the human condition by its own inner logic, finally tells us that the limitations we endure are those endured by Jesus Christ—such is the message of the Gospel.

VII

In the foregoing essay I have attempted to lay bare the 'inner logic' of Barth's theology inasmuch as this structure is constituted by the doctrine of time. In ensuing sections Barth's doctrines of God, Christ, and creation have been analysed from the standpoint of their dependence upon a set of temporal conceptions bound up with the doctrine of the divine act in the eternal 'Now'. This has revealed something of the richness of Barth's synthetic drive in reuniting impulses from many strands of the Christian tradition. More negatively, we have seen the theology of time function as a container within which the act of revelation in Jesus Christ is confined. Wherever the content of revelation and its time draws close to the reality common to humanity, ambiguity results because the 'reality' of revelation must both affirm and deny, recreate and annihilate at the same moment. This ambiguity is consistent with the double-edged quality of much of Barth's talk of man (does he mean men or the man Jesus?) and is based upon the fundamental theological developments which led to the adoption of the 'analogy of faith'. Ultimately the ambiguity must disappear in the face of the overwhelming principle of the divine act and its various (but strictly identical) manifestations.

The complexity of this paper stems from the fact that it has proved necessary to prise apart Barth's 'spiral arguments' and relate the *loci* widely dispersed in his thought together into a single argument. We have encountered a profound theological totalitarianism stemming from the application of the principle of *analogia fidei* in a context bereft of any vestiges of natural theology (and thus of natural reality or the natural order itself). The consequence of the functional identity between this principle and doctrine of being and time that Barth employs is the systematic exclusion of any dimension not immediately derivable from his primal sources of reality. Such a monopoly demands the re-creation of genuine plurality and categorical distinction *within* the structure of the new reality whereby the discontinuity between that reality and the reality normally external to it is reproduced. Thus a new world appears within which the old distinctions of transcendence and immanence are re-created. Whereas in traditional theology the analogy of being was used as a means of relation and differentiation between God and cosmos, Barth's analogy of faith functions within the sphere of faith alone. Time, instead of being or substance as such, becomes the medium of relation and disrelation between God and man, but, as we have seen, its efforts to escape from the confines of Barth's system to posit and structure a reality other than God and his revelation get no further than ambiguity, and ultimately fail, once we perceive the logic of the theology of the *Church Dogmatics*.

The theology of Karl Barth is (despite his own protestations) a reworking of metaphysical theology, albeit in 'biblical' guise. As such it has entranced some and driven others from the Christian fold. One major factor influencing in different ways both the devoted disciples and the disaffected has been the great intellectual offence offered by the assertion of a reality about which so much could be said at such length. As we have seen, this reality is a single one which brooks no rival or opposition. It either exists and demands submission in the 'acknowledgement' of faith or it cannot exist for those who refuse to grant its totalitarian demands.

Through a profound ontological exclusiveness Barth has attempted to preserve Christian theology from the indifference and hostility of a secular world. The triumphalist aggrandizement of his theology was made at the risk of a total disjunction and alienation of his theology from natural reality. The disturbing irony of his efforts is that Barth achieved this alienation by skilled and energetic use of traditional Christian theological categories. His creation stands before us as a warning as to what may happen if the God of the orthodox Christian Gospel is prized apart from the structures of contemporary human life. The ontological dogma of the Incarnation loses its roots in the shared and public reality of the world in which we live; it hovers above us like a cathedral resting upon a cloud. Can such an intellectual presentation of Christianity be entered with anything short of total alienation and lack of personal and existential authenticity? Is such a theology not a merely perfect illustration of (say) the Marxist critique of religion as alienation of the self, but an alienation so profound and complex as to daunt those who might wish to form a judgement upon it in the name of Christianity itself. In almost Proustian manner Barth has re-created a lost world[31]

[31] George Steiner regards Joseph Needham's *Science and Civilisation in China* as the only adequate sequel to *A la recherche du temps perdu* (see *In Bluebeard's Castle*, London, 1971, pp. 99–100). The *Church Dogmatics* might well qualify as a third 'prodigiously sustained, controlled flight of the creative intellect'.

whose demands are nothing less than total and unconditional submission, but whose precepts and potential for the promotion of the interpersonal life of the Body of Christ in the world would appear to be minimal without radical appreciation of its dangers and limitations.

Should we now in conclusion turn away from the theology of Karl Barth in dismay, or even disgust? I think not, for Barth's great gift to the Church is his quite magnificent grasp and representation of materials drawn from the Christian tradition. His work is, moreover, not merely the product of genius or perversity on his own part alone but a phenomenon which illustrates the logic of the disrelation of Christian theological categories and the reality of which they speak from our own culture. Barth was not responsible for this situation; he merely illustrates it and yet manages to conserve and pass on the tradition. To accept or reject Barth would be merely to succumb to the demands of his own theological error. His work lies before us, the stricken, glorious hulk of some great Dreadnought—our task is to dismember and salvage, to exploit what is usable, and to melt down and re-forge the rest into weapons for the continuing theological battle for the truth.

5

Barth on the Triune God

R. D. WILLIAMS

Westcott House, Cambridge

She caught the crying of those Three,
The Immortals of the eternal ring,
The Utterer, Utteréd, Uttering.

(Gerard Manley Hopkins, *Margaret Clitheroe.*)

I

THAT MAN should hear the Word of God is an impossibility; but it is an impossibility revealed to man by that very Word. It is this essential *strangeness* in the event of man's hearing the Word to which Barth's discussions of revelation again and again return; and this sense of strangeness is of major importance in the whole of Barth's analysis of the nature of man's encounter with his Lord, since it at once raises the question of how the impossibility of revelation is compatible with the *fact* that the Word is heard. It raises the question, that is to say, of where the possibility of revelation is grounded. How is it that God can abrogate the principle *homo peccator non capax verbi divini*[1] (*CD* I/1, 407)? There is no ground of possibility in man; that is axiomatic for Barth, not as an abstract principle but as a consequence of what in fact the Word itself reveals about man's God-less condition. 'The insight that "I have sinned . . . and am no more worthy to be called thy son" (Lk. 15:18) is not an insight of abstract anthropology. Only the son who is already recalling his father's house knows that he is a lost son. We know that we are God's enemies first and solely from the fact that God has actually established that intercourse with us.' (*CD* I/1, 407; and cf. 161, 199.) The abstract statement that man is incap-

---

[1] 'Sinful man has no capacity for the divine word.'

able of hearing the Word is a nonsense, in that it presupposes that we know in some way what this Word is from which we are alienated. In pretending to affirm an impossibility, it really affirms a possibility, the anthropological 'condition', the human capacity for hearing so vehemently rejected by Barth in his long discussion of 'The Knowability of the Word of God' (*CD* I/1, §6; 187–247, especially 190–8). And, on the other hand, the revelation of an impossibility is the creation of a possibility: 'If we ascribe to man this aptness [for the Word, in faith] which is not his own but is loaned to him by God . . . then we cannot shrink from speaking of a conformity to God proper to him in faith.' (*CD* I/1, 238.) Conformity in faith, the *analogia fidei* (see particularly *CD* I/1, 243–4): this is the ground of the possibility of hearing the Word, and it is a 'retroactively' established possibility. That is, it depends entirely upon God's creative address to man, the Word spoken out of his freedom, his decision (*CD* I/1, 156–62); so that when we speak of the possibility of hearing the Word, we are ultimately speaking of the possibility for *God* of uttering the Word which is constitutive of man-as-hearer. To ask, 'How can God abrogate the principle *homo peccator non capax verbi divini*? is to ask 'What kind of God is it with whom we have to do?' Or, more strongly and more accurately, '*Who* is our God?' (*CD* I/1, 298–304.)

'In scientific theology we begin with the actual knowledge of God and seek to test and clarify this knowledge by inquiring carefully into the relation between our knowing of God and God himself in His being and nature.'[2] This, from one of Barth's foremost disciples in the English-speaking world, neatly states the heart of Barth's intention in his theological method. And, as Eberhard Jüngel has insisted,[3] Barth considers that to think *theologically* is above all to take seriously the fact that God's being is prior to the enterprise of human theological questioning, that God's being in its character as 'in motion' (*gehende*) establishes theology upon its path. The structures and inner relations of the event or events which

[2] T. F. Torrance, *Theological Science* (London, 1969), p. 9.

[3] *Gottes Sein ist im Werden* (Tübingen, 1965), pp. 9–10; Eng. trans., *The Doctrine of the Trinity: God's Being is in Becoming* (Grand Rapids, Michigan and Scottish Academic Press, 1976), pp. xix–xx.

constitute the uttering of the Word to men determine absolutely what theology is to say about the being of the Lord who
speaks and reveals. Theology (as Dr Ford's chapter in this
volume so fully and painstakingly argues) is regarded by
Barth as an essay in *Nachdenken*, following out in thought the
'order' of revelation. The nature of God is uncovered to the
theological inquiry by undeviating fidelity to the 'story' of God's
movement towards men, that which makes man a knower of God
in the first place; which, it might be said, decisively introduces
the name of God into the language of the world.

The structure of this man-ward movement is, as Barth sets
out in Section 4 of his first half-volume ('The Word of God in
its Threefold Form'), manifold. There is a primary revelatory
occurrence, the determinative speaking of the Word in the
Word-made-flesh. There is the 'recollection' of this in Scripture; 'The prophetic and apostolic word is the word, witness,
proclamation and preaching of Jesus Christ' (*CD* I/1, 107),
and it 'imposes itself' upon the Church in virtue of (and *only* in
virtue of) its reference to and dependence upon the primary
event, upon God's free utterance. And finally there is the
Church's preaching, 'man's talk about God on the basis of
God's own direction' (*CD* I/1, 90), 'on the basis of the
self-objectification of God, . . . which is really only in the
freedom of His grace' (*CD* I/1, 92); preaching can become the
Word in and only in obedience to God's free self-
determination in Christ, and the re-presentation of this in the
scriptural witness. The primary event alone *is* the Word:
Scripture *becomes* the Word in fidelity to Christ, preaching
becomes the Word in fidelity to Scripture, but Christ is 'the
divine act itself and as such' (*CD* I/1, 117). 'If "written" and
"preached" denote the twofold concrete relation in which the
Word of God is spoken to us, revelation denotes the Word of
God itself in the act of its being spoken in time.' (*CD* I/1, 118.)
The concrete and particular event of God's utterance to this
man at this moment occurs in the prophetic and apostolic
experience recorded in Scripture, and in the convicting and
converting proclamation of the Church; but it occurs 'derivatively and indirectly', dependently upon the one direct
speech-act of God in Christ. And it is the unity of that act
which guarantees the unity and self-identity of Scripture and

preaching. At the heart stands the one event, the *Deus dixit*, the fulfilment of time; when Scripture and preaching become the Word, they are 'filled with the fulness of this time' (*CD* I/1, 119).[4]

The unity of the Word of God in revelation is, then, a unity-in-plurality (*CD* I/1, 120–1). The structure of revelation is the structure of a complex unity in which three terms are defined entirely by their mutual relations: each is known only through and in the other two. And the three terms are constituted as *identical* with each other because they enact the same free action of God towards men. 'There is', Barth concludes, 'only one analogy to this doctrine of the Word of God. Or, more accurately, the doctrine of the Word of God is itself the only analogy to the doctrine which will be our fundamental concern as we develop the concept of revelation. This is the doctrine of the trinity of God.' (*CD* I/1, 121.) If the Word of revelation has a pluriform identity, this is something which is of substantive importance for our answer to the question, '*Who* is the God Who speaks in revelation?'

This particular line of reasoning is not wholly clear, and Barth does not trouble to spell it out at any length; but it is a point which is made at a significant stage in the whole argument of the first half-volume, and it is therefore perhaps worth while to try to elucidate it a little. Barth is not, I think, simply suggesting that the triplicity of the Word is an 'external' analogy to the postulated triplicity of God, that one 'gives us the idea' for the other. Rather is he pointing to a basic principle necessary to our understanding alike of the revealing Word and of its Speaker; and that is the concept of the divine freedom. The pluriformity of the Word's revealing activity is an index of God's capacity to be free *for men* in their particular and concrete circumstances. In no sense is he imprisoned in a past revelatory event which can be the subject only of human recollection: he is free to speak the same Word in oblique, 'wordly' mediating realities (*CD* I/1, 156–7; and cf. 117, 138–9, etc.). 'The direct Word of God meets us only in this twofold mediacy' (*CD* I/2, 121); and there is no general concept

---

[4] The pivotal importance in Barth's system of fulfilled time (*erfüllte Zeit*) is the burden of Dr Roberts's essay, where its relation to the *Moment* of the *Romans* commentary is rightly indicated.

under which the Word can be subsumed, since (The Word of God is an act of God which takes place *specialissime*, in this way and not another, to this or that particular man.' (*CD* I/1, 159).

The freedom of the Word is God's capacity to speak not 'publicly' or 'generally', in a single form (*Gestalt*) which is then once and for all accessible to all men without mediation, but in hiddenness which requires his own free decision in every particular instance in order to become manifest. 'Where the Word of God is known and therefore can be known, it must have been spoken and it must have come as a divine call to specific men.' (*CD* I/1, 189.) 'The Word of God . . . is to be understood primarily and basically as decision and then and as such as history too.' (*CD* I/1, 156.) God is not trapped in the historical or secular form under which he speaks; his Word is identical with the form of Jesus (substantially), and of Scripture and of preaching (derivatively) because he elects that it be so. And the pluriformity of the Word is precisely a witness to the fact that he is not so 'trapped', but can actualize his revelation in any and every circumstance, in the utter absence of any human 'condition'. God 'can not only come to man but also be in man . . . and thus achieve His revelation in Him' (*CD* I/1, 450; and cf. the long section in I/2 on 'The Holy Spirit the Subjective Reality of Revelation', especially 206–8, and 223–4).

God speaks; he speaks one Word; but he speaks it and realizes it at once obliquely, concretely, fully, and in manifold particularities. And it is from this analysis of what is involved in the act of revelation that we can proceed to the construction of a Trinitarian theology. '*God* reveals Himself. He reveals Himself *through Himself*. He reveals *Himself*. If we really want to understand revelation in terms of its subject, i.e. God, then the first thing we have to realise is that this subject, God, the Revealer, is identical with His act in revelation and also identical with its effect.' (*CD* I, 1, 296.) The doctrine is an interpretation, and a necessary interpretation, of the basic *Deus dixit* of faith; though, having suggested in the earlier *Christliche Dogmatik* (p. 127) that Trinitarian doctrine dealt with the subject, predicate, and object of *Deus dixit*, God has spoken, Barth felt obliged in this section of the *Church Dogmatics* (*CD* I/1, 296–7) to qualify this in the face of criticism which maintained that he was constructing a 'grammatical and rationalistic proof of the Trinity'. He explains later (*CD* I/1, 299–300) that the reference to a *Deus dixit* is not to a general or abstract concept of the revelatory speech of God; for we have no such concept. We have only the speech which God has elected to utter in the event underlying the scriptural witness, and it is this which compels us to answer the question, 'Who is the self-revealing God?' in Trinitarian terms (*CD* I/1, 303).

II

If, then, we say (as is commonly said) that Barth's Trinitarian doctrine is an explanation of what is entailed for him by the idea of revelation, we shall need to tread circumspectly. For Barth does not consider that he is interpreting an *idea* of revelation, but the concrete structure of revelation as it has in fact occurred and is in fact occurring. To interpret an idea of revelation would be to revert to the 'anthropological condition' for revelation, a prior human model against which events can be measured, a category into which they must fit. And when Barth says so gnomically that *Revelation is not a predicate of history, but history is a predicate of revelation* (*CD* I/2, 58; italics in original), he is affirming that 'revelation' is not one of the categories under which history can be spoken of (if it is, we simply have some kind of Hegelian notion of history *as* in itself revelation; see *CD* I/1, 146–7). 'History', on the contrary, is one of the categories under which revelation can be—indeed, *demands* to be—spoken of. And this implies that *God* demands historical predicates, cannot be spoken of except historically.[5]

To discuss this adequately would require a full treatment of Barth's concept of 'The Time of Revelation', as set out in the *Church Dogmatics* I/2, § 14; and, since Dr Roberts's essay is particularly concerned with this area of Barth's thought, I shall treat it only briefly. Whether the implication of this insistence that revelation is (in theological discourse) subject, not predicate, of the historical, 'worldly' events with which dogmatics has to do, amounts to such a radical devaluation of

---

[5] Jüngel's treatment of the question (op. cit., pp. 76–7, 106–8; Eng. trans., pp. 64–5, 94–6), although compressed and difficult, makes this particular point very clear.

the created order as Dr Roberts argues, I am by no means sure. But we may note (at least) the awkwardness of a scheme which so divorces the substance of revelation from its historical form, in making the latter's relation to the former basically external. Revelation demands, we are told, historical predicates; yet there is nothing *in* these predicates which in any sense makes them 'appropriate' to their content. Despite Barth's vehement disavowals (*CD* I/1, 168–74), it is hard not to conclude that this does indeed make the revealing Word's secularity and historicity 'accidental' to its nature.

Barth in effect admits this in speaking (*CD* I/1, 175–6) of the impossibility of removing the distinction in our thinking between 'secular form' and 'divine content'. This impossibility he (predictably) considers a mark of man's distance from God, who alone achieves the miraculous synthesis of the two terms. Faith does not look for synthesis but for the unity which God's act establishes. Now this is a difficult and rhetorically overloaded passage. While it continues to stress the inseparability of form and content in revelation, it allows no possibility at all of any *unity* between them. The power of God and the freedom of God can make form and content one in effect or operation; but there is nothing here (or, indeed, in the discussion in I/2) to suggest that, even *ex parte Dei*, any more internal or substantial union can ever be envisaged. History, and the *world* as such, are wholly foreign to God: he can act through, but not in, the historical *qua* historical. 'Fulfilled time [sc. the time of revelation] in our midst is the enemy who has forced himself in.' (*CD* I/2, 61.)

Barth is evidently working with a sharply defined model of revelation, whether or not we conclude that it is ultimately determined purely by the revelatory event. It is germane to his whole exposition that revelation is a unitary event, a divinely actuated event, and therefore an *effective* event (*God* responds to God in the human occurrence of faith). In a sense, therefore, for Barth as much as for Bultmann, faith must be preserved from the dubieties associated with strictly historical knowledge, since (for both) revelation and faith are one event, and for Barth they have one primary agent. It is precisely the rigorous definition of this model which raises questions about Barth's protestations that he is interpreting the simple fact of revelation. Robert C. Roberts, in a provocative recent study of Bultmann,[6] has complained at Bultmann's thoroughgoing 'homogenization' of what the New Testament has to say about faith and assurance, the reduction of a family of images and ideas to one clear principle. Barth does not expose himself to quite the same charge; but we may properly ask whether some such homogenizing process is not going on in his treatment of the events of revelation. Dr Ford in his essay questions whether Barth's scheme of Christocentric typology can do justice to the 'complexity of reality'; and this query is exactly the one which I wish to enter against his account of revelation. Did the Hebrews conceive of the Exodus and Sinai experiences as both veilings and unveilings of God? For that matter, did the Twelve so understand the resurrection?

Hardly; but of course, it could be said in reply that it is the *Cross* which ought to provide the paradigm of revelation, since the resurrection is never other than the resurrection of the one *who has been crucified*, and that the Cross most sharply poses the problem of revelation in hiddenness. Barth refers us to Luther for this, and to W. von Loewenich's superb study of Luther's understanding of the Cross.[7] Yet this does *not* in fact resolve the issue. It is one thing to speak of 'revelation in hiddenness': as von Loewenich makes clear,[8] Luther is concerned to maintain a sharp distinction between the 'naked God', *God in se*, and the revealed God, God on the Cross, 'under the appearance of the opposite', in order to guard against any notion that there can be a showing of God apart from Manger and Cross. God *is*, simply and absolutely, in these forms, in the contradiction, the doubt, and the pain. This is, indeed, the essential feature of Lutheran Christology, its almost Monophysite understanding of the *communicatio idiomatum*.

At first sight it looks as if Barth is saying precisely the same. The difference, however, is that signalized in the Reformation debates by the concept of the *extra calvinisticum*: God is present *mit*

---

[6] *Rudolf Bultmann's Theology: A Critical Interpretation* (Grand Rapids, Michigan, 1976, London, 1977); see particularly Part I, Ch. 2 ('Existence, World, and the New Testament') and Part III, Ch. 9 ('Faith').

[7] *Luthers theologia crucis* (1929); Eng. trans. of 5th (1967) German edn., *Luther's Theology of the Cross*, Belfast, 1976.

[8] Op. cit., Ch. 1, esp. pp. 38–49.

und unter, with and under, the contingent and historical, but he cannot be said to be *in* it, identified with it in the way Luther envisages. For the Lutheran, what is involved in the revelation of God in suffering and darkness is a real communication of God; the worldly circumstances of Cross and dereliction *themselves* say something about God.[9] They are not simply a concealing exterior vehicle: the mercy of God is such that the divine *opus proprium* 'translated' into worldly form is necessarily and properly the Cross. And this, I suggest, is not the same as saying that we can only hear the Word in its secular form, as this says nothing (as it stands) about the Word's relation to its form.

In Barth's eyes, such an understanding of a relation between Word and form would be 'trying to do God's miraculous act ourselves' (*CD* I/2, 175). The revelatory event is God's miracle from beginning to end, and its unity, continuity, and *trustworthiness* depend upon God alone. The act of God cannot be uncertain or inconclusive in effect; when God speaks, he 'achieves His revelation', 'He makes himself sure of us, . . . establishes and executes His claim to lordship over us by His immediate presence.' (*CD* I/1, 454.) To say that God's Word becomes fully identical with the ambiguous circumstances in which it is spoken is to prejudice the sovereign freedom of the Speaker. 'God is His own interpreter / And He will make it plain.' As his own interpreter, God lifts for the believer the veil of ambiguous fact. Through the medium of uncertain secularity, the clear witness of God to himself establishes the certainty of faith, which is a standing in this royal road from God to God, by God's grace. Only in face of this 'uncertain secularity' can such faith occur; but it does not occur by a grasping of any inner unity between Word and form. That would be too perilously near to putting the Word at our disposal; and God does not so give himself into our hands, but keeps us in his (*CD* I/1, 176). 'Man must be set aside and God Himself presented as the original subject, as the primary power, as the creator of the possibility of knowledge of God's Word.' (*CD* I/1, 247.) Revelation is a unitary act, and its God-grounded unity in diversity secures for the

---

[9] Ibid., p. 47: 'Is the form of revelation perhaps accidental, or is it not to the highest degree characteristic for the content of revelation?'

faith it effects an absolute and stable character, God's guarantee.[10]

The reason for engaging in what may seem a laboured and
disproportionately long digression on Barth's view of revelation and its *Gestalt* is simply this: that the defensibility or
otherwise of his claim to be interpreting the fact, not the idea
of revelation is of material importance in assessing the viabil-
ity of his Trinitarian theology. If it can be shown that Barth is
actually operating (even unconsciously) with a concept of
revelation defined in advance of his exegesis of the records of
revelation, substantial questions are raised about not merely
the ground but also the *shape* of his articulation of the doctrine.
It will be liable (to say no more) to be seen as a capitulation to
precisely the anthropological determination which Barth
wishes at all costs to avoid; it will be open to evaluation not, as
he would wish, purely on the grounds of its adequacy as
exegesis of saving history, but in terms of the validity or
acceptability of an anthropological premiss. Now what has
emerged from our argument in the foregoing paragraphs
constitutes, I believe, a strong case for regarding Barth's view
of revelation as *not* determined exclusively by the structure of
saving events. Revelation must be such as to be characteristic
of a God who is sovereign and free; and therefore its relation to
any historical circumstance, whether of triumph (like the
Exodus) or of humiliation (as on Calvary) is bound to be
arbitrary—or, if that word seems too pejorative, freely elected.
Thus what can be said about the pattern of events reported in
Scripture as being of saving effect is determined by a prior
consideration of the sovereign effectiveness of the acts of God.
All saving events are alike in containing the dialectic of veiling
and unveiling; and this might well be called (using a term
proposed earlier) a 'homogenization' of these events.

A defender of Barth could respond that, since the revelatory
event reproduces the *Urgeschichte*, the 'primal history', *historia
praeveniens*, of God's act, or the 'event' of God's being, it cannot

---

[10] Professor Sykes adverts in his essay to Barth's expression (as used in *FQI*),
'noetic necessity', and Dr Roberts touches on the implications of Barth's model of
knowledge as 'acknowledgement' (see, for instance *CD* I/1, 205–6 for this). The points
which they make shed much illumination on Barth's understanding of the stable and
'guaranteed' character of faith and of theological reflection from, in, and upon faith.

simply be 'arbitrarily' related to this divine act.[11] But this argument is frustratingly circular; for the *revelatory* event, properly so called, is not simply identical with its historical form. It is the event of God uttering himself and witnessing to himself; and of course this is not arbitrarily related to the primal act of utterance. What remains as unrelated as ever is the circumstantial historical event 'with and under' which revelation occurs. This applies even to Barth's reworking of the doctrine of election in the *Church Dogmatics* II/1 (to which Jüngel devotes much attention), in which the eternal election of the man Jesus is so emphasized. Jesus of Nazareth is the form under which God eternally chooses to determine himself in giving himself to man (*CD* II/2, 161 ff.); yet, even as presented by Jüngel, this does not justify anything like the Lutheran view of the *communicatio idiomatum*. Nor, it seems, does it cope fully with the problems raised by the fact that the existence of Jesus of Nazareth is historically contingent, a point in the interrelated, interdependent system of worldly events, from which it can in no way be abstracted. It is an existence of a certain character, with its own historical singleness, because of its occupation of a certain point of convergence for innumerable systems of worldly causality. The election of Jesus logically entails the election of his 'world'—not in the sense in which Barth speaks of the predestination of all in Jesus, but in a rather more mundane way. And if God does so elect the world of Jesus—which means, finally, the world, *simpliciter*—it is hard to maintain a Barthian insistence upon revelation as highly particularized interruptions of the worldly story. But this raises issues of large generality of which I do not propose to treat here.

To sum up this discussion: I believe there are grounds for caution in accepting at face value Barth's claim that his Trinitarian scheme is simply exegesis of the facts of revelation. We have seen his understanding of revelation to be a highly defined and specific view, a prescriptive programme. In spite of all, Barth is, it seems, determining in advance what can and what cannot be admitted under the heading of 'revelatory events', finally refining the concept so as to make it clear that

---

[11] See Jüngel, op. cit., pp. 87–90; Eng. trans., pp. 74–8.

it really comprises only the witness of God to the speech of God. The revelatory event and experience is not only unitary but infallible, God guaranteeing the divinity of his Word, miraculously grasping man through the uncertain medium of worldly happening and bringing him into the single true event of the divine being. It is Calvin's irresistible grace rendered into epistemological terms.

It remains true, then, that Barth's Trinitarian theology and his doctrine of revelation are intimately connected; and in the next section I shall endeavour to set out this relationship, as Barth conceives it, in more detail. However, it is important to remember constantly that Barth's account of revelation is by no means as 'neutral' as it purports to be. A powerful ideological motive—the need to assert the infallibility and irresistibility of God's self-communication—underlies all that is said about the revealing event. This is not to prejudge the validity of Barth's treatment of the Trinity, not to take for granted that this 'ideological' root is simply to be deplored or dismissed; but no understanding of Barth (or any other writer, for that matter) can begin to be adequate if it simply relies upon his own description, however sincere, of his method and intention.

III

Theodore W. Jennings, Jr., in a recent and very valuable essay in theological method,[12] complains that 'Barth's reliance upon a doctrine of the Trinity and Incarnation as the starting-point of his reflection subordinates reflection to ecclesiastical formulations whose appropriateness and intelligibility it has yet to evaluate.' This is an unfortunate and rather unperceptive comment, though it represents fairly enough a widespread view of Barth; unperceptive, because for Barth the starting-point for dogmatics is not a dogma or dogmas (not even 'all of them together', a further formulation dismissed by Jennings), but revelation, the pure fact that God speaks to man. Jennings allows that theology does involve a 'hermeneutical circle', that it begins in *Vorverständnis*, 'pre-understanding', but fails to see that Barth's is no more

---

[12] *Introduction to Theology. An Invitation to Reflection Upon the Christian Mythos* (London, 1977), 81.

grounded in dogma as such, than is his own. Barth's starting-point is the actuality of God's speaking and being heard; it is not a set of 'ecclesiastical formulations whose appropriateness and intelligibility [theology] has yet to evaluate'.[13] The appropriateness of the Trinitarian confession is precisely what is under consideration in Barth's basic question in the *Church Dogmatics* I/1: what *must* be said of God in himself if he reveals himself in such- and- such ways? if this is the actuality of revelation, what is it in God that makes it possible? Thus the doctrine of the Trinity is not for Barth a 'centre of theology' (as Professor Sykes argues, no doctrinal articulation explicitly holds such a place in the *Church Dogmatics*; though we may well conclude that the level of conceptual control is much higher than Barth admits, whether, with Professor Sykes, we consider this to be exercised by Christological dogma, or whether, as I have proposed above, we find it in an all-pervading epistemological premiss about the nature of revelatory event). Its position in the *Church Dogmatics* is not a matter of its being the most important out of an ensemble of dogmatic formulations. It is placed at the beginning of the dogmatic investigation because its subject-matter is what makes the whole of dogmatics possible: the grounds of the confession that 'God reveals Himself as the Lord' (*CD* I/1, 295–6, 306–7). Thus it contains the question: 'Who is our God?' What (as we might rephrase it) is God's subjectivity like?

'God reveals Himself as the Lord' amounts to saying that God is free; he is free over against man, so that to reveal himself *is* to reveal himself as man's God and Lord. 'Lordship is present in revelation because its reality and truth are so fully self-grounded, because it does not need any other actualisation or validation than that of its actual occurrence, because it is revelation *through itself* and not in relation to something else.' (*CD* I/1, 306; my italics.) Revelation is the statement of God's autonomy, that he is a self-subsistent 'I', addressing man as 'Thou', and in so doing displaying his absolute independence of us, and thus his lordship, ἐξουσία, over us (*CD* I/1, 307). This is what is meant by speaking of revelation as God's 'self-interpretation' (*CD* I/1, 311). He

---

[13] Ibid.

explains to us what and who he is; and he does so by being himself a second time, becoming his own *alter ego*. By nature he cannot be unveiled to (*CD* I/1, 315); but he transcends his own hiddenness and becomes 'God a second time in a very different way, namely, in manifestation, i.e., in the form of something he is not' (*CD* I/1, 316).

Revelation thus establishes two things concurrently. Just as it reveals to man at once the impossibility and the actuality of human knowledge of God, so it reveals God as the Lord, the utterly autonomous, free subject of whom men can have no *concept*, no analogical or connatural knowledge, in revealing him as *our* Lord, the one who is free to be for us. 'He is not tied to His secret eternity and external secrecy but can and will and does take temporal form as well.' (*CD* I/1, 320.) And in revealing himself under an alien form, 'something He is not', he shows himself to be capable of self-differentiation. He is thus Lord as 'Word' or 'Son', in the differentiated form of revelation (*CD* I/1, 320); he remains by nature hidden and free, and so is Lord as 'Father' (*CD* I/1, 324); and he causes men to see the identity of his veiling and his unveiling, which otherwise no man would see, and thus is Lord as 'Spirit' (*CD* I/1, 331–2). God is identity-in-distinction. This is the direct implication of the fact that revelation occurs, it is no 'arbitrarily contrived speculation' (*CD* I/1, 333). The doctrine of the Trinity is implicit (and sometimes, Barth ventures, explicit) in what Scripture reports of revelation, and as such is 'exegesis' of the biblical record; but it is better seen as the Church's response to the question which Scripture poses about the divine identity (*CD* I/1, 333).

To speak of 'identity-in-distinction' obliges us to do full justice to both terms in the expression. If we fail to see that the Trinitarian dogma is an 'explanatory confirmation' of the single divine name of biblical revelation, we should be postulating three objects of faith, and so three gods (*CD* I/1, 348–9). We must, rather, say that the unity of God's essence 'consists in the threeness of the "persons"' (*CD* I/1, 349–50). God's unity is such that it must be threefold; we cannot conceive it on the model of any other kind of unity. 'Singularity and isolation are limitations necessarily connected with the concept of numerical unity in general. The numerical unity of the revealed God does not have these limitations.' (*CD* I/1, 354.) God is one in being three, and this is what makes Christian monotheism Christian (*CD* I/1, 354).

This a point of importance for the understanding of Barth's characteristic doctrinal concerns. As he has already insisted (in the section on 'The Place of the Doctrine of the Trinity in Dogmatics' (*CD* I/1, 295–304), there is properly no preliminary treatise *de Deo uno* as a 'neutral' prelude to a statement of what is specifically Christian. We do not hold the confession of God's unity in common with other monotheistic religions. Without revelation there would be no understanding of the unity of God, and any conception of that unity independently of revelation is vacuous. And what revelation shows as the structure of God's unity is the threefold *repetitio aeternitatis in aeternitate*, 'repetition of eternity for eternity'. 'The doctrine of the Trinity confirms the knowledge of the unity of God, but not any knowledge of any unity of any God.' (*CD* I/1, 353.) Trinitarian doctrine is therefore not 'answerable' to or measurable by any non-revealed system of monotheism.

Leaving aside for the moment Barth's discussion of the notions of 'person' and *Seinsweise* ('mode of being') in Trinitarian terminology, let us pass on to examine the way in which, according to Barth, the structure of the revelatory event specifies the distinctive characters of Father, Son, and Holy Spirit respectively. The event itself Barth considers as the story of 'Easter, Good Friday and Pentecost' (*CD* I/1, 332): and it is noteworthy that this ordering of the three terms of the event is meant to correspond to the order of '*Son*, Father and Spirit' (not, as we might perhaps expect, 'Father, Son and Spirit'). Good Friday is the revelation of the Father: 'The One whom Jesus reveals as the Father is known absolutely on the death of man, at the end of his existence.' (*CD* I/1, 387.) The will of the Father is death to man, it stands in utter opposition to man's 'will to live' (*CD* I/1, 388). And this revelation of God as dealing death to men establishes his character as Lord over human existence, as a God whose power is not coterminous with our limited nature and aspirations. He is not only the death of man, however: this would deny his Lordship over our existence as such, and reduce him to the status of a mere boundary, a 'limit concept' (and therefore, once again, a datum of anthropology). He deals death to men so as to create the new man to whom he can speak, whom he can encounter. *As* dealer of death, he is giver of life. In human death, he shows that he rules and overrules man's life, since man's life is a constant essay in reckoning with, coming to terms with, his death; and God is the promise of that which human life of itself knows nothing of. He is outside it, a power absolutely unlimited by it, and so Lord of life and death alike. Thus it is he who sustains our existence and is its source, its free and self-sufficient Author, its Creator (*CD* I/1, 388–9).

The man Jesus, in all that he does, turns in obedience towards his Father; and his obedience issues in death, so the Father of Jesus is revealed as Lord of life and death, as Creator. This is a difficult and compressed piece of reasoning; but, as I have tried to show, it is closely bound up with the entire structure of Barth's understanding of God and man. God's absolute 'otherness' can only impinge upon human aware- ness, human will, human self-reliance as negation. This may seem to involve a contradiction: God is experienced as the negation of a life of human self-reliance, yet he is equally experienced as the negation of a life directed towards himself, as he is revealed in the death of a righteous man. Here, however, we must remember the peculiar character of Barth's view of revelation. Without the Word, man does not know the negating judgement of God upon his whole existence; in hearing the Word, he is at the same time judged by it and (because of its divine effectiveness) re-created by it. God 'wills death in order to lead our life through it to eternal life' (*CD* I/1, 388). Christ is not a hearer of the Word; but *as man* he places himself in the situation to which the Word is addressed. He knows and does the Father's will in the place where fallen man stands; that is, he does God's will as God's enemy, as a sinner, and so dies of it. This is not made explicit in I/1, and has to be worked out from the general structure of the argument.

If, however, we turn to Barth's major treatment of 'The Doctrine of Reconciliation' in the enormous fourth volume of the *Church Dogmatics*, we find in the section on 'The Judge Judged in Our Place' (*CD* IV/1, 211–83) a full statement of the Son's identification with sinful men. This long, and often

very moving, presentation makes it clear that Jesus' obedience, Jesus' righteousness, *consists in* the willing assumption of
the limitations of sinful creatureliness. Alone among men, he
declines the temptation to 'impenitence', to rebellion against
these limitations. 'In (men's) place and for their sake, instead
of committing fresh sin, he returned to the place from which
they had fallen into sin.' (*CD* IV/1, 259.) His 'free penitence',
wholly accepting the condition and consequence of sin, begins
with his baptism and culminates in the Cross, and in it 'there
took place the positive act concealed in His passion as the
negative form of the divine action of reconciliation' (ibid.).
And later, in a long exegesis of the New Testament evidence
(*CD* IV/1, 273–83), Barth puts it still more clearly: for God's
will to be done, the old man must die, must be totally
immolated; Jesus alone can, as God's man, perfect this
offering, shedding 'our wicked blood in His own precious
blood' (*CD* IV/1, 280).

These clarifications and refinements are absent from I/1,
and it may be argued that their working out in detail implies
some substantial modification of the over-all argument of I/1.
I shall return to the point; enough for the present to note how
significantly Barth's view of the Father is related to the
dereliction of the incarnate Son. The Easter Sunday revelation
of 'God as Reconciler' leads us on—as we might expect—to
what is beyond wrath and death, the unqualified miracle that
God overcomes the enmity of man and *speaks* to him, establishes fellowship with him. Here is the new life created by the
Father freely offered to the world, yet not offered by the
Father, purely and simply. We are not dealing with a natural
law of life-through-death (*CD* I/1, 391), a 'continuation of
creation, (*CD* I/1, 410), but with utter novelty. Here is a
second divine act, the possibility behind the impossibility, the
Word heard and received by the enemies of God. So, says
Barth, we have to do with a second, and in *some* sense
'subordinate', way-of-being-God (*Seinsweise*), God the Reconciler following on God the Creator: an 'irreversible relation',
but one in which each term is wholly necessary to the
apprehension of the other (*CD* I/1, 412–13). In creation and
reconciliation we see two miracles, two modes of transcendent
strangeness. At the beginning of this essay, it was suggested

that the sense of *strangeness* in man's hearing of the Word was one key to understanding Barth's view of revelation; here we see how it functions in establishing the dialectic of Fatherhood and Sonship in God, the tension between the lordship which rules and overrules, and the lordship which restores and re-creates. Only God can rule as Creator; only God can renew and reshape the world he has made. Each mode is divine, and equally divine (*CD* I/1, 414), yet their order is irreversible. But again, God is known as Creator only in the act of reconciliation: the Father is always the Father of Our Lord Jesus Christ (*CD* I/1, 412).

The final term of the triad is (as we have already noted) that mode of being in which God 'makes Himself sure of us'. The doctrine of the Holy Spirit is the answer to the question of how men can confess the lordship of the God revealed in Jesus 'as the beginning and not the end of their thinking about [Jesus]' (*CD* I/1 448). The Holy Spirit is to be distinguished from Christ, because he (the Spirit) is found only after the Good Friday and Easter event, 'in the form of knowledge of the crucified and risen Lord, i.e., on the assumption that objective revelation has been concluded and completed' (*CD* I/1, 451). In the Spirit we have to do with the 'subjective' side of revelation: not that the Spirit is in any sense at all a human capacity (see, for instance, *CD* I/1, 460 ff.),[14] but that it is he who gives to each human subject the miraculous possibility of hearing the Word. The Spirit is emphatically not the bearer of a new revelation (Barth has some harsh things to say later in *CD* I/1, 481 about speculative Russian Orthodox thinkers whose systems cut loose from the givenness of revelation in Christ and appeal to the revealing Spirit for justification), but the realizer of the one revelation in Christ. Once more the theme of the absolute unity of the revelatory act governs what can be said. 'The Holy Spirit is the authorisation to speak *about Christ*' (*CD* I/1, 455, my italics). The freedom of man to hear the Word and so to become God's child is the gift of the Spirit, whose miracle it is to *make* men responsive to the lordship of Jesus and the Father. Man does not become *capax*

---

[14] See also a rather neglected essay of Barth's, *Der heilige Geist und das christliche Leben* (*The Holy Spirit and the Christian Life*) in K. and H. Barth, *Zur Lehre vom heiligen Geist (On the Doctrine of the Holy Spirit)* (Munich, 1930), pp. 39–105, esp. pp. 54–5, 92.

verbi divini and then hear the Word; hearing and capacity to hear are given in one act by the Spirit (*CD* I/1, 457).[15] And the gift of the Spirit remains irreducibly gift, miracle; it does not become a possession. We can understand only, as it were, from God's point of view, 'as it is posited by God' (*CD* I/1, 462). All that can be said of man's relation to God in the Spirit has to do with *promise*, it is eschatological. If this were not so, God would not remain the Lord, our security would be in ourselves, not in him (*CD* I/1, 464–5). The deity of the Spirit, as that of Father and Son, is always to be understood as radical freedom—in this case, the freedom of 'God's future'.

All this seeks to establish the threefold nature of the act of God as exhibited in the event of revelation. But there is more: as we have noted, Barth's pressing concern is to establish the foundation *in* God for these structures, and each section on the manifestation of a person in revelation is followed by a treatment of the eternal aspect of that person's distinctness. The method of these sections is relatively simple, consisting basically in a further application of the principle of the divine autonomy. Thus, God is not Father in virtue of being *our* father and creator: 'He already is that which corresponds thereto antecedently and in Himself.' (*CD* I/1, 391.) He *can* reveal himself as Creator and lord of our existence because he *is* 'antecedently and in Himself' Father, originator, one who is capable of setting himself in relation to what is other than himself (*CD* I/1, 394). 'Father', designating as it does, inter-creaturely relations, may seem an improper word to describe the divine originator; but its impropriety is removed when we consider that our use of terms involving origination is properly dependent upon the divine act of origination (*CD* I/1, 392–3; there is a reference to Eph. 3:15). God's sovereign will to be himself a second time (*repetitio aeternitatis . . .*) is the ground of his fatherhood and of all fatherhood. However, it is essential to remember that he is *himself* a second time. It is not as though God the Father alone is Creator: God as Creator is revealed inalienably under the form of Jesus' relation to his Father, but his is precisely a revelation of *God*, the three-personed God as Creator. 'Not the Father alone, then, is God the Creator, but also the Son and the Spirit with Him. And

---

[15] And cf. *Zur Lehre vom heiligen Geist*, pp. 94–100.

the Father is not only God the Creator, but with the Son and the Spirit He is also God the Reconciler and God the Redeemer.' (*CD* I/1, 394–5.) The knowledge given in revelation is thus 'relativised', but in no way devalued. Revelation remains our only access to the truth of the triune God, and the language which revelation makes possible is only 'improper' in not being exhaustive. The 'appropriation' of the work of creation to the Father is not wrong; but we must understand it from the proper perspective of God's unique unity-in-distinction, the *perichoresis* of the three modes of being. The 'particularity' of knowing God the Father as Creator is essential, so long as we remain sensitive to what God's unity involves. We cannot be modalists (dissolving the Trinity in a 'neutral fourth'): there is 'order' in the Godhead. But it is the order of a 'repetition' of *one* divine subject (*CD* I/1, 395–8).

As to 'The Eternal Son', the same general principles apply in the discussion. Without the 'antecendently in Himself', it is impossible to say that in Christ God reveals himself as himself, reveals himself in the mode in which 'He posits and knows Himself from and to all eternity' (*CD* I/1, 416). The mode in which God is God as Jesus Christ is not something accidental to God's simply *being God*: if it were so, it would not in fact be a mode-of-being-God at all. And, at the same time, if we say that God's relation *to man* in Jesus Christ is constitutive of his simply being God, we introduce an anthropologically conditioned necessity into God, and destroy the gratuity of grace (*CD* I/1, 420–1). And furthermore, if we simply refuse to ask the question about the nature of Christ, appealing in characteristic Liberal fashion to Melanchthon's *beneficia Christi cognoscere*,[16] we fall back upon Christological language as 'evaluative', and such evaluation can only be on the basis of some human standard brought to bear by the theologian. The anthropological condition rears its head, and a theology of revelation becomes impossible (*CD* I/1, 421–2). God is eternally Son because he is eternally himself; that is the burden of Barth's argument. If he is not eternally Son—if he is Son only in relation to us, or if his revelation in Christ begs no ontological questions—he is not eternally himself, and cannot reveal *himself* to us. Either what is revealed is not God; or else

---

[16] 'to know the benefits of Christ).

God is not truly God and Lord, but is ontologically bound up with and conditioned by the world of men, and so cannot reveal himself as the Lord. The basic statement, 'God reveals *himself* as the *Lord*' demands the 'antecedently in himself' of eternal sonship, the eternal self-reiteration of God. He gives himself to be known by us on the grounds of his eternal knowing of himself: 'The Word of God in which He gives Himself' (*CD* I/1, 435). That God reveals himself, becomes knowable in the form of an 'other', Word and Son. For God to be God (as Barth has clearly said at an earlier stage in the same volume) he must be an object to himself (*CD* I/1, 140), he must not need creation as a means of self-realization or self-interpretation.

Barth is, of course, tacitly rebutting anything like a Hegelian notion of the world as the divine self-objectification or 'noetic realisation'. It is illuminating to turn briefly from the *Dogmatics* to Barth's discussion of Hegel in his *Protestant Theology in the Nineteenth Century*[17], where he deals particularly with the Hegelian identification of self, mind, and God, as an enormous theoretical justification for Romanticism (*PT*, 392 ff.), the identification of ego with non-ego. Barth proposes that the key to Hegelianism is its treatment of 'reason, truth, concept, idea, mind, God himself' as *event*, 'life, movement, process' (*PT*, 398–9). Misunderstanding arises in thought when this life is conceived in terms of a state. Reality—including God—is historical, and so true understanding is inevitably historical (*PT*, 400); because historical understanding alone can grasp the movement of truth, the resolution of contradictions in ceaseless process. Truth *is* method, in effect, as far as thinking is concerned, for true thinking is the entry into the world's processes (*PT*, 405–6). Thus God's truth must be apprehensible by the dialectical flow of thought and as *being itself* the dialectical flow of thought at its most fundamental level. 'The truth is God, God, however, is God only *in actu*. This means for Hegel, only as the God who is Three in One, the eternal process which consists in something distinguishing its parts, separating them, and absorbing them into itself again.' (*PT*, 413.) Reality is one; knowledge is established as secure upon this basis, since the unity of all things rests upon

[17] London, 1972, pp. 384–421.

the unity of God, with whom begins and ends the noetic process. We know the world rightly in that the world is God's medium for the knowing of himself.

Barth expounds all this with great sympathy and perceptiveness (and we shall return later to the question of the points at which his own presentation is marked by Hegelian epistemology), but his major diagreement comes over the matter of sin. For Hegel (says Barth), sin is finitude and fate, and its overcoming is as necessary a part of the cosmic process as is its occurrence in the first place (*PT*, 418). There is no *fall*, no radical, mutilating breakage of man from God; indeed, how could there be, since divine and human nature are one, as Hegel makes quite plain in his *Philosophy of Religion?* In such a scheme, the basis of Christian knowledge cannot be revelation, and so cannot be God's freedom. If God is the universal noetic process, all that is is necessary to him. If he is to speak his word, He requires a world with which to utter it. The Word is concrete being, creation is the Word of God.[18] 'Hegel, in making the dialectical method of logic the essential nature of God, made impossible the knowledge of the actual dialectic of grace, which has its foundation in the freedom of God.' (*PT*, 420.)

Once more, therefore, it is evident that, for Barth, the Trinitarian dogma is the only ultimate safeguard for belief in the divine freedom. Without the 'antecedently' of the doctrine of the Son's eternal generation, God is caught in the Hegelian trap, subjected to a necessity which is both his and the world's. He is *obliged* to reveal himself, since 'A mind which is not manifest is not a mind.' (*Philosophy of Religion III*, 35; quoted by Barth, *PT*, 420.) And, theologically, this is not and cannot be revelation in the proper sense. There can be no dialectic of hiddenness and revealedness, only the one organically evolving 'manifestation'. So to insist that God is God *in-und-für-sich-selbst*, ('in and for himself'), whether or not there is a world, is necessarily involved in any confession of 'revealed religion' (to use an un-Barthian expression); and

---

[18] For a useful, if uncritical, summary see James E. Griffiss, 'Hegel's Logos Christology', in *Lux in Lumine: Essays to Honor W. Norman Pittenger*, R. A. Norris, Jr. (ed.) (New York, 1966), pp. 80–92.

any faith which does not rest upon revelation cannot be faith in a free God, faith in God as Lord.

Barth begins his discussion of 'the Eternal Spirit, *CD* I/1, 466–89) with the usual programmatic statement: 'What [God] is in revelation He is antecedently in Himself.' (*CD* I/1, 466.) Scripture clearly testifies that the work of the Spirit in revelation is God's work. If 'man's own presence at revelation' were *not* God's work, man would confront the Word as an object (*CD* I/1, 468). Thus the Spirit is God, and God in another mode than that revealed in the incarnate Word. Barth proceeds to a complex exegesis of the final section of the Nieceno-Constantinopolitan Creed to establish what may be said of the eternal Spirit; and here it is clear that the exposition is halting a little. What emerges from the discussion of the credal statements is a curious and uncharacteristic uncertainty about the person of the Spirit in the 'immanent' Trinity. Κύριον, says Barth, is used 'adjectivally' of the Spirit in the Creed: it is neuter (τὸ κύριον not τὸν κύριον), like the word πνεῦμα itself. And this suggests to Barth that the Spirit's mode of being is—so to speak—'neutral'; it is not involved in the reciprocal relatedness which characterizes the other two modes. The Spirit is the common factor in the mode of being of God the Father and that of god the Son. He is what is common to them, not in so far as they are the one God, but in so far as they are the Father and the Son (*CD* I/1, 469). The Spirit *is* the communion of the Father and the Son (the *vinculum, nexus, donum*, bond and gift and so forth, in Augustinian terminology), their common intra-divine 'act' or 'work' (*CD* I/1, 470). Thus as the intra-drivine act of communion, he can be in revelation the act of communion between God and men (*CD* I/1, 471).

What is curious here is, first of all, the rapidity with which Barth moves into a consideration of the credal text, laying what may seem a disproportionate weight upon a grammatical point. Here—as happens very seldom in the *Church Dogmatics* I/1—he gives the impression of hurrying the argument forward towards a conclusion determined in advance (evidently with a lot of help from Augustine and the rest of the Latin tradition). The notion of the Spirit as *vinculum* provides a good basis for connecting the Spirit's role *ad intra* with his work *ad extra*; yet this can only be satisfactorily stated if the Spirit's work in revelation as *witness* to the Word (elsewhere so much emphasized by Barth) is allowed to drop into the background. Indeed, the whole structure of περιχώρησις (reciprocal movement and communication) in the Trinity, as set out earlier in the volume (especially *CD* I/1, 348–75), becomes problematic if one *Seinsweise* is seen primarily as a function of the other two. If the Spirit is a common *act* of Father and Son, why is it necessary to postulate him as a third hypostasis to account for the divine origin of human response to revelation? As an 'act', the Spirit cannot be a subject of predication in any way analogous to that in which Father and Son are such subjects. Barth, in his treatment of the concept of 'person' *in divinis*, has firmly rejected (*CD* I/1, 355 ff.) any identification of 'person' with 'personality' or 'centre of consciousness' in Trinitarian discourse, and the point is repeated in the section on the Spirit. 'Even if the Father and the Son might be called "person" (in the modern sense of the term), the Holy Spirit could not possibly be regarded as the third "person".' (*CD* I/1, 469.) This is confusing: Barth seems to be saying that, although no 'person' of the Trinity is an independent centre of consciousness in the modern sense, yet the Father and the Son more nearly approximate to it than does the Spirit. And the whole tenor of the argument about the Spirit as *donum* supports such a conclusion. If the Spirit is the communion or love between Father and Son, the implication is that there are two subjects and one 'operation' or, perhaps, 'quality' involved. In the words of a very different theologian, 'The revealed parable of the Godhead is a story about two characters, Father and Son . . . The Trinity is not (in human terms) a society of three, but a society of two.'[19]

This does not seem satisfactory. Barth is, in his introductory sections on 'Trinity', deeply concerned to avoid any appearance of imbalance between the three modes of God's being; all that he says (as, for instance, *CD* I/1, 349–50) about the need to see God's unity as *consisting in* his trinity reflects such a concern. Yet, when he comes to discuss the Spirit, a curious kind of Trinitarianism seems to appear. It is noteworthy that he devotes fourteen pages (*CD* I/1, 473–87) to the

---

[19] Austin Farrer, *Saving Belief* (London, 1964), pp. 128–9.

Filioque clause, and is implacably opposed to the Eastern *ex Patre solo*: without the *Filioque*, he maintains, the internal nature of God as 'fellowship', which is the basis of the redemptive act of God, is not conceivable (*CD* I/1, 480–1). 'The love which meets us in reconciliation, and then retrospectively in creation, is real love, supreme law and ultimate reality, because God is antecedently love in Himself.' (*CD* I/1, 483–4.)[20] Unless the Holy Spirit constitutes, as we might say, the 'lovingness' of God, there can be no ground for God's loving movement towards the world. Something has impelled Barth to qualify his earlier model in a direction which is both more explicitly pluralistic and less precisely triadic, and the oddity of this qualification prompts some further questioning about Barth's systematic assumptions, which we shall attempt to pursue in the next section of this essay. The relative clarity of the treatment of Father and Son is itself put in question by the apparent failure of the same method to produce an adequate theology of the Spirit.[21]

That God is, in himself, Father and Son is a matter which can be firmly established, in Barth's terms, by the simple demonstration that, for revelation to *be* revelation, God must be what he shows himself to be, and must be 'capable' of self-showing. But for God to be in himself what he shows himself to be as Spirit is an idea which immediately raises difficulties; for God as Spirit is his own witness in the event of revelation, God 'making sure' of us, and it is not easy to see how God in himself can 'make sure' of himself. He may perhaps 'utter' himself to himself; but it is distinctly odd to say that he *reveals* himself to himself, and assures himself of his self-revelation. That has unhappy echoes of the Fichtean self-positing *Ich*, which does not know itself until it has set itself until it has set itself against the *nicht-Ich*, and then establishes a balance of mutual limitation within the over-all *absolute-Ich* ('absolute I'), so that the ego's self-knowing is not, so to speak, annihilated by an all-pervading otherness, but is secured by an abiding complementarity between ego and non-ego. Now the whole point of Barth's theology of revela-

[20] And compare with this *Church Dogmatics* II/1, 275, 279.
[21] The near-total lack of reference to the Spirit in Jüngel's book is interesting in this connection.

tion is that revelation is a miraculous act of God towards what is radically apart from himself: it has nothing to do with some kind of interior divine self-clarification. Thus the Spirit's role in the Godhead cannot be the *Offenbarsein* (the 'revealedness') of revelation; and the emphasis has to be moved from revelation as such to communion, the fellowship of the Holy Spirit which God bestows on believers, as a mirror of his own life. But this suggests a problem of a very fundamental nature in Barth's Trinitarian scheme: is the all-important model of revelation or divine self-interpretation really capable of bearing the weight it is given in the argument if it breaks down at this point? It is to a consideration of this that we must turn in our next section.

IV

I have already indicated at various points in the course of this essay that I believe Barth's understanding of revelation and its place as a governing point of reference in theology is, although powerful, fruitful, and attractive, attended by grave difficulties, and not without its own inner tensions. And such doubts about the all-sufficiency of the revelation model have been raised by others. Gustaf Wingren, in a vigorous and provocative study of Barth,[22] has argued that the *Dogmatics* is pervaded by the 'modern' question about knowledge of God rather than the authentically Protestant question about righteousness before God. It is a situation not without its ludicrous aspect to find Barth being attacked for anthropocentrism; but Wingren makes a very serious point, although the compression and polemical intensity of his writing may make it difficult to grasp. Barth's frame of reference, Wingren claims, is a model of two 'beings', a higher (God) and a lower (man), separated by an epistemological gulf: God sends a message to man across the gulf, which both 'itself indicates the difference between God and man, and . . . discloses God's will to fellowship with men'.[23] The fundamental situation is the antithesis of God and man; if the biblical imagery of conflict is to be used, it must refer to the conflict between God and man.

---

[22] *Theology in Conflict: Nygren, Barth, Bultmann*, trans. Eric H. Wahlstrom (Edinburgh and London, 1958).

[23] Op. cit., p. 24.

The Devil, or the active power of evil, or the force of sin which keeps man in slavery, all these are absent from Barth's theology: there is no *Christus Victor* story to be told.[24] The human predicament is ignorance. And Barth, by taking this as axiomatic, aligns himself with precisely that liberal theology which he is concerned to attack; what he and the liberals have in common is a lack of any sense of human bondage. Thus Barth's efforts in the *Church Dogmatics* IV/1 to give some weight to the idea of God liberating or rescuing man are largely vitiated by the unreformed structure of epistemological assumptions still underlying them. The Incarnation is still seen as essentially *manifestation*.[25] ' "Revelation" stands in the place where "justification" or "forgiveness of sins," i.e., the gospel in the essential meaning of that word, ought to stand.'[26] The Pauline (and, we might add, the Lutheran) understanding of law can have no place here. Fallen man's situation, in Barth's eyes, is catastrophic, but not, as for Paul, strictly *tragic*. Barth allows no true knowledge of God in the creation or the law, and so is unable to utter the Pauline cry of despair at man's inability to obey the God he knows as Creator and Lawgiver (Rom. 7:7–25).

Similarly, 'The statement, "the word became flesh", ought to be rendered "the word assumed flesh".[27] Not even in Christ can the gulf between God and man cease to exist, because God can never act *as* man or *in* man, only through man.[28] And the paradoxical issue of all this is that we are left with a system in which human knowledge, not the activity of God, is central. If we do place the activity of God at the heart of theology, we do not have to ask the obsessive question, 'How do we know?', 'Where is all this revealed to us?' Faith implies a readiness to speak of such activity in the world precisely in the *absence* of clear and secure 'revealed' evidence.[29] Salvation is not simply a being delivered from 'false thinking': God has acted to deliver us and make us righteous. There is, indeed, a focal *event* here, but it is an eschatological victory over the power of the Devil, not simply the uncovering of a timeless truth.[30] To

[24] Ibid., pp. 24–5.　　[25] Ibid., pp. 27–8.　　[26] Ibid., pp. 28–9.
[27] Ibid., pp. 30–1.　　[28] Cf. ibid., pp. 123–4.　　[29] Ibid., pp. 35–6.
[30] Ibid., pp. 37–8.

remove the centre of theological gravity from the liberating act of God in the death of Christ is to jeopardize the very notion of God as living and as free to act.[31] Man with his epistemic capacities or incapacities occupies the centre of the stage, and the theological question is about the sources of his knowledge of ultimate truth. The Barthian *Nein* denies that nature can be such a source, and indicates that Christ is so—that is, that Christ answers *the same question*.[32] The burden of Wingren's critique is the refusal to accept this question as self-evidently the correct starting-point for theology.

This is a penetrating and damaging criticism. Even if it is thought that Wingren does less than justice to the Barth of the *Church Dogmatics* IV/1, he has drawn attention to a presupposition in Barth's system which has not, on the whole, been sufficiently examined. In a discussion of Barth's hermeneutics later on in the same work,[33] Wingren explains how the anthropological presupposition of man without knowledge of God dictates a reading of Scripture almost entirely in terms of 'communication' from God to man; whereas in fact the scriptural record points far more consistently to the struggle between God and evil, to a dramatic picture of God engaging in the tragic situation of man. It is a picture at the centre of which is not *Das Wunder der Weihnacht*, the Christmas miracle, which Barth so much emphasizes in the *Church Dogmatics* I/2, but the defeat and victory of Good Friday and Easter Sunday. Wingren notes[34] the way in which the story of the virginal conception of Jesus provides Barth with a vehicle for stressing yet again the utter passivity of man before and in the event of revelation. Christmas is centrally important because it shows so clearly the nature of revelation in Christ, the divine Word present in the negation of human act and ability. Yet, as Wingren remarks,[35] the birth of Jesus is not, *in itself*, of any significance in New Testament preaching, and Christmas is not celebrated by the Church until a fairly late date. Properly speaking, it cannot be more than an introduction to the human life in which the incarnate Word works our salvation.

---

[31] Ibid., pp. 38, 40–1.   [32] Ibid., p. 42.
[33] Ibid., Ch. 6, pp. 108–28.   [34] Ibid., pp. 111–12.
                    [35] Ibid., pp. 120–2.

Wingren implies, without ever stating it in so many words, that Barth has no doctrine of the humanity of Christ.[36]

It is true that the long and subtle treatment of Christ's obedience in the *Church Dogmatics* IV/1 weighs against any such conclusion, and Wingren, as we have seen, is not unaware of Barth's efforts to state a more authentically incarnational scheme of the work of redemption. Indeed Barth's understanding of Christ bearing our condemnation in the same act as that in which he perfects our failed obedience is very close indeed to Wingren's own Christology. Yet here again Barth presses back towards talking about revelation. The obedience of Christ is the way in which the love of God is make *known*: 'space' is made for God's communication in the world by the self-abnegation of Christ. We may refer back here to our earlier discussion of the revelation of God the Father in the Cross. Christ's obedience, says Barth (*CD*, IV/1, 208) 'proves Him to be the Mediator between God and man'. In his obedience is revealed his lordship. This, of course, raises the issue of how the obedience of Christ reveals (as on Barth's presuppositions it must do) some aspect of the divine life *ad intra*; and we are given a very long and tortuous treatment of this (*CD* IV/1, 192–210), proposing the existence of 'above' and 'below', *prius* and *posterius*, command and obedience, in the life of God, while still insisting (*CD* IV/1, 204–5, 208–9) that the divine hypostases are modes of being, and not centres of volition. 'In His mode of being as the Son He fulfils the divine subordination, just as the Father in His mode of being as the Father fulfils the divine superiority.' (*CD* IV/1, 209.) What, if anything, this can possibly mean, neither Barth nor his interpreters have succeded in telling us. The whole movement of IV/1 is towards a very much more 'pluralist' conception of the Trinity than is allowed for in I/1; the attempt to harmonize the two models–or rather, to bring the former into line with the latter—produces one of the most unhelpful bits of hermetic mystification in the whole of the *Dogmatics*. Wingren is right at least in saying that Barth has

---

[36] The importance of this in Wingren's own dogmatic theology is plain from his early work on Irenaeus, *Man and the Incarnation* (Edinburgh and London, 1959; Swedish original published 1947).

failed to carry through any major reformulation of his assumptions in IV/1.

The conclusion suggested by all this is that as soon as the *history* of Jesus, in a fairly simple sense, the detail of a human life and death, is allowed a place of genuine salvific import, the unity, clarity, and security of a scheme based upon a single and compelling act or event of revelation is put in question. It has more than once been remarked (by Hastings Rashdall, for example[37]) that a 'substitutionary' theory of the Atonement—any theory, in effect, which lays emphasis upon Christ's bearing the consequences for human nature of the Father's 'wrath'—implies a strongly, perhaps insupportably, pluralist conception of the Trinity. God must confront God across the gulf of fallenness, from the place of Godless man. Barth puts this eloquently in IV/1: 'It therefore pleased [God] . . . for the redemption of the world, not to alter Himself, but to deny the immutability of His being, . . . to be in discontinuity with Himself, to be against Himself . . . His identity with Himself consisted strictly in His determination to be God, our God, the reconciler of the world, in this inner and outer antithesis to Himself.' (*CD* IV/1, 184.) In the act of reconciliation, God, for our sakes, 'risks' his very identity, his continuity with himself.[38] And if we are to take this at all seriously, the kinds of assumption about the freedom and lordship of God with which Barth is working in I/1 will need radical revision. The pluralism to which the logic of Barth's argument in IV/1 points not only demands a modification of any exclusively revelatory or 'interpretative' reading of Trinitarian doctrine; it also demands a rethinking of the *kind* of revelation with which Christian theology has to deal, and so of the kind of divine subjectivity from which revelation emerges.

Such issues as these have been discussed, with an insight shown by few other contemporary theologians, in the work of

---

[37] *The Idea of Atonement in Christian Theology* (London, 1919), pp. 444–6. I am indebted to Professor Sykes for drawing my attention to this passage.

[38] For a uniquely sensitive treatment of this theme and its implications, the reader is referred to Professor D. M. MacKinnon's article, 'The Relations of the Doctrines of the Incarnation and the Trinity', in *Creation, Christ and Culture. Studies in Honour of T. F. Torrance*, R. W. A. McKinney (ed.) (Edinburgh, 1976), pp. 92–107.

Hans Urs von Balthasar. Donald MacKinnon[39] has indicated the importance, in von Balthasar's treatment of the death of Christ, of the theme of a 'coincidence of opposites' grounded in the eternal Trinity,—the *kenosis* of Christ in his manhood and mortality revealing an eternal self-determination of God which in some manner includes this manhood and mortality, and so includes the whole created order. The place of Christ before the Father, as elect and beloved of the Father, is not an afterthought in the being of God, but eternally in the identity (*Eigentlichkeit*) of God.[40] Our distance from God is itself taken into God, finds place in God; by the Spirit of adoption we enter the relation between Father and Son, the relation of exchange and mutuality.[41] In the Incarnation, God distances himself from himself: the divine, intra-Trinitarian love is enacted and realized in the world by the descent of Christ into Hell. And the separation between Father and Son is bridged by the Spirit, who is the common will and love of Father and Son. The inconceivable self-emptying of God in the events of Good Friday and Holy Saturday is no arbitrary expression of the nature of God: this is what the life of the Trinity is, translated into the world.[42] 'God causes God to go into abandonment by God while accompanying him on the way with his Spirit. The Son can go into the estrangement from God of hell, because he understands his way as an expression of his love for the Father and he can give to his love the character of obedience to such a degree that in it he experiences the complete godlessness of lost man'.[43]

Von Balthasar fully acknowledges, in his *magnum opus, Herrlichkeit*, as elsewhere, his great debt to Barth's presentation of some of these themes in IV/1. And perhaps it requires a theology like von Balthasar's to show us just how far from the schema of I/1 we are led by the implications of IV/1. The

[39] In an introductory essay to von Balthasar's *Engagement With God*, trans. J. Halliburton (London, 1975), p. 7.

[40] H. U. von Balthaser, *Herrlichkeit. Eine Theologische Ästhetik (Glory. A Theological Aesthetic)*, III, 2.2 (Einsiedeln, 1969), pp. 367–8.

[41] Ibid., p. 369.

[42] Ibid., pp. 196–200. For a fuller exposition, the whole of this section (pp. 196–211) on *Kenose* should be consulted, as should the long essay, *Mysterium Paschale* in *Mysterium Salutis* III.2, J. Feiner and M. Lohrer (eds.), (Einsiedeln, 1969).

[43] H. U. von Balthaser, *Elucidations* (trans. John Riches, London, 1975), p. 51.

Trinitarian scheme which can be developed out of the doctrine of the Son of God in a far country is one which must
allow not only for a plurality of agency within the Trinity but
also for the inclusion of the history of man in the being of God.
Such a formulation may instantly suggest the kind of Hegelian
blurring of boundaries against which Barth so violently reacts.
Yet it is Barth himself who struggles to formulate this in II/2
of the *Church Dogmatics* in a celebrated discussion of the
predestination of Christ to which Jüngel draws our particular
attention.[44] God's *Urentscheidung*, his primary determination,
is also the *Urgeschichte*, the primary history, of the act of grace.
'Originally God's election of man is a pre-destination not
merely of man but of Himself.' (*CD* II/2, 3.) Once more, the
ground of what God does in redemption and revelation must
be his self-determination: he elects, before all ages, to be the
God of grace.

The difficult implication—and Barth does not shrink from
it—is that the elected Christ, Jesus of Nazareth, is 'in the
beginning with God' (*CD* II/2, 96 ff.). 'If that primal history is
real *history* between God and man, then the Son of God cannot
be thought of in this history without the man Jesus . . . God's
prevenient being is being *imparting* itself as grace. In the sense
of such prevenient imparting, the man Jesus *has* already a part
in God's eternal being.'[45] The Logos, the Son, is the holder of
Jesus' place (*Platzhalter*) before God (*CD* II/2, 96). From all
eternity, God's self-differentiation as Son or Word is directed
towards the human and worldly object of election, Jesus of
Nazareth.

Does this then imply the eternal existence of *a man*? Not
precisely: Jüngel appeals[46] to the late patristic terminology of
anhypostasia and *enhypostasia* to explain how the presence of
Jesus with God is not simply 'a projection of a temporal
existence into eternity'. The temporal, historical existence of
Jesus of Nazareth would not exist, would not be a temporal
existence at all, without the primal determination of God as
Word; without the Word it is 'anhypostatic', it has no basis or
centre of subsistence. It is thus 'enhypostatised' in the Word,

[44] Op. cit., pp. 81–95 (Eng. trans., pp. 68–83).
[45] Ibid., Eng. trans., p. 80 (in original, p. 93).
[46] Ibid., p. 94 (Eng. trans., pp. 81–2).

it subsists as itself because of the Word. Now these are (as Jüngel admits) terms which Barth himself does not employ; and it seems, indeed, as though Barth's position is stronger in statement than Jüngel's paraphrase. Jüngel in effect proposes a solution whereby God eternally 'foresees' the man Jesus, and, although he denies that the pre-existent being of Jesus is 'gnoseological' or 'ideal' (i.e. presumably, only 'in the mind of God'), it is hard to see what else such a 'foreseen' existence could be.

The point becomes clearer if we return to the discussions in the *Church Dogmatics* IV/2 about the sufferings of God in Christ (see, for instance, *CD* IV/2, 186–8), and about the fellow-suffering of the Father with the Son (*CD* IV/2, 357). It seems as though, in this connexion, we have to do with more than a foreseen contingency, more even than the holding of a 'place'. It is a matter of the suffering and the death of a particular human being at a particular time being true for and in God in his eternity. Because Jesus of Nazareth suffers and dies, the eternal God suffers and endures his own negation in the world; and by enduring transforms death into life, *human* death into renewed human life (*CD* IV/1, 304–9). The divine verdict on the world, the verdict of negation, is affirmed in the Cross; but the world is saved on the Cross because it is God himself who has borne his own judgement and surrounded and penetrated this negation with his unlimited life. God's being is his act; if he acts in an through a man's death, that death is involved in what he *is*.

Does this represent a capitulation on Barth's part to the Hegelianism he so desired to avoid and combat, or to Schleiermacher's understanding of the Trinity as 'the doctrine of the union of the Divine Essence with human nature, both in the personality of Christ and in the common Spirit of the Church?[47] So long as Barth insists, as he does, upon speaking of God's *free* self-determination in the Word, he remains in a different framework from that of Hegel; and so long as he insists upon the divine self-determination as true of God *in se*, he distinguishes his position from Schleiermacher's. For Schleiermacher, the projection of God's differentiated forms in

---

[47] F. Schleiermacher, *The Christian Faith* (Eng. trans. of 2nd German edn., H. R. Mackintosh and J. S. Stewart (eds.), Edinburgh, 1928), p. 738.

revelation into the divine essence itself is the construction of useless, and indeed un-Christian, 'philosophemes', idle speculative constructions.[48] Barth's doctrine of election is precisely a projection into God of the form of his revelation; and, as a doctrine of *election*, it remains bound to his primary doctrine of the freedom of God. God wills to be himself in such a way (as Son or Word) as to make place for the man Jesus. He does not have to be thus. Yet, God 'reveals His very essence in this streaming forth of grace. There is no higher divine being than that of the gracious God.' (*CD* II/1, 356.) He wills freely to elect Jesus; but this is no arbitrary act, accidental to his nature. He is eternally—how might it be said?—'liable' to elect, 'tending' or 'intending' to elect, and so, in some sense, eternally exposed to the suffering of his creature Jesus, to the 'negation' involved in his own judgement upon the fallen creation. Eternally and in himself he meets and contains and overcomes the possibility of negation.

This is therefore a picture in which the revelatory event incorporates in itself the extremest possible risk of its own failure and deficiency. The radical hiddenness of Luther's incarnate God is far closer here than in the *Church Dogmatics* I/1. Revelation includes, at least, tension, perhaps even conflict, between 'Utterer' and 'Uttered', so that the hearing of the Word cannot be conceived simply as the reception of a clear and unambiguous utterance, revealed in what might be called a 'linear' fashion. To put it metaphorically: it is not that we are simply addressed by a speaker; we are drawn into a conversation. In I/1, Barth proposed that the event of revelation, although in a sense pluriform, is most simply and basically the utterance of a subject (the Father) about himself: in Christ, this utterance is projected outwards to men as a true predication about the Father. It is a pattern which corresponds (almost disquietingly) to what von Balthasar characterizes[49] as the Old Testament's view of the God-man relation: God the Lord addresses man the servant across the immense chasm of separation between creator and creature. But, by IV/1, it has become far more difficult to employ so simple a pattern. God's utterance about himself has now to include his

---

[48] Ibid., pp. 741–2.   [49] *Herrlichkeit*, III, 2,2, pp. 365–6.

utterance of a contradiction; indeed, his utterance *is* the contradiction, a divine other which (or who) does not simply 'express', but responds and questions. Merely to put the matter in terms like these shows the difficulty of holding two such models together. It seems that revelation is itself to be discerned *in* the event or transaction between Father and Son on the Cross, the dialogue of Father and Son. Borrowing Hopkins's imagery (from the poem quoted at the beginning of this essay), 'the crying of those Three' is, like that of the seraphim, *alter ad alterum* ('one to another'). And the believer, apprehending the event of revelation, is called upon not simply or even primarily to hear a word, miraculously imported into his consciousness, but to 'catch' that crying, to learn a language and so to join a society, to take seriously the 'strangeness' of revelation in a very different way from that indicated in Barth's earlier proposals, as the manifestation of a life and a system of relations which men are invited to enter and share.

Let us attempt at last to sum up this discussion. Problems begin to appear in Barth's Trinitarian scheme when the controlling model of revelation or self-interpretation proves difficult to apply to a theology of the Holy Spirit. What I have called the 'linear' view of revelation (God—the Word—the hearing of the Word) is no help at all in thinking about God's 'immanent' being *(in-und-für-sich)*, and the idea of the Spirit as *donum*, (gift) and *communio* or *nexus amoris* (bond of love) has to be developed. This has the result of intensifying the sense of plurality in God: not very much sense can be made of 'modes' relating to each other in love. And this becomes still clearer when Barth turns to a serious consideration of the Cross, of God the Son existing at the extreme point of distance from the Father. If this is rightly understood, there is in God, eternally, the capacity for this 'distance' or 'displacement', union with another even across the greatest gulf of contradiction and opposition. God's otherness to himself in his Word is the existence in him of *response*, mutuality, not simply a 'self-expression' of some sort. He is not, in short, *a* self. The basic weakness of a self-interpretative model is its implied conviction that we are dealing with something comparable to an individual human subjectivity, rather than a unity consisting in a system of relations. Barth (as we have seen) insists that the Trinity of God is indeed a special kind of unity; yet his view of revelation in I/1 necessarily dictates that God be thought of as a single self analogous to human selves. If there is one speaker, there can be only one subject; hence the *aporia* of I/1.

The role of the Spirit even in the later parts of the *Dogmatics* remains a difficulty. Barth never wrote a 'Doctrine of Redemption' to crown the threefold structure of the *Dogmatics*, so that we cannot tell how far his excursions into pluralism might have carried him. Von Balthasar's conception of the Spirit as 'going with the Son' into his exile and holding Father and Son together across the gulf of dereliction and death suggests one way in which such a development might be pursued; though this does not, at first sight, go very far towards resolving the question raised earlier, of whether we are not thus left with a model of two subsistents linked by a quality—a very asymmetrical Trinity indeed. However, it may yet provide the ground for a resolution. The Cross is not the end of the Gospel, and this means that what is shown on the Cross as the relation between Father and Son does not 'exhaust' what can be said of the Godhead. If we restrict what we say about God to what we say about Father and Son, we are left with only a relation of potentially radical difference, and *that* relation in itself cannot (by definition) constitute for us a third term independent of Father and Son.

But to confess the Holy Spirit is to affirm that beyond Calvary the life of God is still life. Christ is raised and exalted 'in the Spirit'. And so Barth, writing on 'The Verdict of the Father' in the resurrection (*CD*, IV/1, 283–357), can speak of how very near the Cross comes to a totally alienating, annihilating judgement on the world, to be salvaged only by God's freedom to be Spirit, to resurrect Jesus, and to renew the face of the earth (*CD* IV/1, 306–9). The resurrection, indeed, is not simply the verdict of the Father, but the verdict of the *Spirit* (*CD* IV/1, 919 ff.), the new divine judgement on the whole creaturely and human situation, which is imparted to men in the miracle of faith. The Spirit, *does* present to us the relation of Father and Son, he does not witness to himself; but presents it precisely as a relation which is not closed or fixed, but one into which the human world may be brought. God's being is, in one sense, the act manifested on Calvary; but it is also the act whereby *we* are brought into Calvary, Hell, and newness of life, the inexhaustible resource of God's life. If this is so, God can 'send' his Son into the far country in the Spirit, the Son can offer himself wholly, even in death and dereliction, to the Father in or through the Spirit (Hebrews 9:14), and we are made partakers of the Spirit by baptism into Calvary, whereby we stand before God as Christ did, as sons of one father.

The Spirit, then is the relation of Father and Son, but is not to be thought of as some kind of common possession which the Father takes from himself and bestows upon the Son for the Son to return to him. He is not the same as the Father or the Son, *or* the two together. Against Barth's vigorous defence of the *Filioque*, we may set 'the verdict of the Spirit' of IV/1, the divine freedom to be Spirit 'beyond' the Father-Son relationship. Vladimir Lossky, whose attack on the *Filioque*[50] is the most penetrating and systematic statement in this century of the Eastern view of the Holy Spirit, has argued that the *Filioque* presupposes an abstract monotheism for which distinctions in the Godhead can be stated only in terms of internal 'relations of opposition'. God postulates himself as Father, know himself as Son, and returns into himself in love as Spirit; the Spirit turns the 'dyad' of Father and Son into a primal 'monad' again. Proper Trinitarian theology, on the other hand, sees the procession of the Spirit as 'an infinite passage beyond the dyad, which consecrates the absolute (as opposed to relative) diversity of the persons. This passage beyond the dyad is not an infinite series of persons but the infinity of the procession of the Third Person.'[51] We may compare with this some words from Raimundo Panikkar's obscure but profoundly suggestive essay on *The Trinity and the Religious Experience of Man*:[52] 'Could one not say that in spite of every *effort* of the Father to "empty himself" in the generation of the Son, to pass entirely into his Son, to give him everything

---

[50] See his long article, 'The procession of the Holy Spirit in Orthodox Trinitarian Doctrine' in the posthumous collection of his essays, *In the Image and Likeness of God*, trans. J. H. Erickson & T. E. Bird (London, 1975), pp. 71–96.

[51] Ibid., pp. 84–5.   [52] New York and London, 1973, p. 60.

that he *has*, everything that he *is*, even then there remains in this first procession, like an irreducible factor, the Spirit, the non-exhaustion of the source in the generation of the Logos?'

Barth's Trinitarian scheme seems, finally, to be moving towards a pluralism of this kind; and, although we can have no certain knowledge of what might have been said in a 'Doctrine of Redemption', there is material enough for the construction of a revised model of the Trinity. Jüngel goes some way towards this, but the boldest and most systematic attempt at such a construction so far is Jürgen Moltmann's *The Crucified God*.[53] In Moltmann's conception of the Father whose love 'abandons' the Son to death and dereliction, the Son whose love takes his and all men's 'abandonment' into himself, and the Spirit who is the inexhaustible future opened and offered in the love of the Cross, we have perhaps the fullest indication yet of the potential of the later Barth's Trinitarian thinking. If future Trinitarian systems are to make use (as I believe they must if they are to be humanly—as well as theologically—serious) of the 'dereliction theologies' of Moltmann and von Balthasar, they must engage at some point with Barth's seminal discussions. Theology after Barth is also (as Moltmann never lets us forget) theology after Auschwitz; it cannot now operate without a condemned God, a dying God—'the judge judged in our place'.

v

In this brief final section, it remains to consider some of the possible impulses behind the epistemological position of the *Church Dogmatics* I/1, since it is this position which seems chiefly responsible for the unsatisfactory nature of the Trinitarian scheme there proposed. And, before going any further, it is worth noting that Barth is operating with a particular model of language in I/1, which is never directly expressed but is everywhere present. The nearest thing we have to a clear statement is the section on 'The Word of God as the Speech of God' (*CD* I/1, 132–43). Barth here begins by denying Tillich's idea of speech as symbol—understanding

---

[53] Trans. R. A. Wilson and John Bowden (London, 1974); see in particular Ch. 6 (pp. 200–90).

'symbol' as a designation chosen by men to substitute for a different kind of reality. Speech is an intellectual activity capable of corresponding to reality: *God's* speech, given for our use in his Word, corresponds to God's reality. It is, as Barth explains in his next section ('The Speech of God as the Act of God'), the act of God's lordship. And, if God's Word is speech, it is 'spiritual', 'personal', and 'purposive'. 'Speech, including God's speech, is the form in which reason communicates with reason and person with person.' (*CD* I/1, 135); it may happen physically, corporeally, but it is by nature spiritual, and cannot be reduced to the 'naturalism' of concrete images (*CD* I/1, 136). In God's Word alone, truth and reality perfectly coincide: 'Typical of every other word is an uncertain oscillation between a spasmodic idealism and an equally spasmodic realism' (*CD* I/1, 136), but in God's Word it is truth which comes first and governs reality (the concrete and particular). The Word is also personal, *Dei loquentis persona*, God-in-the-act-of-speech. It is the utterance of the one entirely free subject (*CD* I/1, 138–9). And thirdly, it is 'purposive', it is 'address': 'We know it only as a Word that is directed to us and applies to us.' (*CD* I/1, 139.) God is already object to himself in his eternity, but he freely creates us as objects of address and of love. 'God did not need to speak to us. What He says by Himself and to Himself from eternity to eternity would really be said just as well and even better without our being there.' (*CD* I/1, 140.) His positing of himself as his object is the eternal ground of his positing of the world as object.

What picture of language emerges from a discussion like this? Language here is seen, I would argue, as before all else self-expressive utterance. It is the articulation of inner ('spiritual') structures, the ultimate truth or truths underlying 'reality' (perceived empirical structures). Speech is an externalizing of the *verbum intellectus*, the internal form of thought, which in God is the thinking of himself.[54] Thus the Word, the language, of God is his expressing as object what he knows in knowing himself. In the Word, God literally *utters* himself,

---

[54] The section 'Language and Verbum', in Hans-Georg Gadamer's *Truth and Method*, Eng. trans., G. Barden and J. Cumming (eds.) (London, 1975), pp. 378–87, has a very valuable treatment of the concepts of *verbum* and *logos* in this connexion.

makes himself 'outer', external, *sich äussert*. And so his speaking to man is also primarily self-expressive utterance, this time *directed* towards man (the 'purposive' Word), and it is truth because it is the externalization of God's infallible knowledge of himself. Furthermore, since it is a part of God's self-knowledge to know himself as Lord and creator, his truth is the truth of all created things. Man has no word with which to reply, because he has no subsistence of his own, no truth of his own: all he can do is hear and obey the Word, allow himself to be brought into the single divine act of the expression of divine truth, by the power of the Holy Spirit, and the miracle of faith.

If language is first and foremost self-expression, then God's Word is first and foremost the expression of God's truth; so that to hear the Word is to enter into the infallibility of God's truth. This concern with the appropriation or impartation of infallible truth is, I believe, quite basic to the argument of I/1. At the very beginning of I/1, Barth says that 'All sciences might ultimately be theology', if they so chose (*CD* I/1, 7): science in general works with concepts of truth and certainty which are foreign to the dogmatic inquiry because they stop short of obedience to the one authentic truth; if the scientist bows to this truth, he becomes a theologian. Theology cannot therefore be among the sciences; yet she claims the name and dignity of a science, if only to register 'a necessary protest against a general concept of science which is admittedly pagan', to remind the secular scientists 'that the quasi-religious certainty of their interpretation of the term is not in fact undisputed, that the tradition which commences with the name of Aristotle is only one among others' (*CD* I/1, 11). Theology in fact claims the name of science to witness to the lordship of the Word over true science, and to call the perverted secular sciences to obedience, and so to 'the theological task'. 'Dogmatics', Barth goes on to say, 'is a part of the work of human knowledge' (*CD* I/1, 17); but it is more also, it is the fruit of *acknowledgement*, of faith. It is not and cannot be divorced from the free act of grace which establishes faith on the secure foundation of God's truth. 'It always rests with God . . . whether our dogmatics is blessed and sanctified as *knowledge of the true content of Christian utterance* or whether it is idle speculation.' (*CD* I/1, 18; my italics.)

The implication of this argument is plain. Knowledge properly so called, certain knowledge, is the prerogative of dogmatics in obedience to the Word. Dogmatics is the sole authentic science, because it alone conforms (necessarily conforms) to the truth of its object. It does not thereby deny absolutely the legitimacy of the 'special sciences', but it calls in question any and every claim to finality or ultimate certainty in these sciences.[55] When secular science claims such certainty in its own right, it has become crypto-theology—or rather *ersatz* theology. When it consciously abides within its own limits, looking beyond them for final truth, it is pre-theology. And when it passes over into obedient reflection upon and receptivity to the Word, it is true theology, knowledge of God's truth, 'acknowledgement'. It is shaped by the 'noetic necessity' of *Fides Quaerens Intellectum* (discussed elsewhere in this volume by Professor Sykes). The *Dogmatics* begin with the question of how the *security* of faith and talk about faith is to be grounded, how the nature of dogmatics as pure science can be demonstrated. The predominant concern in the argument is the search for certainty; not, indeed, a certainty which can be tied up in dogmatic propositions, but one which *participates* in the absolute dependability of its object, which is unified with its object, so that 'in the Object of dogmatic statements there is already included human subjectivity'.[56] God is subject as well as object of faith and of theology; his stability in himself, *in-und-für-sich*, is the same stability which holds for propositions about him made in conformity with his self disclosure.

We come full circle. Truth exists, dogmatics exists, the Word is heard. Man is seized by the Word and brought under its lordship, into the event of its eternal utterance. So, first among the tasks of dogmatic science is the attempt to understand how it is itself possible: not merely 'possible' in general, however, but possible as *science*, as certainty, 'acknowledgement'. The particular work which a doctrine of the Trinity therefore has to do is to provide an account of how God can communicate his truth to men; it must describe the

---

[55] See T. F. Torrance, *Theological Science*, Ch. 6, 'Theological Science among the Special Sciences'.

[56] Ibid., p. 351.

divine capacity for perfect self-expression and the perfect communication of that self-expression. The need to assure the 'noetic necessity' of faith and dogmatics demands just such an 'expressive' view of language as we have seen to be at work in I/1, and so dictates what I have termed the 'linear' model of God's Trinitarian utterance. And the consequence of this is Barth's pervasive interest, in the earlier volumes of the *Dogmatics*, in the unity of the revelatory event: an event in which disclosure and apprehension or appropriation are the single act of God in a duality of modes. To allow any positive place of human freedom of response (in the usual sense of those words) is at once to abandon certainty, to say that the eternal unity of God's utterance is, as it were, adulterated by the plurality and confusion of human minds and hearts.

It is surely here that Barth's kinship with Hegel is most evident. The Idealist obsession with what has been called the 'concrete universal' arose from the desire to ground knowledge securely in an ontology of participation: *das absolute Wissen*, Hegel's final synthesis of consciousness and self-consciousness, is the level at which the divisions and contradictions of prior levels are overcome by the finite subject's identification with, recognition of itself in, Absolute Spirit, the one and universal self-thinking thought. It is the finite self's participation in the One. Barth substitutes the Word for the Hegelian pan-unity, and so, by beginning from the total strangeness of God and man to each other, turns the Hegelian system on its head. Yet there is a recognizable similarity of pattern, something of a mirror-image. We may recall Wingren's strictures on Barth's anthropological—epistemological starting-point. The question is still one about certain knowledge, and for Barth it is answered by the possibility of man's 'inclusion' in the one divine speech-act, his participation in the Trinitarian event of God's self-differentiation and self-unification as Word and Spirit.

Perhaps the most fundamental trouble is that Barth (at least in this context) has as little of a doctrine of creation as has Hegel. For Hegel, God and the world are entirely continuous, for Barth, entirely discontinuous. The Fall has, it seems obliterated any theological significance in the created order as such in the Barthian picture; and Wingren is surely right to complain that this (whether accurate of not as a *theologoume-non*) is not the biblical or traditionally Christian, or even traditionally Protestant view. An emphasis upon the compelling, irresistible character of revealed truth leaves almost no room for a conception of free, creative, and *distinctive* human response. Man is free *for* God, free to respond in the Spirit, as Barth explains at length in I/2 § 16, free to know the Word as his master (*CD* I/2, 265–79); but it is a freedom which can only be 'theologised' from *within* faith, *within* the relation of obedience. There is, in the earlier volumes of the *Dogmatics*, little sense of that to which Bonhoeffer was so uniquely sensitive, God's self-abnegation in the face of created freedom, God's 'deference' to the will, even the evil will, of his creatures. God's relation to the fallen world is (as revealed in the Cross) an all but annihilating negation, in Barth's view; yet it may well be asked how this related to the Isaianic Servant, who will not break the broken reed, or to the tempted Christ in the wilderness, refusing (as Dostoyevsky put it) the lures of 'miracle, mystery and authority' as means of imposing the divine truth, or to the Lord who stands at the door and knocks. Even in IV/1, the emphasis is far less on the Son of Man given up into the hands of sinners, God at man's mercy, than on the judgement of *God* upon *man*. Barth will write eloquently of the suffering and dereliction of Jesus bearing the wrath of God; but not of Jesus as 'God bearing the wrath of man', Bonhoeffer's God 'pushed out of the world on to the cross'. We have already noted Barth's denial (*CD* I/1, 176) that God gives himself into our hands; yet the incarnational paradox is that this is precisely what he does. Having created free men, he submits to man's judgement, man's freedom to reject. 'Man's religiosity makes him look in his distress to the power of God in the world . . . The Bible directs man to God's powerlessness and suffering.'[57]

To suggest that Barth is in fact a theologian of 'man's religiosity' is too neat an inversion, too facile and eye-catching a point: Barth is evidently not making a naïve appeal to 'the power of God in the world'. Yet power, lordship, the master-slave relationship, all play an uncomfortably large part in

---

[57] Dietrich Bonhoeffer, *Letters and Papers from Prison* (enlarged edn., London, 1971), p. 361.

Barth's system. No doubt the so-called 'social' analogy for the life of the Trinity has its grave deficiencies, but at least it insists that the divine life into which the believer is baptized is a relational pattern in which 'none is afore or after another', where the predominant model is not address and obedience (significant though that remains), but mutual sharing. Christian Duquoc, in the second part of his magnificent essay in Christology,[58] has given serious consideration to the Freudian charge that Christianity is an inflation of infantile beliefs about the omnipotent father who can solve all problems and heal all wounds. Referring to a celebrated paper by Paul Ricoeur on this subject, Duquoc argues that this is an accurate account only when 'God the Father' is the phantasm projected by 'la toute-puissance du désir': the omnipotent father, that is to say, is the substitute for the failed omnipotence of the self. If, however, the Father is 'symbol', not 'phantasm', a term integrated into a symbolic unity of understanding, self-understanding, and world-understanding, not simply projected over against self and world, it may be less ambiguous, more creative. And Duquoc goes on to explain how the realization of Jesus' divine sonship *in* a human life sets the Father-Son relationship on a new footing for us. 'Elle souligne que la paternité de Dieu n'évoque pas seulement l'origine radicale, créatrice, mais qualifie nouvellement le souci que Dieu porte aux hommes.'[59] Furthermore, since Father and Son are one, in will, act, and substance, the Son has no 'desire' to be what the Father is, since he *is* what the Father is (the Christological hymn of Philippians 2 springs to mind here); and his refusal to 'desire' omnipotence is what makes him human and finite without ceasing to be divine. Free of self-directed desire, he can live authentically as Son and as man at the same time; and from this man learns that *he* may live as Son by accepting his finitude and renouncing the infantilism of desire. 'Le sujet humain, en effet, n'est susceptible d'une relation filiale adulte que dans la mesure ou il est

---

[58] *Christologie, Essai dogmatique*, vol. II, *Le Messie* (Paris, 1972), pp. 327–48.

[59] Ibid., p. 341. 'It emphasises that God's "fatherhood" should evoke not simply the idea of radical or creative origin, but is something which suggests a new characterisation of the loving care which God has for men.'

libre à l'égard de la mégalomanie du désir.'[60]

This is an original and impressive proposal. Like Bonhoeffer, Duquoc is profoundly concerned to answer the question, 'What constitutes an *adult* human relationship to God?' and this is a question which no theologian can afford to ignore. Whatever one's final judgement of Duquoc's suggestions, they at least remind us that our talk about man and God and their relations to one another is being conducted under the cold eye of the behavioural sciences. And, while this fact need not induce in the theologian the paralysing anxiety which seems to afflict much contemporary theological debate, it is clear that what theology has to say about man will inevitably be worked out in some degree of engagement with other contemporary models of man, whether consciously or not. What the nature of human flourishing may be is a weighty and complex issue. For the theologian, it will be defined more or less clearly in relation to the will of God or the purpose of God; but considerations of will and purpose push constantly towards the deeper question of the nature of God. The anthropological question leads into the theological, and what is said about God is of more than peripheral relevance to what may be said about man. And if this is true, Trinitarian theology, in so far as it is concerned with what 'kind' of God Christians worship, is far from being a luxury indulged in solely by remote and ineffectual dons; it is of cardinal importance for spirituality and liturgy, for ethics, for the whole of Christian self-understanding.

This was clear enough to Barth; and if a study of Barth's Trinitarian theology brings us round again to insisting on the point, it will have been a worthwhile enterprise. Barth, almost alone among twentieth-century dogmaticians, undertook to present Trinitarian doctrine as foundational for theology as a whole;[61] and I have attempted to show in this essay that Barth's Trinitarian scheme is indeed tightly interwoven with

[60] Ibid., p. 344. 'The human subject is, indeed, open to an adult relation of sonship only in the measure in which it is free from the megalomania of desire.'

[61] Perhaps the closest comparison is with the Russian emigré theologian, Sergei Bulgakov, whose trilogy, *The Lamb of God*, (Paris, 1933), *The Comforter* (1936), and *The Bride of the Lamb* (1945), represents a vast systematic integration of Trinitarian theology with anthropology. Although the first two volumes were translated into French, they have yet to receive the serious discussion they deserve.

his whole conception of the life of faith. What is said about the Trinity is initially conditioned (though perhaps in ways which Barth did not fully recognize) by certain questions and assumptions about the nature of religious language and religious knowledge; and it in turn conditions the understanding of man's response to God, reflecting back upon the issues of language and knowledge. If, then, the student of Barth becomes aware of weaknesses in the structure of argument and, more importantly, of problematic consequences if the argument is strictly followed out, it is not easy for him to point to any one stage in the discussion and say, '*Here* is the flaw.' He is condemned to the uncomfortable and potentially unfair expedient of suggesting that somewhere in the background a wrong question is being asked. I have indicated in these pages that I consider Barth's failure to be a certain lack of concern with human growth, human diversity, and human freedom of response—with the possibility and character of adult relationship with God; and in reply to the glib 'Barthian' defence, that these matters are not the primary interest of theology, I can only appeal to the orthodox conviction that they *are* of interest to a God who is made known to us in a human life and death.

On what this failure rests, I am not sure: it is possible to attribute it to the kind of preoccupation with 'ontologically' secure knowledge discernible in the early Barth, to a residually Nestorian (or too radically Calvinist) Christology, to covert idealism or covert gnosticism. Most centrally, it may be (as I have proposed) the absence of a doctrine of *creation*, as opposed to a doctrine of the infinite gulf between the created and the uncreated. None of these, however, constitutes an explanation of 'what is wrong with Barth'. The non-Barthian's attitude to Barth has about it something of Barth's own attitude to Catholicism—a fascinated exasperation at a system which is at once compelling and alienating in its range and seriousness, which constantly provokes one to attempt a counter-statement which will be no less serious. Barth's counter-statement to the doctrine of the *analogia entis* is the whole of the *Church Dogmatics*; and, while one may not think that a counter-statement to Barth can or should be another *Dogmatics* (and many would say that, for various reasons, such an enterprise is no longer possible for the theologian), Barth's

great work still sets a standard of engagement and comprehensiveness not easy to satisfy. If we object to a Barthian
Trinitarian or Christological model and its implications for
doctrines of man and grace, we are obliged to examine the
roots and the norms of our own understanding, to find out
whether we are asking the same questions, and if we are not,
at least to explore our own questions with the same committed
passion as Barth does. Barth reminds the systematic
theologian of his obligation to be not only systematic but
theological—in the patristic sense in which Θεολογία designated the whole self's growth into understanding of the
three-fold God who saves. It is a humbling and a salutary
reminder.

6

Conclusion: Assessing Barth

D. F. FORD

University of Birmingham

IS BARTH a fraud? That, crudely, is the first question to be answered in assessing his contributions to theology. The above essays have offered four analyses of parts of his work, praising and criticizing it in various degrees, but it is not uncommon for doubts about his whole approach to theology to go so deep as to question the value even of analysing an achievement which, it is claimed, is so ill founded in anything like what most people would call 'reality'. So an assessment must face this problem before going on to finer points.

The most common form of the doubts is about the grounding of what he says. Is Barth not a 'fideist', one who takes up a position of traditional faith and refuses to allow rational criticism? Is his confident theology possible only because he ignores the problem of its intellectual justification? Epistemological questions of this sort have dominated much modern theology, as Barth was well aware. So why did he not engage with them? The answer is that he did, but that his solution is a challenge to the very presuppositions of the debate. These presuppositions are sometimes empiricist—that we have the right, in theology as in other spheres, to demand that anything claiming to be knowledge be verifiable by neutral public criteria; they are sometimes Kantian—that it is improper in the field of religion to claim knowledge as Barth does, since faith is a matter of practical reason, of value-judgements and postulates; and they are often reductionist in tendency—placing the onus on theology to prove that God is not a projection of our psychological, social, or economic needs, fears, or dilemmas. Barth is first of all concerned to distinguish apologetics from dogmatics. By apologetics he means all those attempts to show a path, whether of argument or experience, that leads to knowledge of God from the outside. His attitude to apologetics is that people in fact come to faith in a vast variety of contingent ways, that the justifications of belief will, from this standpoint, be correspondingly various, but that it is not the job of dogmatics to lay down laws in this sphere. Rather, the 'how' of becoming a believer is a matter of the freedom of the Holy Spirit. What dogmatics does is to try to indicate what there is to be found, whichever way one arrives there. Modern epistemologies generally characterize the object of knowledge in terms of the way in which it is known by the human knower. Barth sees any such formal criteria, which are inevitably based on the norms of other areas of knowledge, as an infringement of the freedom of God to speak for himself, and a presumption that in the face of God one can step aside for a while to assess the situation neutrally. His confidence is that theology's object shines for itself. So theology is merely a reflection, but, since its object is supremely good, true, and beautiful, simply being as faithful as possible a reflection is the best way to convince people. Hence Barth's maxim that the best apologetics is good dogmatics.

The scandal for post-Enlightenment epistemology is, therefore, his concentration on God rather than on ways of proving God, a position which is often incomprehensible to his critics. Barth can do this because he understands himself and all men to be living within the sphere and results of God's action, in a God-centred history. This is his reality, decisively different from one which either denies God's existence, or else keeps his significance in check by effectively privatizing him, making his existence a matter of value-judgement, or decision, or inner experience by autonomous man. Barth's theology is sometimes described as if it took the second of these ways and could not avoid being based on his personal decision of faith. This is to assume that he, with Kant and many others, thinks that no true knowledge of God is possible in faith and that therefore the individual's decision of faith goes beyond the facts. This is not Barth's position, for to him faith involves decision, but is primarily knowledge, a recognition of the facts, and is received because God is present and communicating. It is noteworthy that on the issue of rationality, as in much else, Barth is nearer to Hegel than to Kant.

The result is that Barth is a fraud if God does not exist, act, and speak with freedom, appropriateness, and intimacy. Barth sees an either/or of ultimate significance here, and consistently bases his thinking on what he takes to be the right understanding. This is not an evidently incorrect basis, and he can offer a coherent justification for failing to justify it in terms dictated by empiricists, Kantians, reductionists, and others. The verdict, therefore, must be that Barth is worthy of further assessment.

Yet this is only to say that Barth's refusal to produce a philosophical or natural theology does not disqualify his dogmatics from serious consideration. It does not mean that he has produced a satisfactory solution to the problem of the relation of theology to other disciplines. One result of the essays above has been to suggest that Barth is weakest in these border areas. His tendency is to restrict two-way influence and communication rather than engage in this and try to work out its appropriate form. The result is that, instead of offering a way of handling the manifold mutual interpenetration of theology, comparative religion, history, psychology, philosophy, and the natural sciences, his rigid boundaries simplify the picture by excluding much relevant material.

That, however, might be interpreted *in meliorem partem* as the simplification of an artist who does not want his main design obscured by too many details and too much complexity. Henry Moore's assessment of Brancusi's achievement has parallels with Barth's:

Since the Gothic, European sculpture had been overgrown with moss, weeds—all sorts of surface excrescences which completely concealed shape. It had been Brancusi's special mission to get rid of this undergrowth, and to make us once again more shape-conscious. To do this he had to concentrate on very simple, direct shapes to keep his structure, as it were, one-cylindered, to refine and polish a single shape to a degree almost too precious . . .[1]

This implies that one should focus not on what Barth failed to do but on the content of what he did write. Therefore, while our essays all agree that Barth's exclusions mean an impover-

---

[1] Quoted by John Russell in *Henry Moore* (London, 1963), p. 63.

ishment—in the above quotation Henry Moore goes on to say that Brancusi's restrictions are no longer necessary in sculpture—we have been mainly concerned with the rich substance of Barth's thought. It is rare enough in contemporary theology to find a creative grappling with the giants of the past over the nature of theology, or a hermeneutics that has imaginative literary insight into the form and content of the Bible, or a comprehensive attempt to work out an understanding of time and eternity, or a doctrine of God that is not boring. In order to cultivate these heartlands of theology, Barth has marked out a clear frontier and refused to wage foreign wars. His concern is to provide theological nourishment, and it is worth trying to assess how far he succeeds.

At the simplest level Barth makes sure that the big questions raised by Christianity are not ignored or given answers that are too shallow or that refuse to engage in depth with the biblical and other important material. Chief among these is the issue of the reality of God. Barth has been described by Hans Urs von Balthasar as a 'God-intoxicated man', and this is at the root of his revolt against liberal Protestant theology. In his view, any theology which plays down the sovereignty of God as living, speaking, acting, and interesting is inadequate. He is quite aware that his position is commonly dismissed as anything from anthropomorphism to myth, illusion, or superstition, but sees no way of stating Christian truth except as a challenge to the poverty of speaking about God other than as personal in particular ways.

Complementary to this is another traditional Christian position which is perhaps even more alien to prevailing contemporary ideas: that man is created, is subordinate to God, and finds truly human fulfilment in obedience, thanks, and worship of God. Here Barth is opposing such notions as that autonomy is man's highest state, that worship is a form of self-alienation, that there is an inevitable competition between God's will and man's freedom and fulfilment; and he carries out his opposition programme with such thoroughness that the controversial nature of the traditional Christian understanding of what it is to be human is glaringly obvious. There is much to be said about this alleged 'devaluation of man', but partly the accusation has been made because in its central

thrust he understands man as created, and he is provocatively
Christian in developing this position.

A third, vital, and even more distinctively Christian, issue
that he raises is that of the resurrection of Jesus. He is not
concerned with neutral verification, or with how it might have
happened, but he has the theme of the presence of the risen
Christ running through the *Church Dogmatics*, reaching a
crescendo in its later volumes, IV. 1, 2, 3. I have tried in my
article above to describe the centrality of the resurrection in
his theological method and key doctrines. It is for Barth the
place where the relation of God and man is finally clarified
and where he finds the source of power and light for his
theology. Here again is an uncompromising statement of what
is by no means obvious to the world in general.

In all this and in much else Barth takes up an exposed
position minimally supported by the prevailing culture and
maximally in agreement with mainstream Christianity. His
Church Dogmatics can be seen as a spirituality aimed at
converting understanding and imagination to a habitually
Christian pattern of activity. Its very massiveness, and its
method of spiralling round and round the same central
questions, are ways of reinforcing habits of mind and heart by
giving time for long exploration and rumination. He is dealing
with a whole way of life, a movement that embraces many
levels of discourse and whole communities, and his concern is
to do justice to its richness, insights, and errors through the
centuries. The final question is, therefore, whether he does do
these justice.

Professor Sykes has considered Barth's concept of theology,
relating it to major theologians of the past and to the demands
of the present. His verdict is that Barth, despite himself, offers
a system having what amounts to an 'essence of Christianity'
expressed in a particular Christology. In trying to avoid this,
however, Barth fails to pay enough attention to the diversity of
theologies in the New Testament. Barth's capacity to deal
with pluralism is further hindered by his close association of
theology with a Church centred on preaching. Theological
debate then tends to occupy a disproportionate place in
Church life, it lacks the mediating, testing effect of liturgical
life, and in general lacks the freedom appropriate to a

discipline which should be as systematic and strictly conceptual as possible—and so inevitably consists of several systems.
The main problem Professor Sykes traces to Barth's notion of
'necessity' in theological epistemology which makes such
diversity hard to accept as an enrichment of Church life.

My essay finds the heart of Barth's theology in his reflection
on biblical stories, especially the Gospels. The criterion by
which Barth wants to be judged is that of fidelity to the Bible.
I try to show just how his main theological positions are based
on exegesis, and comment on strengths and weaknesses in his
method. He shows acute sensitivity to essential parts of the
Bible, especially the logic of crucifixion and resurrection in
New Testament faith, and he develops the possibilities of the
stories as pointers to the nature of God and man. Yet there is
also an overstraining of the stories by generalizing and
typologizing in order to arrive at conclusions which seem to
require other modes of argument besides those appealing to
biblical narrative. This doubt extends to his whole treatment
of natural theology, and, once the self-sufficiency of the story
is seen to be his instrument of exclusion, then it is easier to
argue for natural theology's inclusion by having a more open
understanding of the story—its very use of the common stuff
of life invites to dialogue with all the sciences.

Dr Roberts, tracing the theme of time and eternity through
Barth's theology, delivers the most unfavourable over-all
verdict. Partly this is because he places a high value on just
the sort of 'extra-theological' justification which, as I have
explained above, Barth deliberately refuses to give. He also
discerns a radical ambiguity and equivocation in Barth's use
of temporal concepts and in his handling of the relations of
God and man. This is a negative statement of what Professor
Sykes more neutrally called Barth's 'Romantic aversion to
abstract clarity', and what I described as Barth's double-
aspect interpretation of Jesus and his story. The problem here
is in part the perennial one that there is no human overview of
God and man, and no fully appropriate unambiguous language for their relationship; but there is also a crucial
disagreement here between our essays about the adequacy of
Barth's efforts to think of God and man.

Finally, Dr Williams, in his examination of Barth's doctrine of God, concludes that for all its interest and power it is limited by its exclusively reflexive and communicational character and its lack of a full doctrine of the Holy Spirit. This latter point might act as an integrator of many of the criticisms of Barth in our essays. It relates to Barth's neglect of New Testament pluralism, his conception of theology in the Church, his handling of the external relations of theology with other disciplines, his concentration on one set of events, and the pervasive epistemological problem. Yet one must not forget that Volume V of the *Church Dogmatics* on the doctrine of redemption was never written, and, as Professor Sykes says, at the very end of his life Barth was still troubled by the possibility that much of the liberal theology that he had attacked, especially Schleiermacher's, might be more favourably assessed as trying to present Christianity with the Holy Spirit as a starting-point. It is, however, hard to see how Barth's Christocentric concept of human identity could accommodate, for example, the thoroughness of Schleiermacher's or Kierkegaard's wrestling with the problems of the post-Kantian shift to subjectivity. Indeed, the exclusion of such problems is an important motive in Barth's use of biblical narratives, his minimizing of the role of the human spirit in Christianity,[2] and the little attention he pays to Orthodox and Catholic spirituality.

Ten years after his death, Barth's theology is perhaps still the single *corpus* most necessary to understanding twentieth-century theology. Yet few people can or will read all six million words of the *Church Dogmatics*, not to mention the similar quantity of Barth's other writings. So what is the best way to approach him with least danger of missing major elements, and most likelihood of catching the tone as well as the content of his thought? For a very quick taste Barth's late set of lectures published as *Evangelical Theology: An Introduction* (London, 1963), is probably best. For particular topics one might use the tables of contents and indices of the various volumes of the *Church Dogmatics*, or the comprehensive *Regis-*

[2] Cf. G. S. Hendry, *The Holy Spirit in Christian Theology* (London, 1957), pp. 51 f., 96–117.

terband of the German edition. But to meet something of the full force of his thought one needs to read a volume of *Church Dogmatics*. The least advisable would be *Church Dogmatics* I whose polemical hammering home of Barth's doctrine of revelation has understandably discouraged many readers from going further. *Church Dogmatics* II is more mature and is perhaps the fullest doctrine of God of the century. Its peaks are the treatment of the attributes of God under the heading of 'The One who loves in freedom', and the doctrine of election which integrates all the doctrines of the *Church Dogmatics*. *Church Dogmatics* III on creation is not so successful, and many of Barth's problems stem from his inadequacy in this area, though there is powerful and provocative reflection on the nature of man in III.2 and on ethics in III.4. There remains *Church Dogmatics* IV on Christology, undoubtedly Barth's best work. In it he presents three complementary ways into the doctrine, gives his most adequate account of sin, and discusses communal and individual Christian life in depth. This is also the volume where, especially in IV.3, he replies to criticisms of the rest of the *Dogmatics*, including some of those made in our essays.

So it is perhaps his latest work that shows Barth at his best, summing up the main elements in his thinking and replying to well-informed critics. Yet he recants practically nothing, and leaves his *magnum opus* standing like a massive, unfinished, but formally simple and consistent sculpture—a spiral round and round the self-expression of God in time.

Indexes

1. Barth's Major Works

2. Names